I0801287

Praise for David Gurr's Previous Work

Troika

"Gurr makes a stunning debut ... moving right up there with the big boys in the spy business."
— *Publishers Weekly*

"An event in Canadian publishing history."
— Derrick Murdoch, *The Globe and Mail*

The Ring Master

"An extraordinary achievement, a work of richness and virtuosity to which a reviewer can scarcely do justice."
— Alberto Manguel, *The Globe and Mail*

"The most extraordinary book I have read [this year]."
— Lord Robert Skidelsky on his favourite books of 1987, *The Sunday Telegraph*

"Dazzling."
— *Vancouver Sun*

The Voice of the Crane

"*The Ring Master* and, now, *The Voice of the Crane* place Gurr at the forefront of Canadian fiction ... and in the company of such major twentieth century figures as Malcolm Lowry, Thomas Pynchon, Siegfried Lenz, Salman Rushdie, Umberto Eco and Yukio Mishima ... From behind the black curtain comes the voice of a master storyteller, and it is a voice we should listen to."
— Sherrill Grace, *Canadian Literature*

"Gurr now ought to take his place as one of Canada's most formidable writers. This is an extraordinarily complex and inventive book ..."
— Bruce Serafin, *Toronto Star*

UNORGANIZED TERRITORY

Also by David Gurr

Troika
A Woman Called Scylla
The Action of the Tiger
An American Spy Story
On the Endangered List
The Ring Master
The Voice of the Crane
Arcadia We$t
The Charlatan Variations

UNORGANIZED TERRITORY

a boy's own memoir

DAVID GURR

STONEHEWER
BOOKS

ISBN: 978-1-7389933-8-3

1 2 3 4 5 6 7 8 9 10

Cataloguing data available from Library and Archives Canada.

Author photograph by Nicola Gurr
Set in Jenson and Kabel by Ned Seager

Printed and bound by Friesens in Canada

Stonehewer Books | Victoria, BC
stonehewerbooks.com

Stonehewer Books is located on the traditional territory of the Lkwungen people on what is now called Vancouver Island. We acknowledge and are grateful for the unique contributions to our common well-being made by the Indigenous peoples of this land.

For Bun ...

Who shared two-thirds of the voyage,
and is sweet enough to forgive me for the arrow.

Contents

Some Significant Personae 2

A Twelve-Year-Old's View of His New World 3

Death and the Maiden Aunts or A Mistaken Identity 5

Victory or The Last Straw 49

Empress to Empress or A Canadian Pacific Odyssey 71

Victoria Regina or Child's Play in a Little Bit of Olde England 97

Adolescence in a Perfect Eden or Act One: "Tragedy and Comedy" 141

Adolescence in a Perfect Eden or Act Two: "The Age of Indiscretion" 185

Adolescence in a Perfect Eden or Act Three: "Curtain Up" 213

Jane's Letter 289

Lifting the Fog 303

A Note of Appreciation and Acknowledgement 305

About the Author 307

Some Significant Personae

Jane (aka Janet, aka Iseult Harvey) Gurr:
My mother

Jim (aka Jimmy, aka James, aka Hugh, aka Courtney) Gurr:
My other parent

Teddy (aka Harold):
A secret waiting to be uncovered

Angela (aka Bun):
My sister

The Aunts (Dorothea and Elspie):
Jane's guardians

Nan (aka — by Jim — Nanny Goosegog) Harvey:
My aunt

Kythe (aka — by Jim — Old Trout) Mackenzie:
My great aunt

A Twelve-Year-Old's View of His New World

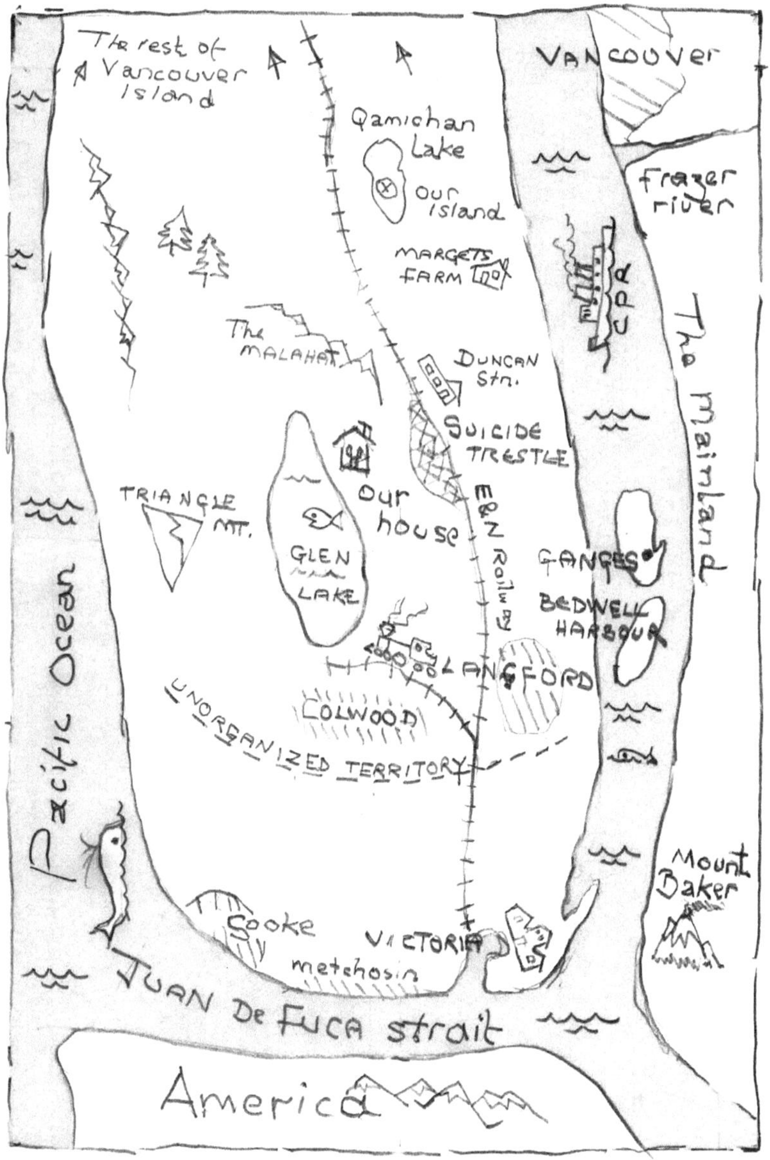

Death and the Maiden Aunts
or
A Mistaken Identity

When I was Willum, I was three years old. I was living with my mother, Jane, in a third-floor walk-up flat in a villa with three front steps and a garden behind it, on Boundary Road in Hampstead.

She was calling herself "Mrs. Howard, a war widow" to neighbours, tradesmen and various suitors. She did it — plus wearing a wedding ring — to avoid the awkwardness of "A baby with 'no husband.'" There was also a man called Jim, or sometimes Jimmy, hanging around. He could play the piano (moonlighting as one half of a music hall act, Singer & Keyes). Jim sold the kind of clothing for ladies that my mother said I wasn't supposed to see at my age.

My earliest memories (that aren't prompted by faded captions above old photographs) come from sensations: taste, and music, and love — for a first beloved dog, a Scottish terrier I unimaginatively called Scotty. I also loved the red label on Heinz Tomato Soup, purchased from a Hampstead corner grocer; eating bananas and Kit Kats wrapped in "silver paper"; and a menagerie of stuffed animals who all had names.

I only remember two other beings from that earliest time as a Willum. The more important was Aunt Nan, my mother's older sister, who took me for outings to see a monkey in Hyde Park, where I ate the Kit Kats and bananas.

The other person was Mademoiselle Jessie Franks. She was a young woman, French by birth or choice, a "fashion buyer" who would travel to and from the continent to get samples of the latest designs in Paris, and bring them to London for cheaper imitations to be made. Her connection to Jim was his Hygrade Lingerie Ltd. brassiere collection.

Jessie brought me two Schubert records on one of her returns from France. I don't know why; we just seemed to like each other at once. She also tried, less successfully, to teach me French, and I used to hug her.

And then …

Paradise began to be lost because of Jim. His "main love" at this time was driving his new Vauxhall car to show off "my son" (as proof of his virility and masculinity) to the most important people in his life — his Savile Row tailor, his Burlington Arcade tobacconist, his Bond Street barber. And while my golden curls were being given their first chop, my heart was broken.

Scotty was stolen. Dog-napped from Jim's new Vauxhall, which, in his virile eagerness to show me off, had been left unlocked.

Scotty being stolen added to an already existing — inexpressible yet undeniable to a little child — feeling of something else taken away from me, forming a rock-bottom seismic sense of betrayal and loss.

Jessie Franks made her last fashion trip from France in the first week of September, as Neville Chamberlain, and thus England, and therefore I, declared war!

"No, No, Nanny Goosegog"

In a time of war between adults bombarding and annoying each other with nicknames ... Jim applied them to everyone, and always pretended he could never keep real names straight on my mother's "upper middle" side of the British class divide.

Aunt Nan's proper last name was Harvey, as was my mother's before her marriage. They were both orphans. The maiden name of their mother — my maternal grandmother, Lillias — was Mackenzie. She came from that "lower upper" titled branch of the family at Gairloch — a psychological class gulf away from Jim's birthplace, Liverpool — on the western edge of the Highlands, across from the Isle of Skye. She died when my mother was three, and Nan eight.

When my mother was eight, their father, my maternal grandfather, Henry Egerton Harvey, died of Graves' disease after being gassed while serving as a major during the first of the world war cataclysms.

The Gurr connection was with Liverpool, by way of Brighton. (My connection was tenuous. Apparently there were an astonishing *sixteen siblings* on either side for both Gurr grandparents. Jim did have a brother, Uncle Reg, with a square face and brow, whom I liked, and an older sister, Nina, horse-faced. The Gurr grandparents were in haberdashery and first-generation militant Seventh-day Adventists.)

We will never know why Jim caused Nan to suffer and rage life-long against his calling her "Nanny Goosegog." He saddled me with "Dai-Dai," a Welsh diminutive that he picked up as an adolescent after being exiled from Liverpool to work in the fields with a "Dafydd" on a down-at-heel farm in Wales near a town appropriately called Mold. As Jim hardly ever cracked a book, I have also never discovered why he decided to alternate "Dai-Dai" with the Dickensian "Mr. Snodgrass" but I hated both of them.

He used the "Snod" when he played the Bath Crane Game — hauling me out of it, dripping wet, clutching desperately onto one end of the towel; him pretending the crane was collapsing, then hoisting me up again — after which I had to be kissed by his bristling moustache, ending the hoist with:

"Wasn't that fun, *Snod?*"

The Snod was atrocious: I also hated the moustache. I merely disliked *Dai-Dai* and felt it was not my real name, but couldn't say why.

However, as it coincided with not being called Willum anymore … to my adult self it's obvious: my psyche was torn away from a name associated with natural warmth, to something artificial that I didn't want and couldn't respond to naturally. Of course my mother had agreed to this change of my whole identity, but the infant couldn't possibly assign a sense of outrage to her. It all went to Jim, and I felt some sense of it throughout his life.

Compounding the name-changing mystery was the lack of any christening certificate for David: yet somehow it was a given that I was a baptized Church of England member in good standing.

This clerical error brings us to the Aunts.

Luftwaffe Bombers and Scarlet Runners

"The Aunts," ALWAYS CAPITALIZED: my mother's and Nan's guardians. There were two of them, Elspeth (Elspie) and (Doodlie) Dorothea. In reverse order, one was fat and the other was thin. Each was the daughter of a bishop, Victorian-Edwardian era with all its attendant gaiters and House of Lords regalia familiar from any Trollope novel.

William Thomas Harrison (1837-1920) was Bishop of Glasgow and Galloway, and lived in a house called Olivers (because Oliver Cromwell may have lived in it, originally). Henry Bernard Hodgson (1856-1921) was Bishop of Saint Edmundsbury and Ipswich, and lived in a house called Barton (because his father had been vicar of Barton in Cumberland, presumably).

The Aunts therefore lived in a house called "Barton Olivers." (Just Barton Olivers at first; later it was called Barton Olivers "One," because by then they lived in Barton Olivers "Two," on the Dorset coast, where I first came face to face with the power of the sea.) Barton Olivers One was in Gloucestershire, on the Welsh border, outside Monmouth.

They were not related to each other, nor by blood to my mother. The connection and intersection of families was formed at school. Thin Elspie and fat Dorothea each had a sister (Rhoda and Marjorie, similarly proportioned but less important in our story). My grandmother, Lillias Mackenzie, also had a sister, Kythe, my great aunt — who is important, but not yet.

All six of these Valkyries went to Cheltenham Ladies' College — founded in 1853 — a private education which was still unusual for girls of their "breeding" but born of necessity. The titled heads of their families may have had money. Daughters lower down the tree did not. Or at least the Mackenzie pair didn't.

How much the Aunts had squirrelled away was a mystery, as was anything from my gassed grandfather's estate, but it was enough to buy and run a pair of Barton Olivers. And somebody found the cash for my mother's and my own costly English private education. It certainly wasn't from the tips tossed at Singer & Keyes.

THE FIRST AUTUMNAL AIR RAID SIRENS OF 1939 were a false alarm, but they triggered an over-anxious first evacuation of children from London. While my parents stayed put in Boundary Road I was sent to someone called Nurse Crowe at the "White House" in Reigate, safely twenty-two miles south, in Surrey.

I was about to write that nothing happened that first time, and I was brought back with no memories except of a wonderful summer garden to treasure or hide in — but there was what my mother called "the Bean episode."

At the end of a glorious September the White House garden had all the usual late flowers of a herbaceous border — dahlias, chrysanthemums, Michaelmas daisies — as well as vegetables like cauliflowers and Brussels sprouts. There were also teepee structures supporting Scarlet Runner beans. So late in the season, the last pods had been left to form seeds for next year.

For some inexplicable reason, Nurse Crowe reported, I had torn open the pods and eaten enough of the large purple beans inside to make myself violently ill. Again, today's child psychologist would make short work of renaming the Bean episode an "Evacuation from His Mother in London Episode."

Two Little Runaways

MY NEXT EXCURSION to the Surrey countryside was to protect me during the Battle of Britain in August 1940, age four and a half. No bombs fell on me — which was good. However, as the White House and its scarlet runner garden lay directly beneath the flight path of all the German bomber fleets on their way to butcher London, the subliminal thought was always there — *Bombs Could.*

Presumably it was this thought which prompted the Runaway episode.

I tried to escape from Reigate's safety with a girl called Lucy, another evacuee. A single photograph shows the runaways, age four, perfectly dressed: David in his grey shorts and jacket, neat tie, wool socks pulled up, and school cap; Lucy in her flowered dress with a collar and bow, buttoned shoes; both criminals caught standing with their tiny leather suitcases at the White House gate.

Why we would wish to run away is obvious. How we thought we could make it to London, and who caught us, and why they thought it was a good moment to take an adorable snap for the family albums remain riddles of war.

The Runaway episode, or the temporary pause in the daylight bombing, eventually brought me back in early October 1940, to the family bosom at Boundary Road just in time for the real Blitz to blow the lid off it — and destroy the houses on each side of us.

Bombed flat!

Light at the End of a Tunnel

In January 1941, Jimmy-and-Jane (as all their London West End friends called them) had almost decided enough was too much. For him, driving an ambulance through blacked-out streets. For my mother, extinguishing incendiary bombs as they fell on us, smothering them with sand as they landed with their flaring phosphorus in our tiny villa garden behind Boundary Road.

We left town.

Memory becomes my own, not reinforced by photo albums, on February 5th, 1941, my fifth birthday. We travelled on a night troop train, slowly. With the compartments full of soldiers, there were only dim blue lights overhead to reveal tense adult expressions as we waited in a tunnel for explosions to cease outside.

At the end of the tunnel, or thereabouts, was Barton Olivers One. I couldn't see it as we arrived by night. The Aunts had most generously decided that the Gurr family should shelter with them for the duration, in the comparative safety of the countryside near Monmouth.

(Events swiftly showed that comparison, if not odious, can be dangerous: Monmouth was on the Luftwaffe's flight path to Liverpool; jettisoned bombs dropped in the field below us, on the banks of the winding River Wye. I played mud pies happily in the craters, accompanied by two grazing donkeys.)

In daylight, the house was — is, it still stands — a small Edwin Lutyens, post-Edwardian manor, stone-faced, with shingled roofs. There was some dispute whether Sir Edwin himself did the drawings but the desired effect was the same: pleasant and comfortable, with wide fireplaces and an entry hall with a gallery landing. Broad, flagged steps went up and down, to and from a stone-balustraded portico and the lion's head knocker on the oak front door.

There was a large garden, with a croquet lawn and rotating summerhouse beside a goldfish pool. The road to Monmouth ran in front of the house, between it and the river. Behind the house was a large hill. Shortly after our arrival there was snow, and magically, the Aunts provided a toboggan. Escaped from Reigate and London, reunited with his mother in time to build a snowman, five-year-old David was in heaven.

The Princesses' Chamber

PARADISE LASTED UNTIL THE END of that post-Edwardian summer of love, which gives us a moment to catch up with why everyone got there, and what they did there.

After being soundly educated by Cheltenham, Elspie and Dorothea started their own All Saints Nursery College, on the outskirts of Harrogate, to train nannies for the households of empire. The nannies needed children of empire to train on.

Most of these were legitimate scions or daughters of imperial administrators and generals serving the Raj in India, or minor royals from assorted Balkan states. Inevitably, some of the All Saints cribs and prams had to be filled by less fortunate — or legitimate — babies.

One of these improper little bastards might even have been Elspie's child. His name was Kiff, from Christopher, the first name of Dorothea's brother, an ostrich-plumed colonel in the Royal Household at Windsor Castle. Later, as an honorary "Uncle

Christopher," he used to grope my sixteen-year-old mother "in 'Naughty Uncle' games around the bishop's dining room table."

Be that as it might have been, on the premature death of my maternal grandmother (only in her early thirties), and with my grandfather, the travelling actor, fighting to breathe after poison gas in France, the Aunts became guardians; Nan and Jane went as their wards to live at All Saints Nursery College. Nan became, for her first career, a "jolly hockey sticks" gym teacher, before transmuting into a highly skilled physiotherapist in Harley Street.

Jane went to Cheltenham Ladies' College — before she was asked to leave at the age of sixteen, after inexplicably being given a 250cc BSA motorbike by the Aunts as a non-graduation present, which she then rode, unchaperoned, for visits to the officers' mess at Colchester.

THESE LOOSE ENDS ASSEMBLED on the croquet lawn at Barton Olivers One as two worlds collided. By the time I arrived there, two Slavic princesses, Irena and Tatyana, were also in residence, inhabiting a mystery chamber of perfumes and rustling fabrics — which brings us to the bedrooms.

The princesses' chamber was next to the bedroom assigned to my parents. I had a nursery room beyond it. The Aunts' bedroom was on the other side of the landing where they slept together in a brass bed. (After Jim said something about that, I heard my mother exclaim to Aunt Nan: "I don't believe they even knew what the word lesbian meant!")

The princesses' exotic presence was magnified by the June arrival of a dashing swarm of young officers in Army and Air Force uniforms, most of them sporting moustaches and medals. Jim also had a moustache and a bowler hat and a sample suitcase containing his Hygrade nighties and knickers.

Although those had already begun to pique my interest because of the rustling noises from the princesses' chamber, a bowler hat looked out of place in croquet or cricket. This social disadvantage was somewhat offset because, after the games, Jim as Jimmy at the grand piano levelled the playing field; his anecdotes of a bisexual West End backstage scandal involving John Gielgud and Marlene Dietrich made him the life of the party.

They did not endear him to the Aunts, who were already dubious of anyone in trade, more so of his black "lounge lizard" Brylcreemed hair, and utterly appalled by his backstage music-hall anecdotes. They resolutely called him James.

He fought back by building them a chicken house on top of a cesspit behind the summerhouse, dressed as a pipe-in-mouth, country gentleman in jodhpurs and a mustard-yellow waistcoat, striped tie and cufflinked shirt. This good work was undercut when, for no explainable reason, he referred to the penis of a randy cockerel as a Japonica — the designation he used for everyone else's from that time on.

The dashing young officers got their own nicknames, like "Nanki-Poo" (after a raucous drawing-room rendition of *The Mikado*, barroom lyrics by Jim and courtesy costume items furnished by the princesses).

My mother seemed particularly playful with an army captain "dasher": owner of a real first name and a racing-green MG Sports with wire wheels. He was called Anthony Paul and he had been a fellow ward of the Aunts, with my mother, at All Saints. A dashing owner of a particularly fine RAF moustache was introduced as "Timmy Vaughan, he was your godfather."

The how-and-why of a "godfather" for me — with no baptismal certificate for "David" to go with him — remains part of the mystery. I liked Timmy Vaughan. Three months later he was shot down and killed.

The summer sun around which these uniformed luminaries revolved was Jane. As she put it herself to Aunt Nan: "Men were attracted to me like bees to honey."

Actions speak louder. She got pregnant and I went to school.

"Mr. Do As You Would Be Done By"

THE SNOWMAN HAD MELTED, and daffodils waved on the tobogganing hill. James — as Jim — with bowler hat and sample case set off every Monday (which for some unexplained reason made me happy) to sell his Hygrade knicker offerings to High Street haberdashers wherever they hadn't yet been bombed out. He returned on Fridays (which then made me cross) in time for Jim — as Jimmy — to play the piano for the weekend RAF bees buzzing around Jane when they weren't teaching me to hold a cricket bat on the croquet lawn.

Summertime happiness was watching a pond frog sitting among the golden kingcups in front of the summerhouse, as Aunt Dorothea read *Pilgrim's Progress* to me.

The summerhouse's Edwardian construction deserves its own moment in the sun: it was the first structure that I really noticed. About fifteen feet square, it was built of wood with a shingled, peaked roof and a copper weathervane of a cockerel on top. The back wall was solid; the two sides had shuttered windows that could be opened, as could the whole front wall, which folded back on huge hinges.

The inside was like a comfortable drawing room, with a sofa, two chairs, a table with an oil lamp, and a carpet on the floor. The entire structure sat on a turntable which had a giant cogwheel with its teeth facing upwards. Underneath the summerhouse floor was an attached and matching cogwheel, with its teeth facing downwards. The crank handle was big and cast iron, but I don't remember exactly where I stood to turn it and make everything go round to face the sun.

Dorothea also did the flower beds in the garden around the summerhouse, telling me the names (always Latin, *Antirrhinum;* never common snapdragon) or showing me how to prune a rose. Elspie did the vegetables (destroyed by her inability to cook) and the tidying: helping her with which led to the first Bird's Nest episode.

The Aunts employed Victorian aphorisms to moderate unruly infant behaviour: *Mr. Do As You Would Be Done By*, or *Little Birds in Their Nests Agree*. (Always capitalized, and anyone who has ever watched baby birds being fed by a parent and heard of Darwin's theory of survival of the fittest knows how inaccurate that second one is.) Age six, I had been helping Elspie clean a gutter above the garage door. She was using a garden hose to flush it: my part of the task was to stand on the closed lid of a rainwater barrel and operate a tap.

Suddenly, a small bird dive-bombed Elspie's head. A nest of sparrows had been built in the gutter. The eggs had hatched. All the nestlings' beaks somehow managed to yawn open and cheep deafeningly at the same time, as water began flooding them out of their home. I turned off the tap. Elspie said, "Turn it on." I refused. There was a row. I was sent to my nursery. The birds were drowned out of theirs.

"Doubting Castle"

My only sexual education had been the randy cockerel and Jim's penile misuse of *Japonica,* neither of which made anything clear. I had never been to kindergarten, nor played with other children: the single child's name I remember from my first six years is that of Lucy the runaway.

My friends to talk to, and play with, were stuffed animals. A photo shows them lined up on the summerhouse bench beside me: Ellie the Elephant, Eeyore, Pooh, Piglet, Penguin, Panda and Rabbit, with my Donald Duck gas mask placed at the end.

I couldn't officially read or write, but unofficially I could follow along because Dorothea read aloud to me almost every day, beginning with books left over from her Victorian childhood in the All Saints Nursery.

Horrible *Eric, or Little by Little,* was the worst one. It was supposed to teach something called Purity for Boys. Aunt Dorothea explained that all the important words in books like Eric's had Capital Letters to make me remember them, and some words like "&" or "&c" let you not have to write so much and save time.

I didn't dislike Kingsley's *Water-Babies,* Mrs. Molesworth's *Tapestry Room, Golden Fleece Greek Myths (illustrated),* or Charles Lamb's *Adventures of Ulysses.* Although some, like Mrs. Molesworth, are still on my library shelves to earn their keep as antiques, few of them stayed in my mind. The illustration of "Perseus Holding the Gorgon's Dripping Head" certainly did for a considerable while. Two others that never left are Wilde's *Selfish Giant* and Bunyan's *Pilgrim's Progress.*

"The Slough of Despond" Revisited

I FELL INTO IT ON MY FIRST DAY OF SCHOOL: whenever I return to it, all other memories of Monmouth Grammar are pretty much wiped out. I had never been alone in a public toilet; more brutally, I had never seen a male urinal. This one was a long trough, used in common by all "caught short."

Six-year-old David didn't only need to urinate, and didn't know where else to go. I was wearing shorts. I dropped them and sat on the edge of the communal trough. There was "a scene." In the six months following that horrific incident I somehow learned to write with a steel nib dipped into an inkwell on a wooden desk. I suppose there was arithmetic.

The exciting visits by the dashing young officers ended, as did so many of their lives. Their place was taken by an eighteen-year-old called Robin Maxwell. I remember Robin's name because I thought of him as my first adult friend.

Robin gave me rides in a trailer he made to attach to his bicycle, and showed me his mouth-watering collection of balsa-wood planes, like a Fairey Albacore biplane torpedo bomber, meticulously painted, suspended from the ceiling of his room. Then he left to join the naval Fleet Air Arm to fly a real Fairey Albacore off an aircraft carrier and be killed.

Occasionally there were treats: Aunt Nan came to visit and tried for the first time to teach me to swim in the River Wye. She did not succeed. The occasion was recorded in a nude photograph which prompted Jim to point out, whenever he saw it (which was too often), my "hollow buttocks," whatever darkly Freudian thing that meant.

Elspie was the world's worst driver as well as worst cook — on one early automotive occasion, visiting Liverpool with my mother, she had got her solid-tired Trojan car stuck in tram tracks and had to go all the way to the depot to be lifted out. Petrol was severely rationed, but on some weekends she would drive us erratically in a Humber she called "Blue Peter" to the Forest of Dean, or to landmarks like Raglan Castle, for the adults to take photos, and allow me to have my favourite Heinz Tomato Soup (with its red label) kept warm in a thermos flask.

A Proper Bunny for a Proper (Half) Sister

Of course I thought she was a whole one. She was christened Angela Dorothea Elspie. I wrote a card with the steel-nib pen dipped in schoolroom black Indian ink from the inkwell on my desk:

Dear Mummy hope you are well with baby sister

It was the first, and remains the only, sample of my handwriting kept by my mother from my first eighteen years. Perhaps we can blame that maternal oversight on all the moves.

Postpartum, mother and daughter moved back from the hospital in Monmouth to the second floor at Barton Olivers, and into my parents' bedroom (next to the princesses' chamber) which for the rest of his life Jim described — in Aunt Dorothea's voice and with a tone of awe at his accomplishment — as:

"This is the room where she was conceived."

I doubt that Dorothea ever said such a thing in her life. The absolute fact that Angela and I had different fathers was never alluded to while we were growing up. Nor can I say there was any manifest display of preference by our parents for one sibling or the other.

Coincidentally with Angela's beginning to say a first word, my (now our) mother decided to make a special stuffed toy "just for her." It was created out of an old dead black creature, which once hung around Dorothea's neck. Though described on its faded label as "Marten," it looked and felt like dead cat.

Angela called this toy *Proper Bunny* — the first to have that name because the fur from the original owner quickly disintegrated under the conditions of its new use: our mother had to make at least one replacement, but each was always referred to as Proper Bunny.

After Angela grew her first teeth the nomenclature became even more peculiar because of Jim's use of nicknames. Baby sister's two front ones protruded slightly. Jim immediately compared these incisors to a rabbit's, and as swiftly called his baby daughter "Bunny Rabbit."

The next move happened abruptly, before the end of my first spring term in 1942. Jim was "called up." Although he was thirty-seven, selling lingerie was not a "reserved occupation" and his age bracket had come due. For reasons that were never made clear, he chose to volunteer for the Royal Marines — a decision for which I have always cut him a lot of slack. Even though he ended up in the Pay Corps he endured the entire and gruelling process of becoming a Marine, a survival test that a host of younger men failed.

At the same time as this latest parental bombshell, the Aunts decided to sell their house. Their sisters (Fat Marjorie and Thin Rhoda) lived in a cottage in the hamlet of Swyre, in Dorset, and the two pairs wanted to dwell closer to each other. My mother and baby Angela accompanied them immediately: I did not.

The plan had been for both children to be looked after by Nurse Crowe, again at the White House in Reigate, while the adults got settled. Instead, my mother said later, baby Angela "created such a fuss. She screamed until she was blue in the face."

I was left alone on the platform at Paddington Station while the train taking my mother and sister (now calmed down) steamed west.

"I felt awful, but you didn't seem to mind," my mother added. "You just held Nurse Crowe's hand and walked away."

The boy called David *minded*. Whenever his mother made one of her abruptly inexplicable absences, he experienced the kind of overwhelming sadness that first happened when Scotty was stolen from Jim's new Vauxhall car. I just didn't have the words for it then.

Sugar Plum Fairies & Opium Poppies

Barton Olivers Two was on the edge of a cliff, in deepest Dorset. The Aunts drove to it in Blue Peter; mother and baby sister travelled by Great Western rail. How I first got down there from London I don't recall, but the house and subsequent events while I lived in it became indelible.

You may know the West Bay end of the cliff on which the house perched because it formed the backdrop for the TV series *Broadchurch*. In 1942 I saw a post-Victorian brick villa, three stories high and a cellar beneath, with no vegetation for miles around. There was another similarly sized villa beside Barton Olivers, and a small bungalow beside that, but both of these buildings were uninhabited when I arrived.

Our end of the cliff was almost a mile from the village of Burton Bradstock, which was three miles from the town of Bridport, where, for the second time, I somehow went to school: the last of summer, 1942.

The development of memory in children is almost as mysterious to me as the Horsehead Nebula. I attended that Bridport school for a year and a half, growing from the age of six to eight, and if it weren't for a single photograph I could recall nothing about it.

The picture shows me in a rabbit costume with floppy ears, wearing a doctor's stethoscope. There are one or two other animals and some little girls in ballet fairy costumes. The school was private, in a small house, two stories, and had rhododendron bushes, in the midst of which we were performing. I associate the Waltz of the Sugarplum Fairies with that experience, and have loathed *The Nutcracker* ever since.

Barton Olivers Two loomed enormously out of place. A three-foot-high ornamental red-brick wall separated the domesticated lawn and feathery tamarisks from the wild clumps of sea pinks growing in front of it along the road. The wall had decorative holes in it to allow glimpses of the sea, and then grew higher along the sides of the property, reaching eight feet at the back to protect a vegetable garden from the southerly gales that hurled their way up the English Channel.

This walled garden was the setting for a sad and extraordinary scene. It had flowers as well as vegetables: among them opium poppies. My mother had a particularly close female friend from girlhood, the same age, and in our first Dorset summer Lefroy came to visit us.

The details are impossible to unravel, but the opium poppies were rare, and Dorothea was apparently collecting their flower heads to dry out for seeds. Somehow Lefroy discovered and ate them.

I only saw the aftermath when, with my mother and Elspie on either side of her, Lefroy was walked round and round the garden to keep her awake. After the Poppies episode she revealed to my mother that she had cancer, and a short time later she died.

A Postcard Hardy Village

The Aunts and the evacuated Gurr family had this Thomas Hardy landscape to ourselves — almost. The coastal picturesqueness had been jarred by the arrival of a searchlight battery and an anti-aircraft gun. I loved the gun immediately but had little time to enjoy it: on its first firing the sandstone ledge supporting it gave way, depositing it on Hive Beach beside the mackerel fishermen's planked boats.

Happily the searchlight remained intact, manned by a small group of soldiers. To my astonished delight, my mother miraculously acquired enough of their castoff clothing, and somebody's Singer sewing machine, to make me a uniform that matched theirs in scratchy, coarse-khaki discomfort. It felt horrible, but because she had made it specially for me, I loved it, and as long as I also wore my child-sized soldier's tin helmet to stop shrapnel falling on my eight-year-old head, on some magic occasions I was allowed to swing the searchlight beam. Magic to me: lethal for the Nazi bomber trapped like a silver-moth in the light.

How those southwestern counties of Devon and Dorset looked in the early years of the Second World War has been perfectly described by John Fowles in his novel *Daniel Martin*. The conscription of young men from the fields to the armed forces, and the strict rationing of fuel, meant that the fields and village life around Barton Olivers Two had reverted to the Hardy century before. Clydesdales, with plaited manes and tails, pulled the ploughs; elderly mackerel fishermen from the village had to man their oars.

To be less lyrical: the fishermen cheated over the petrol rationing, and nothing ploughed the fields behind and beside our house because they were all land-mined, with scarlet skull-and-crossbones signs saying *Keep Out*.

Except for the soldiers at the searchlight and the fishermen on the beach, people did keep out. Consequently, our isolation must have seemed extreme to the adults; to me it was bliss. Unsupervised, I was free to crawl out on the sandstone ledges of the cliff to try and recover eggs from the gulls' nests to add to my egg collection.

Looking back, I'm ashamed of it, and of the birds' agitation when I stole their future progeny. As a boy I was proud of acquiring the skill to reach into the burrow, remove only one egg, take it home, stick a needle in both ends, blow into one, and with luck watch the eggy contents blow out of the other, leaving behind a perfect empty shell to label and admire.

The old fishermen took me with them whenever I asked, helping them to set their nets, recover the lines, lift lobster pots — treating me, an observer might have said, almost as an adopted grandson.

BURTON BRADSTOCK WAS STILL a postcard Hardy village. When I walked down to it, after descending a steep hill at the start of our cliff road, I came to a rustic bridge over the River Bride, with a smithy beside it and a leather-aproned smith to shoe the Clydesdales.

Sometimes he even let me hammer the red-hot metal on his anvil. There was a village pub, the Dove, where Jim-as-Jimmy and his piano-playing helped business enough that the publican bent the rules and let me in as well for lemonade.

Of course there was a village church, St. Mary's, and a vicarage, described in *A Topographical Dictionary of England* by Samuel Lewis in 1848: "The living is a rectory, with the curacy of Shipton-George ... The church is an ancient cruciform structure, in the Norman style. There is a place of worship for Wesleyans."

The current very Church of England Rector was Mr. Dittmar. As the daughters of bishops, the Aunts' connection got us more than a foot in the door: it got me into a pew every Sunday morning.

And there were village children — which means that we have arrived at the 1940s British class divide. At seven, I couldn't recognize it, although I was vaguely aware of it: there were occasional "la-di-das" at the way I said things, a mock bow and snigger if I addressed the blacksmith as "Sir" — but as I genuinely liked the boys I was playing with, and appreciated the way they showed me such things as "girdling" for trout (tickling them with my fingers) in the pool beneath the bridge, they usually seemed to tolerate me.

The divide appeared for the first time when a boy called Brian took me to his home, a cottage at the foot of the hill. His mother got cross with me for no reason. She shouted "Blasted evac, do be get your own bloody school" and began to slam their front door. I offered my normal, polite apology to an adult, and explained my recent transplanted arrival at Barton Olivers. As she heard my piping voice and the name of the house, the mother's face changed to a smile:

"Never 'ee mind, m'dear. Youm come along in."

Decades later, I understood why she changed. My accent did the magic trick; other child-evacuees with Cockney accents, whom I didn't know about, were also billeted in and near Burton Bradstock.

Nor did I consider myself an "evac." I just lived in a large house on the cliff that happened to belong to the Aunts, and went to a small school. I didn't realize it was private. The Cockney bomb-driven children went to the local council school. The village mothers took it as a given that people like the daughters of bishops landed among them or departed as they wished. The children accompanying such higher beings were therefore not considered as a drain on scarce village-schooling resources, or on rations for food, as "evacs" were.

"No Bing Crosby, Please"

Mealtime with the Aunts had its own higher rituals. Grace at both ends was obligatory. Even our Daily Bread had its own Capitalized Liturgy which (once the requisite brown and/or white loaves were in place on their cutting board) Elspie and Dorothea took turns reciting before slicing, for each diner, in turn:

Brown or white, thick or thin, crust or crumb, half or whole?

As there were never fewer than half-a-dozen diners for breakfast (each with a different desired colour, thickness, whole or half slice, and finally, interminably, inner-or-end), this cutting process took long enough for my breakfast soft-boiled egg to get harder, as well as cold.

Compared to city-dwellers' wartime rations, some rural resources were more plentiful. Fish, game birds like pheasants or ducks, and rabbits sometimes appeared for the table to augment our ration books. Elspie still kept chickens, who now lived in the walled vegetable garden behind the house, and who sporadically provided eggs.

The conversation at table had proscribed limits: except for special bulletins from the BBC, no war; no politics; no mention of the aristocratic owner of the surrounding land, Lord Pitt-Rivers, whose father had sat with their fathers in the House of Lords. He had recently been arrested as a Nazi sympathizer and — according to headlines in the *Daily Mail* that I wasn't supposed to read — "liked going to supper with Goering."

The Aunts of course only took *The Times,* but we had added Doreen to the household. She was a girl from the village (the niece of the wife of the publican of the Dove) to help look after my new baby sister as a sort of nanny, and she sometimes brought the forbidden *Daily Mail,* wrapped around fresh fish.

Another prohibition was crooning in general (Dorothea believed it responsible for society's moral disintegration) and, because of his popularity, Bing Crosby in particular.

Three things brought the household to stand at attention: the Easter hymn ("Jesus Christ Is Risen Today"), the Hallelujah chorus at Christmas, and the national anthem after an address by the King. Any Churchillian words from the prime minister were received with complete silence, and sometimes a tear.

In the spring of 1943 this High Church solemnity was shattered. The Americans arrived.

The Big Red One

His name was Sergeant Richard Baier of the United States 1st Infantry Division, and he came bearing Spam and a shoulder-patch insignia, with a scarlet number 1, for my battledress jacket.

How mother first found Dickie B buzzing around her is an open question. If propriety was being observed it was probably at one of those Jimmy piano-playing evenings in the Dove pub. The 1st Division had set up a training camp just outside Burton Bradstock and its young soldiers, away from homes in New Jersey or Nebraska, quickly and surprisingly became emotionally connected with the Dorset villagers' lives.

As did Sergeant Dickie B and my mother.

(Eighty years later, poignant photographs and letters on the Internet record the depth of that connection when it was severed. In the words of another American staff sergeant, Don Wilson: "It was a deeper, more painful feeling than when I left Penn Station in New York a couple of years before.")

FAMILY CONNECTION HAD BEEN TENUOUS for Jimmy-and-Jane from its inception, to say nothing of mine. War and the Royal Marines made fidelity a very dodgy subject. She excused it to Aunt Nan: "He was at their camp in Dawlish. There were long separations. Everyone's having affairs. People turn a blind eye."

No doubt. Selfishly, I was just happy to have my mother without Jim. When he came back on leave there were parties at Barton Olivers Two, as there had been at Barton Olivers One (the Aunts considered it their patriotic duty), but the rank structure attending them had changed.

Instead of moustachioed young officers, the party guests now came from the ranks of the Royal Marines and the 1st US Infantry. Jim was a corporal — he had refused to let his name go forward for a commission — and would also bring with him Marine pals.

Fun and games weren't just for adults. I had a seventh birthday and got presents. Because not much else was available, these were nearly always books: *Doctor Doolittle, Swallows and Amazons,* and my favourite, *Just William.*

A Tortoiseshell Ear Trumpet

For my seventh summer we also got a second beloved dog (the first being the dog-napped Scotty), and a first goat. The new beloved dog was a result of a first visit to Thin Marjorie and Fat Rhoda: the Aunts' matching pair, in their cottage at the hamlet of Swyre, three miles away via Common Lane. Naturally, their cottage was about three times the size of those of the ordinary villagers.

Our arrival was greeted by the matching sisters, who fell fondly on each other's thin or amply matched bosoms before taking us into their drawing room to meet an extraordinary trio.

The human in the trio was someone called Great Aunt Hetty, who looked as old and fat as Queen Victoria's picture at Barton Olivers Two, dressed sepulchrally in black (mourning for her late husband — yet another bishop) and crowned with a black lace cap. She also clutched a tortoiseshell ear trumpet, the first I had seen, and fascinating in its own right.

This terrifying apparition was seated in a wicker-basket-tricycle-chair, for invalid transportation. Squatting at this antique vehicle's right side was an extremely fat and drooling Pekingese. On the other side of the tricycle chair was a moth-eaten, white cockatoo. The cockatoo had its own low perch and a baleful eye.

Introductions followed slowly via the tortoiseshell ear trumpet, interrupted by the Pekingese breaking wind which the adults attempted to ignore. I tried to hide a giggle. The parrot suddenly launched itself across the room and savagely bit me on the leg.

This unsettling pattern was repeated throughout the visit. I never imagined that something wonderful could come of it.

The name of the wonderful something was Sammy, a treacle-and-cream-coloured Pekingese puppy, with whom I fell instantly and totally in love. Impossible as it seemed, Sammy was the grandson of the obese drooler belonging to Great Aunt Hetty, and the Aunts presented him to us as a gift.

The aforementioned goat arrived from the village as a kid. It was supposed to grow up and provide milk for baby Angela. That never happened — it would have needed impregnation and there was no billy in Burton Bradstock — nor did it get a name, but it provided a lot of amusement in its hopscotch games with Sammy, and also cut the grass.

"*Just William*" WASN'T MY ONLY ROLE MODEL for bad behaviour that summer. A young female friend of Jane's had also moved from London to raise a six-year-old male offspring called Ben, in the farmyard safety of the Dorset countryside. To the Aunts' open disapproval she was raising him with no physical punishment, in what she called a free marriage.

Their farm was in the valley between Barton Olivers Two and Swyre. The male half of the free marriage had somehow escaped conscription — perhaps because of his costume: floppy corduroys secured with a string, and a floppier orange silk scarf around his neck. His spouse, Ben's mother, had sandalled feet, wore flowers in her hair and peasant-smock dresses to the ground. Together they laid the hippie groundwork for California, *circa* 1967.

Despite this — perhaps to get a better class of present — Ben's birthday was a strictly Georgian-English affair: adults in the drawing room, children in the nursery. This led to my Tea Party episode.

I refused to be separated from my mother with the grownups and their teacups in the drawing room, and go to join my baby sister and the other younger children for mugs of milk and dipped rusks in their farmhouse nursery. In a move that Just William would have been proud of, I sat down on the drawing room carpet. My mother told me to leave. Ben's mother suggested that I leave. There were disapproving stares above all the teacups.

I stayed put.

I had no psychological insight about Oedipus and sibling rivalry — and in my own defence my seven-year-old's behaviour, when set against Ben's, still doesn't seem extreme. On more than one occasion he defecated on carpets, followed by No Physical Punishment.

Always Turn Off the Light

The nursery at Barton Olivers Two was the attic, originally the servants' quarters. An exciting, almost hidden, winding set of rear stairs led up to it. A front room was for happy play with toys like a Victorian rocking horse, or unpleasant study of school subjects that I don't remember.

The attic had a window looking south to France across the sea. To the east lay shingled Chesil Beach and the long peninsula of Portland Bill, with wrecks of galleons from the Spanish Armada lost off shore.

The wall opposite the window, above a wooden desk, had a large lithograph called *The Death of Nelson at the Battle of Trafalgar*, with the dying Admiral being kissed by Hardy (the naval captain, not the Dorset author), and in calligraphy above them, his immortal signal, *England Expects Every Man Will Do His Duty*.

The back room was smaller, for sleeping, and had a deep purple, almost black ceiling, with silver stars and a crescent moon hand-painted by my mother. Somewhere there was a fireplace which warmed towels after baths.

One bath time ended with the Electrocution episode. Jim had been back on leave and wanted to play the hated Crane Game of hoisting me dripping out of the tub, to be kissed by his hated moustache.

I didn't want to play. "There were words": another Aunts expression. Still dripping wet, I left the bathroom and as strictly advised — because of wartime blackout, "Always Turn Off the Light" — I obediently did, and was zapped with the full British current of 220 volts.

It was an accident. It shouldn't have been possible. The light switch was on the outside of the bathroom door, in the hall. The obsolete switchbox was surface-mounted on the wall. The electrical connections inside the box could only be harmful if the switch cover was unscrewed. Somehow it had been, and my fingers touched the wires and then wouldn't let go.

Jim was still inside the bathroom. My mother heard my screams, rushed from somewhere and managed to drag me free without being electrocuted herself. There was an inquisition which answered none of the questions.

Too Much of Everything

While we children played in our nursery, below us the Aunts had their own leisure pursuits. As befitting daughters of empire (as well as of bishops) their hobbies were not small-scale. Elspie did her jigsaws but these required a surface that seemed as big as a ping-pong table. There was one of those in the cellar, which allowed my mother to play ping-pong games with Dickie B down there whenever he dropped by with Spam.

One end of the cellar formed a huge cupboard, containing spare silver sugar bowls, jam jars, and salt and mustard pots, all lined with blue glass, the result of downsizing from two bishops' palaces. There was too much of everything at Barton Olivers. Turkey rugs (Persian carpets) lay three deep on the floors.

Still on the subject of adult play, Dorothea had her stamps. These filled several huge albums. They started with a Victorian Penny Black and seemed to hold every empire stamp ever issued since then.

The Clockwork Drummer Boy

Christmas in 1943 was heralded with bagpipes — on the gramophone; and after our usual standing up for Handel's *Hallelujah Chorus* — because Great Aunt Kythe had arrived mysteriously from Scotland to give me a kilt in the Mackenzie hunting tartan. In a handwritten note she made a point of stressing that its deep blue and muted green pattern "Is the Ancient like your Ancestors. Not the Modern."

I thought Great Aunt Kythe was already ancient. (Like the Aunts and their sisters, all these strong women were actually in their mid-sixties.) Nor did Kythe seem Scottish. Her voice was more "cut-glass upper class" English than the fluting Archbishop of Canterbury. She also had buck teeth and no chin. None of that mattered. There was the wonderful accompanying pair of black, patent-leather shoes with silver buckles (real, but not ancient) that reminded me of Long John Silver in *Treasure Island*. Unfortunately, in exchange for my kilt and shoes, I had to sing.

Reluctantly, in my piping soprano: "Oh where and oh where has my Highland Lassie gone." I was childishly tickled pink by my Highland Plaid costume, although far from understanding Kythe's reason for giving it. Stuff about ancient ancestors wasn't bad, but my focus was on the rest of Christmas.

The Aunts did it straight from Dickens. The tree — somehow rural Dorset provided a fir — was decorated not with electric lights but wax candles, each of which had to be started with a match. An arsonist's delight, but I was entranced. The table cutlery setting, with Georgian sterling silver and Wedgwood china, was something you might find familiar from watching *Downton Abbey;* for me its centrepiece was a Victorian clockwork drummer boy, who really drummed.

I didn't think 1943's Christmas could be capped, but by New Year's Eve it was. Jim had returned — which always annoyed me — but so had Dickie B (with his usual abundance of US Army gastronomic supplies to augment our rations), and assorted other adults of various ranks in military and Dorset society.

One of these luminaries had brought pheasants to be roasted for the Eve supper. First they had to be "hung" and then plucked. I was allowed to help with the hanging and plucking — but not to keep the magnificent tail feathers, which led to a tantrum and storming upstairs to the nursery, vowing never to come down.

Of course I did. The opportunity to "bring in" my first New Year's Eve couldn't possibly have been missed, and when I got to the bottom of the stairs, my mother was standing there with a fantastically wonderful, "Red Indian" headdress she had made from the plucked pheasant's feathers. I wore it with my Ancient Mackenzie hunting kilt and Treasure Island silver buckle shoes, and marched around the adults while we all sang *Auld Lang Syne.*

The lyrics of the fourth verse, which only people like Kythe ever sing, are these:

We two have paddled in the burn
From morning sun till night
The seas between us roar and swell
Since the days of auld lang syne

It was prophetic. I was about to make an acquaintance with one man out of an armada, yet one that I have not forgotten; just one of so many, swept in that stream of time which would soon swirl him and them across that sea of the English Channel in front of Barton Olivers, leaving them on a beach in Normandy … and me these eight decades' worth of auld memory.

"Something Very Special"

THE INEVITABLE HANGOVER ON NEW YEAR'S DAY: my mother and Great Aunt Kythe had a row. My mother's voice said it was something to do with "the damn kilt putting ideas in his head." She didn't mention the shoes. There were tears by Kythe followed by "one of my angina attacks." (It would be the first of many.)

Kythe went back to ancient Scotland, and January storms hurled their giant waves against the cliffs. I listened to them crashing as I lay in bed and looked at the picture above me — of Nelson dying on his gun deck, as Hardy kissed him, while *England Expected* less fortunate others *To Do Their Duty* by having their arms or legs chopped off by surgeons (and no anaesthetic) in the *Victory*.

Between extreme neap tides that washed right up to the base of the cliffs, I walked west along the beach looking for live machine-gun bullets, or treasure (to go with my silver-buckle shoes) which might have been washed up from the Armada's Spanish galleons sunk by Francis Drake. Instead of treasure, there was the tragic wreckage of modern war: bits of rafts, globs of black oil, a canvas life jacket snagged on a rock. (Irrational fate spared me that dead body.)

February 1944 brought milder weather and my eighth birthday. Aunt Nan gave me *Swallowdale*, my second Arthur Ransome book; but the most excitement was discovering a horned mine washed ashore a quarter-mile east on Chesil Beach. I hoped the naval disposal crew would blow it up with a giant bang. Gallantry and expertise defused a dud; it didn't help their nerves.

March brought more winds, and soldiers around the village. Between April showers we went on flower walks to find bluebells, primroses and cowslips, and even a rare green-winged orchid. At the beginning of the last week in May I walked home from school to find a tank parked across our almost private Cliff Road at the bottom of the hill.

A soldier in the tank said: "You can't go there."

I said: "I live there."

He let me pass the tank. When I got home, there was a Jeep in front of our wall. I thought at first it was Dickie B's, but then I saw that instead of an American Army white star, it was painted with a red square and a number. At Barton Olivers One, the dashing captain Anthony Paul had taught me that the red square meant a British Armoured Brigade.

As I would on any day after school, I walked through our gate, up the brick path, said hello to the goat grazing on the lawn, and went into the sunroom. An officer was talking to the Aunts, my mother and Doreen, who was holding Angela's hand. Sammy wagged his tail at me.

My mother said: "We all have to listen to something very special."

The officer said, more or less, that for about two weeks, or thereabouts, we weren't allowed to go anywhere, or make telephone calls to anyone, and if we did, we would all be taken away and not allowed to come back. Then he saluted, got back in the Jeep with the red square and drove off.

That night, while I slept, the two empty houses beside us filled up with soldiers. When I looked out of the nursery window the next morning, I could see them. They were carrying grapnel hooks and rope ladders. Their faces were painted black.

The final rehearsals for D-Day, and its Omaha Beach, were *On.*

G.I. Joe

I HAD A UNIQUE PERSPECTIVE on this stupendous event. After breakfast, as I couldn't go to school — and couldn't even go further along Cliff Road than the bungalow, or go down to the beach beside the searchlight, before armed sentries stopped me — I walked instead to the edge of the cliff, and crawled out along one of the sandstone ledges to look for some more seagull eggs.

I had barely got as far as the first nesting hole when there was a loud roar from a cloud of smoke out to sea. A soldier with a painted face yelled up at me:

"That's a Duck."

(Actually spelt DUKW: "D" for the model year; "U" for utility-amphibious; "K" for all-wheel drive; "W" for dual rear axles.)

First one, then several more "Ducks" — nothing like a bird; a sort of cross between a jeep and a boat — loaded with more of the soldiers with black-painted faces, emerged from the smoke.

The "Ducks" drove out of the water onto the beach almost directly below me, but slightly to the west. I heard a sudden whoosh, and something whirled up past my head. It was one of the grapnels on a rope that I had seen the night before. A rope ladder whizzed by me, then several more. The soldiers started to climb up them.

THESE AMAZING SCENES, which seemed staged for my personal enjoyment, went on for several days, and were filmed by military photographers: their end product was used in the movie *The Longest Day*, and if the camera had been a little to its right, they would have had to remove a small boy from the footage.

Historically unique as it was, and is, the thing that remained with me on the deepest level was the emotional connection between myself, that very young English boy, and the American soldiers who met each other for so brief a time.

I think it was their ages. The youngest would have been eighteen; most in their early twenties; a handful, perhaps sergeants, might have been older than thirty. The youngest would probably have had a brother or sister of my age back home; the majority would have photos of girlfriends, or young brides; the ones with new wives might have left them with an infant, or pregnant; the sergeants, perhaps with a boy my age.

And all of these men — sons, brothers, husbands, fathers — the Rangers of the US 1st Infantry: all of them were truly about to be the first of the first when, in a very short time remaining, they had to scale their cliff in Normandy.

I MET THE SOLDIERS by "accident-on-purpose" because I let Sammy run in through the open gate of their house next door. Just talking to them should have got me arrested. No civilian adult would have been permitted to speak to them. A soldier at the open front door patted Sammy. I asked if I could go inside their house to see how much different it was from ours.

He said: "Security's tight as a duck's ass. But sure, kid, why the hell not?"

The villa's internal design was almost the same as Barton Olivers but its rooms, which had been completely empty, were now crammed with narrow cot beds. The spaces between them had so much equipment piled up there was scarcely room to walk, and none to sit down. The soldiers had to use the cots as sofas if they wanted to relax. Some of them were playing cards, or writing letters, or strumming a guitar.

One was plucking a small stringed instrument that I didn't recognize, and singing quietly a song, that I didn't know either. I halted in front of him and saluted, because I was wearing my battledress and tin hat.

He stopped playing and saluted me back, which made all the other soldiers laugh. I asked him what his instrument was, and the name of the song.

"A balalaika," he said. "It's Russian. The words are sung by the Volga Boatmen. Until you get the hang of it, how about you hum along? I'm Joe."

He was a G.I. Of course he was Joe, and my memory of our first exchange of greeting can't be exact; but that an American Ranger, on his way to destiny at Omaha Beach, was playing Russian words and music on the eve of D-Day is true. He played me cowboy songs as well, but the "Volga Boatmen" was my favourite.

Why? It couldn't be the foreign lyrics. A large part was its melody, which became harmony, and music is undefinable anyway. What sank its grapnel hook into my heart was the timbre of Joe's voice and the expression on his face.

And then they were gone.

The Pigeon

Joe had warned me the night before — which must have broken every security regulation in the book — and I clung to him and wept, which almost made him cry, but in the morning both the houses beside us were back to empty.

Endless fleets of towed gliders flew over the skull-and-crossboned minefields behind us. Great guns of the invasion battleships thumped loud enough to shake the windows of the sunroom, even though their sixteen-inch barrels were with my US Rangers, fifty miles away.

That night a historic gale swept the channel, shaking slates from our roof down into the garden. I went to look out of the nursery window and found a carrier pigeon huddled on the sill. There was a red band around one of its legs, holding a tiny yellow pouch.

I ran to get my mother. We opened the window slowly upwards. The carrier pigeon let us wrap it in a towel. The same army officer in the Jeep with the armoured brigade marking, who had first told us we were prisoners, came to collect it.

He said: "This one's pretty special." Then he set it free.

A Seagull in the Chimney

THE SUMMER MONTHS OF 1944, which marked the beginning of joyful liberation for occupied Europe, were the end of Dorset rural freedom for me. A defiant attempt to keep doing what I wished, and go where I chose when I wanted, was the Drainpipe episode.

It was caused by Queen Boadicea. I had been reading about her in H.E. Marshall's *Our Island Story* and decided to recruit Brian from the village to help me re-enact her gallant but doomed last stand against the Romans. There was a lot of good battle costume material in the cellar cupboards of Barton Olivers, but I couldn't think of any way to reproduce a decent chariot with swords on its wheels.

Druids only needed a white sheet and blue poster paint for faces and bits of bodies not covered by the sheet, and in an unmined field above the searchlight at Hive Beach there was a convenient tree.

It wasn't an oak, and it had been blasted by machine-gun practice, and there was no mistletoe, but there were still some leaves. I told Brian we had switched from Boadicea to woad-painted Druids at the summer solstice.

The time of sunset on Midsummer's Day in Dorset was about half-past nine. Nursery bedtime was frozen at eight o'clock. My mother kissing us good night seemed to take forever, because baby Angela (she was now two) hated to go to sleep. Eventually she did. My mother left us.

Getting dressed again only needed shorts, shirt and sandals (the blue poster-paint and Druid sheets were already at the tree). Our nursery on the third floor was too high for my escape route; I had to creep down to the bathroom on the second floor — the location of my previous electrocution — open its window, and use the cast iron drainpipe attached to the outside of the house wall to complete my descent. There was one more obstacle: the brick wall shielding the vegetable garden. But I had planned for that as well, by digging a tunnel beneath it, and covering the entrance with an old potato sack.

My escape was flawless. Brian met me on the other side of my tunnel. The sheets and blue paint were still safely hidden under a root at the tree. We put on the sheets, and applied the paint to faces and other visible body parts. The actual Druid ceremony was a bit anti-climactic (as there weren't any ancient Briton worshippers to appreciate it) but we danced around and chanted. Logistically, I considered it a complete success.

It would have been, if my sister hadn't woken, been frightened by my absence, and howled for help. The reception committee of my mother and the Aunts met me as I lifted the potato sack to re-emerge triumphantly into the vegetable garden, via the tunnel.

There were consequences. Bedtime discipline was reinforced by an extra patrol from Doreen before she went down to the village. The adults had heavy conversations with me about not playing so much with Brian. Instead of fighting Romans I grew a lettuce to exhibit in the village fête. It won a blue First Place ribbon — but as all the prizes were awarded by the vicar, Mr. Dittmar, while the Aunts looked on, my being attached to the daughters of bishops probably had something to do with it. At some point in all this post-Druid dreariness there was the Marmite Elspie episode.

You already know that Elspie's cooking at Barton Olivers One was not inviting. It hadn't improved at Barton Olivers Two. A child of eight made no allowance for the hardships that wartime rationing imposed on any cook. I only resented that Kit Kats and bananas had vanished long ago.

Elspie was preparing some sort of stew for our supper. I knew it would be tasteless, so I simply went into the kitchen and asked her if she could add Marmite to it: "Please."

All hell broke loose.

(Marmite is a dark brown paste, yeast extract. Marmite with anything is to the mass-market British palate what peanut butter is with jelly in North America. Many Canadians find it disgusting; however, it hangs on in places like Victoria. Elspie's cooking needed any help it could get, but in fairness, the rationing shortages didn't make anyone's food preparation easy.)

Ingratitude. Dreadful boy. Village influence. No discipline. Spare the rod. The invocation of Victorian child-rearing practices went on for a week. I was saved by a seagull falling down the kitchen chimney to block the stove.

The seagull was alive. I don't remember who finally managed to wrap it in a tea towel and get it out, but coping with the miraculous seagull emergency took Elspie's mind off Marmite and me.

So I thought; especially as, in a wonderful treat, Aunt Nan arrived for a rare visit from London. She seemed the same to me — my favourite person after my mother — but apparently I struck her as disappointingly different. I had just finished telling her about my Druid ceremony adventure with Brian, including the blue poster paint for our faces, when she said to my mother:

"Good God. What's happened to his voice?"

She didn't mean puberty, six years early: it was my Dorset accent. It had been unwittingly acquired (probably as defence against my earlier "la-di-da" voice, when I called the blacksmith "Sir"). I'm sure that by now I called Brian by his vernacular, "Britch": in the village children's play world we used our first names or nicknames. And perhaps I described our Druid ceremony in dialect as a "girt" one instead of "great," and almost certainly said "she" or "her," as applied to a farm wagon, instead of neutral "it."

My vocal qualities had been observed more favourably, and earlier, by Dorothea, the musical half of the Aunts combination. After my "Lost Highland Lassie" soprano act in exchange for Great Aunt Kythe's ancient Mackenzie kilt, Dorothea had decided that I could be taught to sing properly.

"Doodlie" herself would be my coach, providing accompaniment on the Barton Olivers baby grand. What began with *Good King Wenceslas* had by now worked itself up to *O for the Wings of a Dove*.

Aunt Nan's visit at first seemed to be ending with a super surprise: I was to go back to stay with her in London for a holiday.

The surprise got less super when I discovered that the exciting London holiday would include an audition at St. Paul's Choir School so that I might even have to sing in the cathedral.

This already terrifying prospect wasn't helped by the fact that my arrival, in July, coincided with the arrival of the first V1 "Doodlebug" flying bomb to hit London.

The shock for Londoners was a double whammy. After nearly three years of calm, compared to the nightmare of the full Blitz in 1940-1941, people had been able to sleep in relative peace. Now the Doodlebugs could not only arrive by day or night, you could hear them do it. Their jet engines roared until the moment they didn't. When they stopped ... after five seconds' dread silence ... there was going to be an inevitable, one hell of a bang.

O for the Wings of a Dove

In June 1944, I arrived at Aunt Nan's flat in Harley Street to be told that a Doodlebug had landed in front of it the night before. The explosion had blasted an aluminum coffee pot through a mercifully open window. Astonishingly, the pot was undamaged, and she used it for decades thereafter.

The musical part of my dreaded St. Paul's Choir School audition — more *O for the wings of a dove* — was apparently successful, but I flunked mathematics: something about two trains leaving to go somewhere, and how long if (A) was slower than (B), or stopped for coal at (C), and so on, *ad infinitum*.

To make up for what adults supposed was my huge disappointment in not having to face the terror of singing in St. Paul's Cathedral, Nan presented me with an astonishment: a fabulous replica of world speed record holder Malcolm Campbell's racing car, *Blue Bird*. Nan found it in the street after a Doodlebug bombing, undamaged. It was two feet long and left me speechless.

July in Dorset became August, and fields of golden grain next to the deserted US 1st Army camp began to be harvested slowly by Clydesdales pulling threshing machines. Not only the GIs had left the West of England: Jim and his Royal Marine pals had gone east.

There had been no advance warning, and no word of his destination. The troops guessed (because tropical uniforms were issued) that it meant war in the Far East against Japan.

I had wept on D-Day for losing my G.I. Joe. In the heedless manner of a young child, when Jim left, I was happy. Now I had my mother all to myself. She said to Aunt Nan that she "felt relief at his departure."

She had a lot of other moving things on her mind. Our time with the Aunts had come to its end.

Sammy is Stolen

Not quite. On the day of the paternally truncated Gurr family's unexpected (by me) departure from Barton Olivers Two, Elspie and Dorothea stole Sammy. They didn't call it stealing but there is no other word for it — although a lot of words were exchanged in a furious row with my mother.

As usual, Dorothea was the chief criminal. She claimed that Sammy had never been given to us. He had only been a temporary loan from her sister, Fat Marjorie, who now wanted Sammy back. This outrageous betrayal was being egged on by Great Aunt Hetty with her ear trumpet.

I tried, unsuccessfully, not to cry and said, "That isn't fair." My sister, Angela, threw one of her screaming-till-she-was-blue-in-the-face fits. Neither childish display did any good. Sammy had to stay at Swyre.

With adult hindsight, I might agree that the additional difficulty my mother would have faced in finding accommodation for a pet as well as her children made it logical to leave the pet behind. I wasn't an adult then. For a second time in my young life, a beloved dog had been stolen from me. It was a long time until I let my heart get so close to a dog again.

Victory
or
The Last Straw

Even by Mother's standards the reasons for our moving are vague. She said at the time, "It's just that you need to finally go to a good school."

The "good school" was Sherborne Prep, and certainly I needed a more structured education than Burton Bradstock could provide. But Great Aunt Kythe Mackenzie's "Of course it was so that you would lose your *appalling* Dorset accent" was nearer the mark.

Nearer still, I'm sure, was the maternal extramarital relation with Dickie B. There had been "rows about it" between her and the Aunts: Dorothea's raised tones of "*an American sergeant*" had reached three floors up to the nursery (although it never stopped Elspie from accepting the sergeant's surplus American groceries).

Clearly the overriding pressure on everyone was simply the war. There had already been five years of it, and despite D-Day triumphs, the Far East showed no end in sight.

The three of us "took rooms" in what the Aunts called "an ordinary suburban house" in Sherborne. It was owned by an ordinary suburban couple who had a son about my age.

It had a small, ordinary suburban garden, with some Orange Pippin apple trees and a tree house, and was the place where I first learned to ride a bicycle. The husband taught me — I think he was a teacher — by holding the bike as I pedalled and he ran up and down the road, supporting me.

A Dash of Pedophilia

AND SO TO SHERBORNE PREP. I was only there for two years, a span so short that it always surprises me for the permanence of its impressions. For most boys physical punishment was the main one. For me, it was architecture.

Sherborne Preparatory School ("preparing" eight-to-ten-year-olds like me for the ordeal of entering Big School) circa 1944, was in a large house, grey stone, Virginia-creepered, and had only been there since 1850; nothing to write home about. The Big School at Sherborne had already been humming with male adolescents for four hundred years, and was built accordingly.

The abbey at the heart of the school, and the town, was older still, founded in 1100 *Anno Domini*, give or take a century or two. All those buildings are of local Ham stone, to which great age has given a patina ranging from rust, through bronze, almost to pink, depending how the sun strikes it.

Unforgettable, and so I haven't.

The physical punishment shouldn't be blown out of proportion, although I don't think I ever did anything bad enough to deserve my two bare-bottomed thrashings with a cane. The thrasher was a red-headed Ulsterman called Fred Lindsay.

(His son, Robin, succeeded him as headmaster, and notorious sadist; abusing countless boys from the 1950s until 1998 — when he was declared a "fixated paedophile" by a Tribunal, but never charged. The prep school was then turned into a charitable trust.)

For the first year I attended as a day boy, and we weren't completely separated from our previous Dorset life. Sherborne is only twenty-five miles from Burton Bradstock: I couldn't ride my new bike to it but somehow we went back and forth to Barton Olivers for short holidays, probably by bus.

In October, my mother had the first news of Jim since his departure.

East of the Cape of Good Hope, fate had thrown the dice: his troopship convoy divided in half. One steamed on to Burma, and a fifty percent chance of Royal Marine annihilation; the other half, plus Jim, dropped anchor at Ceylon (now Sri Lanka) where he avoided live ammunition, but in a devilish bargain was struck by malaria, and a mysterious hand-rot, which returned at intervals to make him suffer the rest of his long life.

In the second film that I remember — a Hollywood version of Far East war called *The Story of Dr. Wassell,* starring Gary Cooper — the images of ambushes and amputations without anaesthetic showed the possible battlefield fate he had avoided. For months afterwards I had nightmare reminders of "Butchery by Savage Japs in the Jungle" as advertised by lurid posters outside the cinema.

It isn't possible to convey to a Smart Device Generation — with visual imagery hitting users' eyeballs and metabolisms 24/7 — the impact film had on me then. But before I saw *Dr. Wassell,* and a handful of *Rin-Tin-Tin* silent shorts at school, there had only been

Disney's *Reluctant Dragon* that I was taken to by Jim after baby sister Angela was born.

My third film followed soon after *Dr. Wassell:* it was *Jane Eyre,* with Orson Welles this time, instead of Gary Cooper. It had a nightmarish legacy that was even more pronounced than butchery in the jungle: somehow I got in to see it without my mother. Consequently, when the madwoman with her scissors burst shrieking through the door of her tower prison, I ran screaming from the theatre.

Otherwise, Sherborne life was peaceful. The town — and another small grammar school — had suffered terribly from a random drop of three hundred bombs by the Luftwaffe in September 1940, but mercifully nothing since. I played cricket (badly) and rugby (adequately) as a featherweight scrum half — until a torn cartilage in my left knee, at age ten, came back to haunt me even longer than *Jane Eyre.*

And we had swimming in the nude, for which activity the prepubescent prep minnows shared an outdoor pool with the adolescent giants from the Big School. Because of the war, women had temporarily replaced male staff in many teaching positions. This was fine for English and history, but more awkward for teaching swimming and supervision in the showers.

Our aquatic supervisor was Miss Snow, with her keen eye for male anatomy. That Miss Snow kept her focus on the phallus was made clear when she accused me of peeing in the shower. Because she also taught Latin she used *micturating,* and I'm sure I did — everybody did — but to differentiate my tiny stream from the combined flow required observational power of a high degree.

She honed it at the swimming pool. She would select a nude

minnow to get on her back (she wore a suit) at the top of the slide in the shallow end, then swim with him towards the diving board at the other side, which kept her eyes directly on the newly hairy groins of the Big School adolescents going off their deep end.

Miss Snow repeated the trip with me several times, which may have turned her on; but it was an unheated outdoor pool, in rainy May, in England, and I had to wear coarse wet canvas water-wings against my naked skin.

I didn't learn to swim at Sherborne, either.

Camping in the Mad Professor's Garden

VICTORY IN EUROPE DAY, on May 8th, 1945, lives in my memory because, while the town of Sherborne painted itself red with bunting and Union Jacks, my sister Angela, age three, did the same with lipstick all over our bedroom walls.

We had moved from the bicycle-and-apple-tree house of the jealous suburban wife to the centre of the town and into the home of "the mad professor." I don't know how mad he was, but he had buckteeth and straggling grey hair, and would knock on my mother's bedroom door at all hours to inquire about the heat.

Mama wasn't with us for VE Day because she went up to London to celebrate victory with her sister Nan, and a million others, cheering outside Buckingham Palace. She had managed to get former nanny Doreen to come from Burton Bradstock to babysit. Doreen must have been cheering locally, and didn't see my sister get hold of mother's lipstick to play with.

Sherlock Holmes might have been able to study the enraged scarlet scrawlings, and give us a summation of the criminal motive behind them. I think it was because Angela's usual "blue-in-the-face screaming fits to get attention" never worked with Doreen. The lipstick all over his embossed Victorian wallpaper certainly got the mad professor's attention when he spotted it in one of his landlord's late night checkups after my mother returned.

We didn't get evicted, for which I was glad because I needed the mad professor's back garden to set up a V for Victory camp. Dickie B had given me a US Army pup tent and I had made a friend from school.

His name was Blackman — the village children's friendly usage of first names was left behind with my Dorset accent — and I can't remember what we thought we were going to do with the camp: possibly guarding German prisoners of war, but with only two protagonists that recollection doesn't seem feasible.

Instead, I have my first memory of sleeping outdoors under canvas and the stars. The sky was vast, but the mad professor's back garden could have been fitted ten times into that of either Barton Olivers.

The obvious fact that the war *wasn't* yet over was brought home to us next day in English class. It was taught by Mrs. MacDonald, the only teacher I remember liking in my first half-dozen school years. The day was sunny, we were having an outdoor rehearsal for a play, *The Wind in the Willows*, and I was doing Badger. Some boy got carried away and shouted something triumphal about VE Day.

"Not for those of us with their people fighting in the Far East theatre," Mrs. MacDonald said. "Isn't that right, Gurr?"

This put me in a quandary. While I was delighted to be tarred with a brush of heroism at a safe distance, I was even more delighted at Jim's absence; which, unreasonably, and despicably, I hoped would never end.

"Badger" was my second trip on the boards (my first named part) but I spent three-quarters of the play lying underneath a ground-sheet covered with leaves, before I emerged to say something to Toad, in a grumpy voice, which the rest of the class seemed to enjoy.

My voice brings us to the centrepiece of the town of Sherborne: its abbey.

I thought it was my warbling all the *ah-ah-ahs* for the carol "Gloria in Excelsis Deo" — while wearing a yellow paper crown at the school Christmas concert — that caught the abbey choirmaster's ear, but it might have been the Aunts telling him that I was a St. Paul's Cathedral reject. Either way, becoming a soloist involved a lot of practice, which allowed me to absorb unconsciously the magnificence of the abbey's architecture.

The centre of my conscious attention and that of the other choirboys was the tomb of the two king Æthels — in Latin class their "ae" combination was drawn to our attention "as an example of a ligature." (They were two of the five sons of Æthelwurf, King of Wessex. The name of one of the two sons ended in *bald,* and the other one in *bert;* and whichever Æthels they were, they lay under a green, bottle-glass cover, set into the floor, that we had to walk over to get to the choir stall. When the angle from sunlight was at a certain point, it would strike the green glass, and we'd peer down hoping to see an Æthel skull. We never did.)

Getting back to the war:

It ended. Jim returned, and I was tossed into Pilgrim's Dungeon of Giant Despair, otherwise known as boarding school.

"You Have to Allow for Rationing."

The clichés of that English boyhood imprisonment all happened: the occasional undeserved thrashing; the water in dormitory washbasins being frozen in the morning; the flannel shirts that scratched like barbed wire; "Frenching" a bed with the sheets halfway down so that you couldn't get into it ... all these proven ways of strengthening boyish character were applied — but I blamed my boarding misery on the meals.

The food was vile.

Powdered eggs, with water added, were called "scrambled." Mutton, from a sheep that had died of old age, then been boiled, was called "lamb." Complaints to parents by letter invariably received the reply, "You have to allow for rationing." Allowing for it didn't make it taste any better. "Tuck boxes" of treats from home, like cakes or chocolates, which might have helped before the war, didn't now, because they were also rationed to extinction.

My transition from day boy to boarder began after VJ Day.

"The Jap says uncle to Uncle Sam" was the caption in one crude cartoon. It was celebrated by the three of us in a trip to West Bay (at the *Broadchurch* end of the Barton Olivers cliff), where the fishermen's boats were decorated with flags and we got free rides.

The Second World War really had ended.

Through that historic autumn of 1945, from Monday to Thursday I slept in the school dormitory, which still had its frozen washbasin and other unpleasantnesses, but at least I knew I could go home to rejoin my mother on Friday.

On the four nights that I was imprisoned, I regret to admit that, in order to remove attention from my own shortcomings, I joined in bullying someone else because he had a funny surname: Pine-Coffin.

Somehow, I had acquired a tiny China dog that was covered in luminous (radioactive) paint, and so could glow in the dark. We used the glowing radioactive dog to terrify Pine-Coffin. Even worse, in daylight I made friends with him so that I could be taken out on weekend joyrides in his father's zippy sports car.

Jim returned from Ceylon in time for my tenth birthday. He took my mother away to London, leaving me in despair, seven days a week, and seven nights a week without her bedtime kiss, for endless months.

The conditions of my eventual release are vague. There were some end-of-term holiday reunion trips by train to London — in a first-class compartment, but unescorted by an adult: not something that many parents would permit today. When I came back to school I refused to eat ... which at first led to a thrashing ... but later into the solarium, under the care of Matron ... and finally, on doctor's orders, to where we came in:

The bosom of my family, near Boundary Road.

Horsemeat for a Honey Bee

Old Mrs. Fairlambe's 30 Ferme Park Road, adjacent to the Alexandra Palace — "Birthplace of Television" and where I walked Honey Bee, a golden cocker spaniel — was a better accommodation than the mad professor's, but only just. In bombed-out London, 1946, as old Mrs. Fairlambe relayed through her daughter, young Miss Fairlambe, many times a week: "With our gas bill, remind them they're lucky to get it."

A third-floor attic: microscopic kitchen with a gas stove (no fridge); combined living-dining, perhaps ten feet square; parents' bedroom the same; something left over for my sister and myself. No bath or toilet *en suite:* for those functions we descended a long flight of unlit stairs to a gloomy landing. The toilet had a clanking chain. The bath was heated by a gas geyser that devoured shillings, kept track of minutely by young Miss Fairlambe for her mother's accounts book.

Old Mrs. Fairlambe was only a voice, thinly antique, with a Cockney base inadequately disguised by a middle-class emphasis on pronouncing the letter "h" — which always dropped off under stress.

I never saw her until *she* dropped off.

THE FIRST DEAD BODY that I ever saw was Old Mrs. Fairlambe's and she was lying on the kitchen table. The news of her position was given to us by young Miss Fairlambe, who always wore black anyway and looked like the Wicked Witch in *The Wizard of Oz.*

Old Mrs. Fairlambe kept well, because it was December 1946, described in *Daily Mail* headlines as "The Coldest Winter of the Century."

Fleet Street hyperbole, but cold enough that we had to stand in the road to collect water from a single hydrant — insulated, presumably — and carry it back to our third-floor flat in jugs. The frozen soil of north London also delayed the removal of old Mrs. Fairlambe from the kitchen table for a week. Mercifully, young Miss Fairlambe kept the door to the hall closed most of the time, while leaving the kitchen window open to maintain the required refrigeration.

London meant another new school. University College School, UCS to its inhabitants, was very new — compared to Sherborne. It had been founded in 1830 by Jeremy Bentham, philosopher, reformer, but known to us schoolboys only for having himself stuffed.

The colours on my new school cap were maroon and black. The architecture and landscaping matched it — red brick, black iron fence, strips of grass and squares of more black with asphalt. They were nothing to write home about, but thank God, now I didn't have to. The daily journey from home near Finsbury Park to the western side of Hampstead Heath was five miles, and I made it by bus, London double-decker, not escorted by an adult.

I was never thrashed by my new headmaster, Mr. Vogel: called "bird brain" by boys behind his gowned back. The only other teaching name I remember — "Dixie Dean, the Fairy Queen" — didn't deserve it. Mr. Dean taught English well, and took us to *Puss and Boots* (a pantomime).

This was my fourth school in five years: by the end of one more year, I had somehow picked up a smattering of algebra and geometry, geography and history (ancient and modern), and the same with languages: Greek and Latin, French and German.

I suppose you could use that word — a smattering — about sports. If we add the word "competitive" ... it takes us back to a Parents' Day at Sherborne. Jim was in civilian clothes, so it must have been after his return from the Marines. He wanted to show off his son (D.H.C. Gurr on my name tapes) as he had to his Bond Street tailor and barber before the war. There was a team race, either sack or egg-and-spoon. Whatever its category: my friend Blackman and I came in dead last. Jim felt it as a personal reflection, turned his back on us, and walked away in mortification and disgust.

Which unfortunate reminder subjects me into reliving a truly disgusting moment that almost put me off running for ever. It was a cross-country hare-and-hounds, following a marked trail through Hampstead Heath. My gastrointestinal system had been upset from the moment of Jim's return. Halfway across the heath it gave way altogether, coating my white shorts and bare legs — I will spare us the rest.

I got back to the school, was washed, and later taken to a specialist at St. Thomas' Hospital, who gave me a green-labelled bottle with a vile-tasting medicine that helped with the problem on future occasions — which always coincided with Jim's return from his Hygrade gowns-and-knickers-selling trips. His old job as sales manager for Hygrade, at Leicester, had been kept for him, and "strings got pulled" hard enough to get him — and therefore us — an extremely rare, new postwar car. Rationing of everything was still acute: I would be sent to hold a place in a queue, sometimes for whale meat (for our supper: it tasted horrible), sometimes for horse.

It lay in great slabs, with slimy streaks of green and purple, dotted with flies; just to look at it made me feel ill. The horse slabs were labelled not for human consumption, but the warning was ignored by many people. I stood in line for hours to buy the horsemeat because we had acquired a third beloved dog.

She was a golden cocker spaniel with an illustrious pedigreed name, but Jim decided that she would be called Honey Bee. I walked her in Alexandra Palace Park and liked her for her glossy coat, but never let myself love her as I had Sammy or dognapped Scotty.

I was at UCS long enough to have another friend. His name was Rau — but I didn't realize at the time that Rau was Jewish, or that a majority of the students were Jewish, and the staff, like Mr.

Vogel. Forty years later Tom Rosenthal, my publisher at André Deutsch Ltd., was astonished at my ignorance. "UCS is the Jewish answer to being kept out of the Public Schools. Everybody knows."

(In the UK, what "everybody knows" is that these famous "Public Schools" are the most private of all.)

So MUCH TO LEARN. Rau's father was an eminent ornithologist, but I knew only that he was somehow in charge of birds at the London Zoo, which meant that he could give me wonderful feathers for my Indian headdress collection.

We went to the zoo once with Jim and his brother, Uncle Reg, and thanks to Rau's father, got a view of the aviary backstage. To my delight, a parrot — once again it was a white cockatoo, like Great Aunt Hetty's — flew at Jim and began to savage his Bond Street tie. I laughed. Jim fumed. Uncle Reg chuckled and puffed on his pipe.

Speaking of fumes and Ferme Park Road: we also lived through one of London's killer pea-soup fogs. About fifty yards from our house there was a small corner shop which sold Dinky Toys and Player's cigarette cards. I used to walk past it on my way to and from the double-decker bus for school. Coming home at about five o'clock one November evening, I took a moment to look at the toys in the window, and when I turned to leave, realized I didn't know where I was.

A gaslight — and yes, the street was still lit by a man touching lamps, using a flame on a stick — only a few feet above my head was barely a yellowish blur. I don't know how I found my way across the street to get home: it was probably from bumping into the red pillar box at the corner, then counting the number of house gates to our door.

Memory is its own fog.

Somewhere in this time interval, there was a bizarre juxtaposition between my seeing *The Wizard of Oz* and the newsreels from Auschwitz and Belsen. I wasn't supposed to see them. When the first horrific images were printed in the newspapers, Jim made a point of keeping them from me. I only saw those scenes of bulldozers pushing emaciated bodies into graves because my parents had forgotten that newsreels would be shown before the main feature of the Munchkins dancing with Dorothy along their yellow brick road.

Wartime newsreels would get audience participation: cheers for battles and Winston Churchill. The images of heaped stick-figures being bulldozed in the death camp got gasps and sobs from the adults around me. I closed my eyes, but the dead people tumbling in their striped pyjamas stayed in my head.

An Amalgam of Squirrel Nutkin and Just William

For Christmas 1946, we had a small relief from battered London, and went for the holiday to a first cousin of my mother's, Anne Jackson, somewhere deep in the Surrey "stockbroker belt."

Cousin Anne had married a stockbroker; consequently they had a pleasant stockbroker house, a bit like a smaller Barton Olivers One, with comforting woodwork and furniture, and a large snow-covered garden. To my surprise, the Jacksons had gone on a stockbroker's skiing holiday, which meant that we had the house to ourselves. They had left us a Christmas tree. I don't remember any of the presents. There was a piano, but as Jim performed best for a group, our Surrey family Christmas was subdued.

We got back to Ferme Park Road to find that while everything else in London was deep-frozen, a black market turkey which Jim had managed — "strings got pulled" — to get sent from Ireland had been left unrefrigerated too long, and had thus decomposed. The stink in our unventilated flat lingered for weeks.

A WONDER OF CHILDHOOD is how children make do. In lieu of walled gardens or visits to castles, I turned a large wicker armchair upside down, covered it with a sheet, and it became an Arabian Nights tent for my sister and me to play in. With my Meccano set I built more interesting things, like cranes and tanks.

(War machinery prompts me to add a schoolboy's view of bomb damage as a playground. While I was at UCS, bombed Hampstead — a nightmare minefield to parents — for Rau and I was a Treasure Island of ruined deserted ballrooms, staircases, and garden solariums to explore. It appalls me now, but we particularly liked knocking down ancient brick walls and breaking Victorian greenhouse glass.)

Bedtime at Ferme Park Road gives the only hint that I might eventually have a narrative streak. I began to construct serialized stories in my head, to tell them aloud to Angela every night. They were a derivative and predictable mix of woodland animals and venues plagiarized from Beatrix Potter, Enid Blyton *et al.* — but they did the trick and put her to sleep.

Then I had to put myself to sleep. After I had finished telling Angela about a flying creature who was an amalgam of Squirrel Nutkin and Just William (both my special heroes) in its misbehaviour, I would remind myself of the Barton Olivers nursery ceiling with its stars and crescent moon. And I would conjure up an image of my mother bending over us, with the dark waves of her hair like Veronica Lake's — but looking like that *before* Veronica Lake did it herself — to croon a lullaby, or assure me that she "wouldn't be gone long," on a date with whichever uniformed bee happened to be buzzing her at the time.

I conveniently blanked out the memories of how suddenly cold my mother's manner could become if I clung to her neck for too long. She would push me away and say "That's enough for this one."

Her on-and-off behaviour was a legacy from being orphaned, and thus deprived of displays of affection herself. She continued calling me "this one" in front of other people to the end of her life. I loved her nonetheless.

"The Great Hereafter"

Our last summer in England — though no-one in the Gurr family had the slightest inkling of such a finality yet. This is somewhat surprising, given the magnitude of their next transatlantic step.

After the record-breaking frosts that had kept old Mrs. Fairlambe for a week on her kitchen table, the summer of 1947 became unusually hot for the British Isles. The public swimming pools in London were overcrowded, and infantile paralysis (polio) justifiably frightened parents. I was forbidden to attend.

For another summer season I didn't learn to swim.

Instead we went to the heart of Hygrade Lingerie, in Leicester, to attend a séance. The firm was owned by a no-nonsense man called John King. His wife was the believer in nonsense — or "the Great Hereafter" as she called it, having "lost a loved one in the Great War."

How I came to be included in the experience is equally beyond logical explanation. I remember a dim Victorian room with a table draped with a velvet-tasselled cloth, and some kind of glowing lamp in the centre. Nobody interesting showed up, and Mrs. King said: "Sometimes they are very difficult." John King gave me a half-crown tip for "enduring everything."

Following the Great Hereafter we went south: the Aunts' holiday territory. But this time we stayed with another formidable woman.

Gushy's Green Bum

Her name was short for Mrs. Gushworth, perhaps a widow, though her marital details were vague, and she had a cottage for rent at West Bay. Gushy had an ample figure, maternal manner, and deeply Dorset accent.

On our arrival, she broke the ice by showing us the toilet. It was in its own small stone outhouse and the seat had just been repainted, gloss-green enamel.

"Especially for youm', my dear," as she told me the next day, between gushes of laughter. "Do be doing 'er myself, my dear, I was, and bless me if I didn't forget and plunk me down on 'er before 'er was dry. Me durn bum was green for a week."

The cottage had no electricity, so we had to read and go to bed by candlelight: its lack of modernity, and Gushy's dialect, really did put us back in Thomas Hardy's world. More wonderfully for me, West Bay still had a working railway.

The station was right beside the cottage, and once a day a tiny steam engine would puff and chuff its way to a halt, before the final bump from buffers at the end of the line. Of course the engine driver knew Gushy, and on a few magical occasions he let me into his cab to pull levers and turn control wheels for the two-mile run to Bridport and back.

Sex first reared its head in West Bay.

An older local boy said he had something to show me in a machine gun pillbox halfway up the cliff. We reached it by following a sheep track marked by their droppings, to find that the machine gun was gone, replaced by a stinking recent heap of human shit. What he wanted to show me became the first time I saw a human erection.

At UCS, after showers, boys of all stages of development would leap into a communal hot-water bath, where mock battles took place between Cavaliers (uncircumcised) and Roundheads (the other kind, like me) — but these phallic standoffs never led to anything rampantly red, and aggressive like this. There was an unsuccessful attempt at coercion "to do something" in the machine gun emplacement. It had a threatening overtone that stayed with me, but "nothing happened" and I left quickly.

I didn't tell my parents about what didn't happen in the machine gun pillbox. Instead, I got a surprise invitation to stay with Great Aunt Kythe for two weeks in Cornwall. I hopped on a proper — that is Great Western — train, and travelled unescorted, one hundred miles west across two counties.

The Snipe

Kythe Mackenzie was one of those extraordinary women who, for better or worse, allowed the British Empire to exist. She had either worked for, or known, or had unacknowledged sexual relations with (or all of that at once) a list of names that included Lord Haldane, Ivor Novello and Edwina Mountbatten — the last Vicereine of India. There were others too but, in the one act of my mother's that I cannot forgive, on Kythe's death she burned all her letters and thus a trove of historical fascination.

In the late summer of 1947, Kythe was living with a friend called Wynn Roberts, who owned a property somewhere on the south coast of Cornwall. It was close enough to the sea that I could walk to a sandy beach. We could also drive to Tintagel, on the north coast, and back in a day.

When my train arrived at Plymouth I was met by them both — because Kythe couldn't drive — and went off with Wynn at the wheel of her car (some kind of convertible with the top down) to her home. It had a Cornish name: a very pleasant Georgian house, painted white, on a slight slope facing south, with "one or two hundred" acres surrounding it. There was a cowshed for some Jersey cows, and a stable, but no horses at that moment.

For me, the most interesting building was a small summerhouse (that didn't rotate) now only being used for the storage of miscellaneous objects: striped croquet mallets and balls, archery bows and arrows, straw bull's-eye targets, and leftover taxidermed birds in glass cases.

I use "leftover" because the main collection of glass-cased birds was in the house: pheasant, partridge, and several kinds of duck (Wynn Roberts never added the letter "s" for the plural of any game). But the creature I instantly fell in love with was a stuffed badger. It lived at the top of three shallow stairs leading from a central hall to a lower sunroom. Whenever I had occasion to pass it I would sit down beside the badger and pat its striped black-and-white head.

During the day I watched an old farmhand milk the Jersey cows, and then helped him carry the pails to the dairy. Most of the milk was sold, but some was kept to make clotted Cornish cream for the house.

Wynn Roberts made the cream herself. The milk was first poured into a wide enamelled pan, perhaps eighteen inches across; it rested in a larder, then was put on an old cast iron stove and heated gently. As the curds formed on top, they turned a dark crusted yellow, then were skimmed off and put in jars.

I had never tasted anything so delicious. On my first evening in Cornwall I ate so much clotted cream that I violently threw it up. Kythe was annoyed, Wynn Roberts was amused.

In and around all these Celtic Cornish experiences, Kythe mixed her own fact and fiction by showing me a Mackenzie of Gairloch family tree. It started with the Earls of Ross and Cromarty, and meandered through various levels of butchery, piracy and lechery via Robert the Bruce to names inked in at the end, after her own name, by Kythe.

"So, as you can see, you are descended from Blood Royal."

I couldn't see it, but I loved the idea. And as a Cornish parting gift, Wynn Roberts gave me — as I couldn't take the badger — what I had most coveted in her summerhouse: a snipe, in a glass case.

On the long train ride back to London I wasn't looking forward to the autumn term at UCS, until, on arrival at Paddington station, my glum mood was brightened by momentous news:

The Gurr family was going to build a house.

The Green Belt and Cleopatra

Apparently, Elspea and Dorothea owned a piece of property in Sussex: part of a subdivision that had already received planning permission for houses to be built on it. They had once thought they might eventually "need to be in something smaller than Barton Olivers." Now they had changed their minds and decided, with remarkable generosity, to give the land to us. An architect had already been commissioned to sketch out a bungalow.

Plans of the house were laid out on the kitchen table at Ferme Park Road — ours, not Mrs. Fairlambe's. More than seven decades later, I can still see the drawings in my head. Some bits were shaded pink, others green, with details for a chimney, and shrubs dotted around.

We were all ecstatic. The rest of London, and the nation, had also worked itself into that emotional state in anticipation of the Royal Wedding. Preparations for the two great events went hand in hand, and then ...

Ours went belly up.

The new Labour government (which I felt had unfairly kicked out Winston Churchill) decreed that the land for the Gurrs' dream house would become part of a protected "green belt" to preserve the countryside from urban sprawl. Nothing could be constructed there.

As Jim put it for the rest of his life: "This was the last straw."

The Wedding was booked for November 20th in Westminster Abbey. The day after, Jim announced we had tickets for Canada.

Goodbye to Aunt Nan

Liverpool was endless herrings and occasional treats of meringues, accompanied by a diet of endless December rain.

For three weeks, while we waited to take passage, we really did eat herrings almost every night with grey, still rationed bread and margarine, because there seemed nothing else that my parents' ration book could obtain.

We — my mother, Jim, Angela and Honey Bee — had two rooms. Accommodation was very scarce; the Blitz of Liverpool's dockland had been as bad as London's.

Nan arrived from London for the last few days. We said our goodbyes at the foot of a gangplank. I hugged her. Everybody wept.

We boarded the *Empress of Canada* and entered a new world.

Empress to Empress
or
A Canadian Pacific Odyssey

THE BREAD WAS WHITE. It seemed so unfair. It arrived as we sat down for our first meal aboard the *Empress of Canada* and the sight of it caused a profound shock. We hadn't realized how unlike real bread the grey cardboard we had got used to was. From an eleven-year-old's perspective, that length of wartime had been my whole life.

And after the bread came real food, with real taste: oranges, roast beef, anything we wanted. As I looked out of that thick glass window of the *Empress'* dining room, I realized, with an almost mature consciousness, on one side of the glass was the grey-bread reality of postwar England; on our side, we were already in Canada.

But Aunt Nan was on that other side.

As the *Empress* cast off — first her mooring lines, then her tugs — and finally began to move under her own great turbines into the stream of the Mersey River, Nan's waving figure receded into the wet twilight of Liverpool. There was no way of knowing when, or even if, we would meet again.

Milking Experience Preferred

Honey Bee yanked me physically back to the here and now. Pet animals were kept in a special part of the ship, where our spaniel had her own custom-made kennel- cum-travelling cage, and several times a day she needed to be taken for a walk. Our first one, that evening, was smooth sailing; next morning, it wasn't.

The Mersey and the Irish Sea were behind us, and the North Atlantic in December was heaving all around us. The unique smell of flying salt and half-burnt fuel managed to be everywhere, and added to the action of twenty thousand tons of metal being tossed in three directions simultaneously — the *Empress* had no stabilizers — it made me feel most unwell.

It took about thirty-six hours to find my sea legs for the first time; my mother about the same; Jim and Angela much longer. The North Atlantic weather was so rough that my mother almost had her arm broken when a chair in the dining room snapped its holding chain and crashed across the cabin, carrying her with it. She spent the rest of the voyage with her arm in a sling.

(I would eventually find myself in the Gulf of Alaska, in another midwinter, in a hurricane, by which time I had read Melville and Conrad. After writers of their calibre I can't add anything profound about the authority of the sea. Like the cosmos, it exists; like the wind, it changes its mind; when it gets up on its high white horses, human beings can only say their prayers and hang on tight.)

On the fifth day, I sighted land. Jim's piano-playing skill had returned when he got over his seasickness, and he persuaded the captain into allowing me to blow the foghorn for this hugely exciting occasion. My sighting was the southern tip of Newfoundland, and it looked cold.

So did Halifax the next morning. I have a vague impression of a large cold shed. The next thing of interest for me was a train.

The longest time I had spent on a train until now was the overnight ride with Jim and the soldiers on our escape from blitzed London to Barton Olivers One. This first leg of our Canadian Pacific Railway adventure took almost twenty-four hours just to get us to Montreal.

About one-third of that time was daylight, and all we could see was snow. When we arrived at Montreal, Jim took us to a large department store and bought us all fleece-lined, knee-length leather boots, to keep out the snow. Then we took a horse-drawn sleigh ride, and then we got back on the CPR train for another half-day of snow which ended at Toronto.

So far so good (and cold). Apparently the Gurr family had changed worlds so that Jim could sell wool, instead of lingerie, for the firm of Patons and Baldwins. At that time P&B was still very big in everything to do with knitting, not just in the British Empire but worldwide, and Jim had a personal introduction from either a Paton (the name behind the Paton's Rose knitting pattern) or a Baldwin (ditto of the Baldwin's Beehive).

I grasped little of this at the time. (The explanation from my mother lay fifty years ahead.) My Toronto memory was of us all inexplicably standing on a sidewalk — we called it a "pavement" — wearing our sheepskin leather boots outside a house, being screamed at by a woman that we were "all bloody well locked out" for being "goddamn Limeys" and "not getting your damn deposit money back either."

Then a kind Toronto policeman arrived. Our mother explained

that we had paid the screaming landlady a week in advance for our room while Jim looked for a new job on a dairy farm. The kind Toronto policeman told the screaming landlady that he was on our side about the money, which made her give it back to us.

I hadn't realized that we were going to a dairy farm. More astonishingly: nor had Jim — until *after* not getting the anticipated sinecure with Patons and Baldwins. Instead, he found a card tacked up in a federal government office in Toronto.

Employment Opportunities in British Columbia
Dairy farm in Duncan: Milking experience preferred

With his knicker salesman's glib gift of the gab he informed the employment opportunities people that he had "grown up as a skilled dairy farm boy in Wales": this, plus a postwar government preference for British subjects as immigrants got him the job.

Those same British subjects "getting first crack at scarce jobs" was the cause of our Toronto landlady's diatribe against all "goddamn Limeys," and why she locked us out on the street.

A Happy Canadian New Year

We went back on the train for Christmas. This immense stretch of our Canadian Pacific odyssey took five days and four nights. Our parents somehow managed to find presents that were uniquely North American.

One was some kind of purple or red liquid plastic that you could blow through a straw to make balloon bubbles that floated, or stuck with static to the seat upholstery, until they popped; also a Slinky, which really needed stairs for its effect; and Lifesavers — "candy," not "sweets" — in a Sweet Story container that looked like a closed book, and held a dozen assorted flavors (I hated Wint-O-Green). And finally, pick-up sticks (which were never designed for playing on a moving platform).

And, best of all, comics. Incredible North American comics. *Superman* and *Captain Marvel* made *The Adventures of Rupert Bear* seem back-to-the-nursery stuff.

If there were other families with children on board, we didn't meet them. The conductor and porters made a fuss over us. Jim was his usual life-of-the-party in the club car, dropping names and making acquaintances with "big fish in business."

We got out at Winnipeg to have our pictures taken (wearing our sheepskin leather boots) in front of an old-fashioned steam engine, with a "cow catcher" on its front; then back on board for two days across a snow desert that the conductor showed us, from a CPR map, was the prairies.

In the middle of one of the prairie provinces, I was standing out on the platform at the back of the observation car when I saw a solitary man dressed all in black sitting forlornly on a cart, without a horse. The conductor said: "That's an Indian."

My first sight of one of North America's original inhabitants and landowners looked sad: nothing like the people in Westerns who wore headdresses like the one my mother had made for me from pheasant feathers.

Which brings us to our luggage: We had brought almost nothing.

We had no household effects except a small oak end-table (which somehow arrived in Canada two months late). For myself, my Meccano set — for a surprise going-away present Wally West, Jim's trumpeter pal from the Marines, had made me a beautiful wooden box with a hinged lid to hold it all — and the pheasant headdress, my Arthur Ransome and Doctor Doolittle books, my Museum of Natural History postcards of birds and animals, plus, happily, Panda and Rabbit — but not, sadly, my Blue Bird car, nor the taxidermied snipe in its glass case.

We left the sadness of the Indian on the prairies for the heart of the Rockies at Banff. The only mountain I had seen until then was on a postcard of the Matterhorn sent to me from Zermatt by Nan when she took a Swiss skiing holiday in 1946.

The rock massifs surrounding Banff were the real thing, "and then some" (a new Canadian phrase). The conductor told us that we had to wait at Banff because the snow in the Kicking Horse Pass was so deep that we needed a third belching steam behemoth added on to pull us through it. Unfortunately most of that dramatic crossing of the Great Divide happened at night, so we saw little of it.

The next morning we saw the Pacific. At least, I thought it was: in fact, we were looking at Burrard Inlet and Vancouver harbour, where we climbed down from our CPR train and took passage on our penultimate part of that transportation empire: a CPR ferry called the *Princess Kathleen,* which was to take us out of the inlet and seventy nautical miles across the Strait of Georgia, to Victoria on Vancouver Island.

(That way of getting from Vancouver to Victoria was the best there has ever been. As described at length in the CPR brochure: "Passengers will stroll from the Heart of Business in Vancouver, to board at their leisure, at 10 o'clock in the evening, to sleep in a luxurious cabin between clean sheets, and wake in the morning to find themselves served a full breakfast in the Dining Room, with Crisp

Tablecloth, Silver, and China, then stroll ashore at 9 o'clock to find themselves conveniently in the Heart of Business and Government in the Provincial Capital of Victoria.")

I WISH I COULD DESCRIBE OUR "CONVENIENT ARRIVAL" on December 31st, 1947, and what I thought of the imposingly capitalized "Provincial Capital," but I can't. Too much was happening and we hadn't stopped travelling. We got off the CPR's *Princess Kathleen* only to get on yet another CPR branch line called the Esquimalt and Nanaimo Railway: E&N for short.

We really were on our last leg — in both senses. I do remember that this E&N train was still hauled by steam (the final steam run on Vancouver Island was in 1949) and the seats in the single carriage were upholstered in wicker. The journey north on Vancouver Island took about one hour, but because it was dark, once again we couldn't see the scenery.

The station at Duncan seemed tiny — not even as large as the one at West Bay — and it was cold; light snow mixed with rain. Some people introduced themselves but that information didn't sink in. There was adult discussion. At the end of it we stayed for New Year's Eve, and its night, at the adjacent Tzouhalem Hotel. Even the noise of some Duncan residents celebrating the eve in the Tzouhalem's "beer parlour" (the Canadian for pub) directly underneath us couldn't keep me awake.

In the morning the snow had become torrential rain but to celebrate New Year's Day, the Gurr family ate a week's worth of English rationing for a Canadian breakfast, put on our sheepskin boots and then, with great excitement, climbed into a Canadian car large enough to take all of us to our first Canadian home.

A Near-Death Experience

It was called Margetts' Farm because its owner was Captain Margetts (Canadian Army, retired) who insisted on being addressed by his title and so I never remembered his first name.

His wife and co-owner (as we later discovered, "the farm was mainly her money"), was Mrs. Margetts, who said to my mother, "Just call me Gwen." They had a son my age, Peter Margetts, with blond hair and a pudgy face, who didn't say to call him anything. The grownups said that after we were settled in, "Peter will show you the ropes," whatever that meant.

The Margetts owned (jointly) one hundred acres of cleared, south-sloping land, adjoining Lakes Road to the east. What was described on the local Duncan map as "a small creek" ran across the southern boundary. When I first saw it, in still torrential, Duncan-January rain, the small creek was running bigger than Burton Bradstock's River Bride in full flood.

The Margetts family lived in a comfortable house at the top, northern end of the property. It was a white exterior mixture of stucco and wooden siding, one-and-a-half storeys, with a cedar-shake roof and basement half below grade, typical of both the era and the area, although of course I didn't know that at the time. It seemed a pleasant place for us all to inhabit, if a bit crowded for two families.

"You will be in the cottage," said Captain Margetts. "Peter will show you the ropes down there. I have to start the milking."

Peter Margetts led us — wearing our squelching, sodden, sheepskin boots (built to keep out only frozen water) — as we carried our suitcases downhill along an equally rain-soaked path which flattened out at a small orchard, slightly flooded. The few trees were leafless. A small unpainted wooden building with a sagging roofline sat among them.

Peter Margetts said: "The cottage. That's it."

"It" had a tiny porch, which allowed us to put down our suitcases and get out of the endless Duncan rain. The front door from the porch opened directly into a minuscule kitchen containing an old cast iron coalstove, and no other appliances.

The design of the cottage was a backwards L shape. The small bit was to the left of the stove, and had only one room. It was not more than six feet square, and had a single window divided into four small panes. There was also a twinned bunk bed, but only the bottom part had a mattress. One of the window panes had a pellet hole through it.

"This is your room," Peter Margetts informed me, before pointing at the pellet hole. "I did that with my BB gun. I guess it was a mistake."

Off the kitchen towards the long part of the L shape was a combination dining and living space, perhaps ten feet wide and fifteen feet long. Beyond this area was a bedroom for our parents, with two single beds and, just outside their door, a cot for Angela.

We were one hygienic step up from Gushy's cottage in West Bay: there was inside plumbing. As an architectural afterthought, a miniature bathroom had been attached to the wall behind the coal stove; the latter heated water for an improvised bathtub arrangement partly sunk into the floor. The old iron coal stove provided the only warmth in the cottage because there was no fireplace. In one other modern improvement over the peasant world of Gushy's Dorset, there was electricity, which meant we could listen to the wireless — now called the radio.

As New Year's Day was a Thursday, we had a long weekend to settle into this cramped arrangement. The deluge of Duncan rain continued on Friday and into Saturday morning, at which point Vancouver Island's temperate climate switched abruptly to what the CBC radio announcer called "an Arctic outflow."

Everything froze up — including our sodden sheepskin boots; which meant that we couldn't wear them when we needed them. On Saturday night the temperature dropped to zero Fahrenheit. To try and keep us warm as we slept, Jim put extra coal in the stove.

At some point I woke up because I felt cold. And then I felt strange, but I can't describe the strangeness. I got out of my bunk bed to go and find my mother. My legs wobbled when I walked and I didn't know where any light switches were located, but somehow I got past the stove — which gave off some small light because it was still burning — and through the dark living area beyond it.

Honey Bee was asleep on her cushion in a corner of the kitchen. I patted her head. She didn't stir. Angela still seemed to be sleeping in her cot. I shook her to ask if she felt strange too.

She wouldn't wake up. My parents' bedroom door was open. They were both still asleep and Jim's bed was the nearest one. I shook him but he wouldn't wake up either.

I shook my mother and at first I thought — I don't know what I thought by then. Certainly fear, almost panic. Thank God, she *did* wake up.

Sort of.

She was groggy and wobbly in the same way that I was. She couldn't wake Jim either. Instead, she picked up Angela and holding her in her arms, with me following, carrying Honey Bee, we went up the now-frozen path to the main house, to get help.

It was pitch dark and we had to hammer on the front door for what seemed to be quite a long time before anyone opened it. I think it was Gwen Margetts but the rest of what passed into maternal legend as "the Jim recovery operation" was for me what they call a blur.

The cause of our near-death experience, you will have realized, was carbon monoxide poisoning, and people called our escape miraculous. In fact, both halves of the equation were due to poor maintenance. The monoxide gas got out of the old stove because it had a crack in the side. I got out of my room because of Peter Margetts' "mistake": the BB pellet hole in the window that hadn't been repaired let in just enough fresh air to keep me alive.

To assign life and death to building maintenance is flippant. That a hole in the glass, no wider in diameter than the thickness of a Ritz cracker, should have been present in that pane of glass, and that the pane was in my bedroom, beside my bed, not in the kitchen, and that the opening in the glass was sufficient to let me wake up ...

In my book that chain of circumstance was a miracle.

Going to School and the Movies in Duncan

It was my fifth school: roughly one a year since the unhappy toilet inexperience of a urinal at Monmouth Grammar. This time it was called St. Ann's School for Boys and, as you may guess from the name, run by nuns.

Dear Reader, by this time it should come as no surprise to you that, given my Church of England religious footing by Sherborne and the daughters of bishops, I was as ignorant of Roman Catholics as I had been of Jews. (When the Sherborne Big School rugby team played away, against the Catholic Downside School, Sherborne's headmaster — who had taken holy orders himself — cheered his rugby boys on with the cry: "Lose to the Papists — don't come back!")

St. Ann's didn't have a rugby team and had, instead of a headmaster, something far more formidable: a Mother Superior. I had never seen one (nor an ordinary nun for that matter), but the starch of her headdress was a pale shadow of her icy personality.

I was under her tutelage because the Margetts were Catholics and Peter Margetts went to the school. I only went to half of it because when they said prayers any non-Catholic, like me, was left outside. I don't remember having anyone else beside me on those many-times-daily occasions of endless, muffled Hail Marys sounding through the solid closed door.

During those long, cold, usually rainy intervals, sitting on a damp wooden bench, a sense of dislocation and loneliness that I never expressed to anyone came to keep me miserable company. Looking back, in general, Canada was clearly good for me. The stomach upsets — like that ghastly time on Hampstead Heath, which needed gulps of a foul-tasting medicine to settle — completely stopped. But so much was not quite the way it had been; and the arrival of books for my birthday from Aunt Nan made me miss her a lot.

More happily, I got a new CCM bicycle from my parents, which let me escape my Catholic education and head into Duncan — where we can glimpse what it was when I rode "downtown" in 1948.

THE RAILWAY LINE and the Tzouhalem Hotel with its beer parlour patrons you already know about. There was a grocer's shop with the strange name Overwaitea (the grocer had an advertising gimmick of selling eighteen ounces of tea leaves for the price of sixteen: you can figure out the rest) and a Sunny Bray Dairy, with a man I knew as Harry, who took milk from Margetts' farm and still delivered it to homes using a horse-drawn cart. And there was a cinema, now to be called a movie theatre.

"Going to the movies" brings us to the Duncan population. In 1948 — a time before Indigenous recognition and reconciliation — there were two principal ethnic groups who kept themselves apart even during a kids' afternoon matinee of *Bugs Bunny* cartoons.

The whites sat in the privileged downstairs and the Indians had what was considered the less desirable balcony above them — which seemed strange to me. In a London film palace like the Odeon Marble Arch, where I saw Stewart Granger hoist Vivien Leigh (Cleopatra) in her carpet, the front of the balcony was the most desirable. While the Duncan allocation of seating left much to be desired by enlightened standards, the original tribal inhabitants (the loggers used the derogative "Siwash") got some of their own back on Saturday nights when those of the originals who had over-imbibed unloaded the consequences over the front balcony rail onto the heads of the loggers in the red plush seats below them.

Duncan white society had its own demarcation, which was most clearly marked off around nearby Quamichan Lake. The western end of the lake had large tamed lots, ten acres or more, owned by admirals and generals retired from serving the empire, and now in charge of Duncan's local politics and Boy Scouts. Many of these properties had croquet lawns, tennis courts and rhododendrons which would have been at home back Home, as their expatriate owners (and my parents) referred to the British Isles. Anywhere around Duncan that wasn't tamed for rhododendrons and dairy farms was still the bush, as most of Vancouver Island still is.

Not all of the bush belonged to the loggers. The land on the other side of the flooding creek at the bottom of Margetts Farm was called "the reserve": the day after the Arctic outflow ended, I met a boy there (before I had any idea what he, or the land he stood on, was). I didn't see him at first. My main attention was on several huge fish with strangely hooked noses in the creek.

The fish I had seen being caught by the old Burton Bradstock fishermen in Dorset — mackerel, plaice, flounder, an occasional large skate — would have been breakfast for these giants. The other astonishing thing about them was their colouring: it ranged from pink to deep red with white patches near the tails. Most of the fish were swimming sluggishly but a few seemed to be dead.

I think it was at this point that I noticed the boy standing on the other side of the creek, and I said something like, "What on earth are they?" At which he looked at me ... and after a long pause replied, as though talking to an idiot:

"Salmon, they're dyin' eh."

His name was Jack, and although we met many times — and he taught me the spawning cycle of the salmon, and the names of West Coast plants, like the salal that grew in the underbrush, and the adjacent mountain, Tzouhalem, named for a great chief of the Cowichan people — I regret to tell you that I never found out whether Jack was his first or last name.

It would be wrong to leave the impression that everyone in Duncan in 1948 was a narrow-minded bigot. Gwen Margetts was the exact opposite, and as a result, my mother was able to witness an event that by law in British Columbia was forbidden: a potlatch.

As I understood it (after my mother came home and described it), this ceremony was a sort of huge birthday party where everybody wore robes and masks and gave each other expensive presents, because a local Cowichan princess was getting married (like our Royal Wedding before I left London).

Whether or not potlatches should have been illegal — the government rationale was that they led to excessive drinking and immoral behaviour, and bankrupted all the parties involved — the fact that the tribal elders trusted and respected Gwen Margetts sufficiently to invite her to attend was a remarkable testimonial. For my mother to be able to witness such a rare thing so soon after our arrival in Canada was a one-in-a-million opportunity.

William Tell and "A Lady Without Any Clothes"

Opposite the dying salmon, to the south, the Margetts' other neighbour to the north was Old Ma Kettle. At least that was what Peter Margetts called her when he took me to visit her.

Old Ma Kettle was extremely old, with straggling grey hair, and lived in the kitchen of a cedar cabin because there didn't seem to be any other rooms in the cabin. Living in the kitchen with her were several chickens pecking on the table and one gobbling turkey on the floor.

There may also have been a rabbit under a galvanized washbasin but I was too surprised by my first impression of the kitchen's inhabitants to confirm the rabbit, and I didn't get a second look. Old Ma Kettle hated all children, and especially Peter Margetts whom she blamed for the mysterious loss of a pet rooster. She had an unpleasant-looking dog on a chain outside the cabin and implied she would release it if Peter Margetts — and presumably me — ever returned.

I can't prove that Peter Margetts was responsible for two of my subsequent actions that had severe consequences.

The first was when I shot my sister with an arrow. It was after my twelfth birthday and I had given myself a bow which I had made from a piece of cured yew (as described in a present of the *Illustrated Adventures of Robin Hood*). I was proud of the bow; when Peter Margetts suggested re-enacting William Tell and the Apple, it seemed a good idea at the time.

Things began to go wrong when, instead of a toy arrow with a rubber sucker on the tip, I decided to use some birthday money to buy a proper arrow with a steel tip from the sporting goods shop in Duncan.

Angela had had her sixth birthday. I don't know how I persuaded her to allow us to tie her to the apple tree. She was certainly reluctant but I didn't actually use force. I think she gave in after I told her she was a princess, like the Cowichan one at the potlatch.

My steel-tipped arrow struck her just beside her right eye.

It could have been horrific: thank God it was not. My home-made bow had considerable power, but my young arm didn't, and the range was quite far. There was a little bit of blood, and Angela screamed, and all hell broke loose when my parents found out. But before we proceeded from crime to punishment for the shooting, there was the Down in the Valley episode.

Again it involved Peter Margetts, at its start, and my sister for the crunch. We were building a fort in the hayloft when he said that his parents had told him that I had "a real good singing voice," and he knew "this great song I could sing for people" that would get a belly laugh in any audience. The lyrics to generate this amusement in all who heard it were as follows:

Down in the valley where the green grass grows,
There lives a lady without any clothes,
Along comes a man with a walking stick,
Pulls down his trousers, and pulls out his …

The remainder followed the cycle of procreation (as exhibited by the dying salmon in the creek) via walking-stick — rhymes with prick — insemination, through three-monthly increments (*the belly begins to swell*) to a successful (*the baby pops out*) birth experience for the unclothed female, before the trouser-lowering part repeated itself (*the baby begins to shout: Down in the …*), *ad infinitum*.

When I repeated it to my sister, she didn't understand it. When she repeated it to Jim, he beat me with a leather belt.

It was the first time, and I thought I might have deserved it for the arrow by her eye. But not for a singsong. My mother apparently agreed, but her reaction seemed out of proportion. She and Jim had a furious row in their bedroom. Her eventual explanation: "I told him if he ever touched you again like that I would take both you children and never come back."

The why and how of Jim's exaggerated reaction to sex, and my mother's to my protection, are beyond a child's reach.

Punishments and Crimes

The belt was unpleasant but I liked my other items of Canadian clothing that I was given for my twelfth birthday. They were a pair of brown corduroy knee britches, and a sheepskin-lined, leather aviator cap, with mock goggles and ear flaps. When I wore the cap I became Biggles, intrepid fighter pilot, defeating the Hun.

These bits of costume and all the other new things, like my first Baby Brownie camera, a cap gun (and a toaster and better wireless set — now radio) that the Gurr family needed to furnish the cottage, came miraculously from a thing the size of a telephone book, called the Eaton's catalogue. New food miracles like Rice Krispies and Grapenuts cereals were delivered courtesy of the Overwaitea grocery store.

(Writing about the corduroy britches produces the shivering realization that for the entire North Atlantic crossing in mid-December, and the snowbound vastness of Canada, and the Arctic outflow of Vancouver Island, I had been wearing my grey flannel shorts from school. No bloody wonder I always felt cold.)

The January blast from the arctic had been an exception: February and March in Duncan were mild. Domesticated snowdrops and daffodils appeared early and, in April, wildflowers — cream-coloured Easter lilies, and purple shooting stars — magically carpeted the grass beneath the native Garry oaks, which Peter Margetts said got their modern name from "a Mad Trapper who worked for the Hudson's Bay Company."

And in one Garry oak sat a magical bird. I spotted it for the first time through the same pane of glass that had the life-saving BB pellet hole, and took its picture with my Baby Brownie, but black and white couldn't begin to reveal how magical it was. At first I thought it was a crow; it was about the same size and did look black, but suddenly a cockatoo's crest stood up on its head, and the sun came out, and the feathers were a blaze of blue.

Gwen Margetts told me that this plumed and crested miracle was called a Steller's jay but she didn't like the harsh "cack-cack-cack" noise it made. I wanted to hear it because the sound usually preceded sight and meant one of them was close, and I loved it.

Just in time for Easter, the barn swallows returned. I saw the first one swoop into the hayloft next to what Captain Margetts called the "milking parlour" on Good Friday; by Easter Monday there was a small flock.

On Tuesday we went back to school at St. Ann's and I found the swallows there as well, but a lot more of them, and they were already hard at work constructing or repairing mud nests under the eaves of the chapel and other outbuildings. Finally — through the endless Hail Mary hours of sitting as a lonely Protestant outside the chapel door — I had something interesting to watch.

I watched them for two days and then, on what, given the spot on the religious calendar, should have been a glorious third day, I saw two labourers with ladders approaching the side of the chapel. They propped the ladders under the eaves, and to my horror and rage began methodically knocking down the swallows' mud nests. Then, as the other Hail Mary boys came out of the chapel, the labourers moved their ladders to the stable.

I was going to shout something about telling them to stop but at that point the Mother Superior also left the chapel and, to my relief, went over to stop the labourers.

Except that she didn't.

Worse, she pointed her starched headdress towards the barn to include that in the butchering. I can't say that she made the sign of the cross, but her ecclesiastical approval was obvious. The labourers genuflected inappropriately. She walked back to her office.

I followed her. At this distance I can see the unconscious connection to Elspie and the sparrows in the gutter at Barton Olivers One. At twelve, I only knew that I thought it was wrong.

I knocked on her office door.

She said: "Come in."

I said something incoherent like: "The swallows' nests, they shouldn't be doing that."

She said: "Why not?"

I said — yes, I really did say: "It isn't Christian charity."

She said: "You are expelled."

Howling for a Field Marshal

Duncan Grammar School (my sixth) was run on the honour system, not only because of its British academic antecedents: it was owned and administered by Mr. Honour, who was also its headmaster.

I was only there for two months, and the single memory I have from my days at Duncan Grammar is playing with Dinky Toys in a sandpit during the lunch hour. I also played marathon hours of Monopoly with John Sandys-Wunsch in a tent. I was there because I had become a Wolf Cub.

My mother had remembered that I had already been a Wolf

Cub for some fractional time in Dorset, and she thought it would be good for me to renew the opportunity to "do my duty for God and the King." That was accompanied by a Cub or Brownie pack's ceremonial grand howl, with our two-fingered salute and our piping little *Dib-Dib-Dib* (or possibly *Dob-Dob-Dob*) promise to *Do Our Best.*

I had forgotten the dib-dib (or dob-dob) words, but they soon came back under the "Akela" pack-leading tutelage of Mrs. Seeley, who was married to Colonel Seeley (British Army, Retired) in a house on Quamichan Lake, where our juvenile Wolf Pack assembled at five o'clock on Thursday afternoons. The Seeley house was on the east side of the lake with rhododendrons but no tennis court, and was thus only mid-level in the Quamichan societal pecking order.

After two or three grand howls, and getting my single badge (Naturalist: "name five kinds of trees"), Mrs. Seeley decided that I had remembered enough dib-dibbing to become a Quamichan Boy Scout, and that John Sandys-Wunsch (who had a whole sleeve of badges) should ascend at the same time.

The Sandys-Wunschs (pronounced Sans-Winch) lived at the top end of the lake in society, though the bottom (south) geographically. An exalted neighbour was Admiral Rollo Mainguy, vice-admiral of the Royal Canadian Navy. Many of the Duncan names of that era seem amusing relics of empire in the twenty-first century, but they could represent lives of exceptional service.

John Sandys-Wunsch's father was not an approachable man when I tried to say hello. John said, with awe, that he was recently retired as an Assistant Commissioner of the Royal Canadian Mounted Police. He had started with the RCMP's frontier predecessor, the North West Mounted Police, during which time pursuing Gold Rush criminals John told me that his father had been shot in the head by a Mad Trapper — or perhaps it was a berserk Gold Miner — before killing his assailant.

As well as that, John pointed out photos that portrayed his dad as a colonel in the Camel Corps with Lawrence of Arabia, an escort for the Duke of Windsor and the King of Siam, winner of the King George V's 100 Shooting Competition at Bisley in Surrey (which enabled him to nail the Mad Trapper, or Gold Miner), and so on through a long list of decorations for gallantry. His current call to service was as president of the Cowichan Valley Boy Scouts. Such men and their achievements were not figures of fun. I met two more of them almost immediately.

Colonel Maxwell Dopping-Hepenstal, DSO, Croix de Guerre, CBE, and much else, had retired from leading the Gurkha Rifles to become a founding father of Duncan Scouting. I only noticed him that first time as a little old man with a terribly scarred face, apparently from burning. I couldn't imagine that our connection would become surprisingly close.

In his capacity as Chief Scout, the colonel would shepherd us to Victoria for a national jamboree to salute the new Governor General of Canada, Field Marshal Earl Harold Alexander of Tunis.

The field marshal's final military command had been leading the Allied armies to victory in Italy. Now he was reduced to standing in the garden of Government House in Victoria, solemnly saluting us back as we gave him our grand howl. He actually shook my tiny hand, which impressed me considerably.

We went to Victoria and back by hired bus, which meant my first time "over the Malahat," via the island highway: the single road running (or clutching at straws) for 150 miles along the lower half of the island's eastern coastal strip. All the roads on Vancouver Island were designed for wagons, and so followed the line of least resistance: as there is almost no flat land on the island, this meant that all roads had some resistance.

The Malahat part of the island highway — over a mountain of that name, up to 1,200 feet, then hairpin-twisting down Goldstream Canyon to sea level — had the rest of the resistance, and in 1948 was considered a nightmare by even fairly good drivers. By day the views are spectacular, and a clear sky allowed me to see my first volcano, Mount Baker, snow-capped, a hundred miles to the east.

I THINK THIS WAS THE FIRST TIME that I began to comprehend and appreciate the landscape I had come to. The sad feelings of dislocation from my other world of Aunt Nan and double decker buses seemed to fade when I looked at the Malahat and Mount Baker. I was amazed by all the trees.

To win my naturalist badge from Mrs. Seeley I had found a single specimen of each of the five kinds (arbutus, dogwood, Douglas fir, hemlock, red cedar) near Margetts' farm, but now I realized that trees were everywhere. And if they weren't standing in forests, they were changed to logs, in huge stacks beside the road or on gigantic logging trucks; or, as a footnote to what they had once been, in monumental piles of sawdust beside mills. The furnace in the Margetts' house even used sawdust for fuel: it was fed into a large hopper with a funnel, which Peter filled through a chute from outside.

Most people in British Columbia in 1948 still thought that the supply of prime lumber from the forests was infinite. And if it could never run out, they might as well just use the best bits for their house and chuck the rest away.

Lumber from the Pacific northwest was graded into three categories: "Select" (clear of nearly all knots), "Construction" (some tight knots), and "Economy" (take your chances).

When I stood beside the sawdust furnace in the Margetts' basement and looked up at the basement ceiling, because it was unfinished I was also looking at the underside of the kitchen floor. The exposed two-inch (thick) by ten-inch (wide) Douglas fir floor joists supporting the Margetts' kitchen floor had no knots in them. Almost everything wooden in the Margetts' house — cedar shingles on the roof, the rafters supporting it, the ceiling and floor joists, the vertical two-by-four studs which framed the walls, their exterior sheathing and siding, the subflooring planks and the finished fir flooring above it — all these at that time would be "Select."

And everything except the finished fir flooring was "rough cut," which means that a dimension of two inches thick *was* the full two inches. Today, framing lumber is "dressed," meaning smooth to the touch, and although a framing stud is called a two-by-four it's half an inch less in both dimensions.

This long-winded explanation can be summed up by saying that the Margetts' house was fantastically strong, and there was colossal waste of wood.

Something Stronger in the Milking Parlour

On Margetts' Farm, summer arrived and Duncan became surprisingly hot. Big and beautiful swallowtail butterflies undercut their first impression by landing on fresh cowpats dropped by the waiting cows outside the milking parlour.

The dairy section, with the cream separator, was a little cooler.

Most of the Margetts' herd were black-and-white Holsteins because they gave more milk, but an additional Jersey and Guernsey pair provided something much richer for the family — and a few others, at a higher price.

Captain Margetts drank something stronger than milk in the parlour. I never saw him doing it but in April I heard Jim tell my mother that he had found an empty bottle with a label saying LCB Rye, and at that milking a cow's udder had been injured because the machine hadn't been fitted properly. Jim mentioned it to Gwen. Margetts denied it.

My mother said, "There was a row."

The LCB was the British Columbia government's Liquor Control Board, which had its single store for the whole Cowichan Valley on Station Road in Duncan. Children had to stand outside while adults stood in front of a counter and told the clerk behind it what they wanted from a watered-down collection of booze offerings during strictly limited hours. This rationed severity was a legacy from provincial prohibition, which had ended in the 1920s.

In July, Jim found another empty LCB Rye bottle under the captain's milking stool which had somehow been "kicked over." Apparently there was another, more serious "row."

The hot weather made us all thirsty and the adults cross. It also meant that there was less water in the creek, but still enough for Jim to give me yet another abortive swimming lesson. The bank was muddy and the water only waist deep. He once again drew people's attention to my fearfulness and "hollow buttocks."

I didn't learn to swim but, despite that, went out in a canoe with John Sandys-Wunsch (and no life preservers) to take possession of an island in Quamichan Lake. You can still see it on Google but the lake looks like a green meadow from the resultant algae, fed by runoff from septic tanks in surrounding, non-stop subdivisions that have also obliterated Margetts' farm.

The island was small, screened by thick banks of reeds, providing a place for leaf warblers to build their marvellous woven nests. The postage stamp of dry land had a few alders and one small Douglas fir, providing a place for us to beach the canoe and build a fort. I mention it because John Sandys-Wunsch had discovered that the island was still owned by the CPR — a microscopic leftover from that transportation giant's previous ownership of the entire eastern strip of Vancouver Island.

As we were building the fort, one of us had the brilliant idea that, since it was worth nothing to CP, we should write a letter offering to buy this real estate relic from them — at what John called "a nominal fee." Accordingly, we returned to retired Assistant Commissioner Sandys-Wunsch's study, where — beneath the framed portraits of him escorting the King of Siam, and Lawrence of Arabia's Camel Corps — on a piece of former RCMP stationery, and John's father's Remington typewriter, we pecked out our CPR offer of our nominal fee.

It was one dollar, and John Sandys-Wunsch actually mailed it. But before we could receive word of the keenly awaited counter-offer from the Canadian Pacific Railway, I was once more on one of its trains: with the Gurr family heading south in wicker seats, and still by steam, on the E&N, because Jim said we were moving to Victoria. We arrived just in time to miss afternoon tea at the CPR's West Coast flagship:

The Empress Hotel.

Victoria Regina
or
Child's Play in a Little Bit of Olde England

THE POLICE IN THE PROVINCIAL CAPITAL still wore the helmets of London Bobbies, and "Afternoon Tea at the Empress" was poured into Royal Doulton teacups, but by the time I arrived in the summer of 1948, those identifying markers for "A Little Bit of Olde England" had already become a tourist marketing cliché.

Fine Dining at the Poodle Dog Café

THE EMPRESS HOTEL overlooks a civilian harbour. A statue of Queen Victoria looks back at it. The old girl wears her imperial crown but when I first saw it I thought she had a lace cap on her head; seagulls had crapped on the metal of which she is composed. Behind her are the Parliament Buildings, with a gilded Captain Vancouver standing on its dome. Strings of low-voltage fairy lights illuminate the buildings after dark but we didn't stay long enough in the hotel to see them on that occasion.

Jim's success as a salesman — when there were successes — was his easy ability to make acquaintances out of strangers. The failures usually happened when he "came on too strong," either from giving the new acquaintance too many flowers too soon, or letting his carefully cultivated BBC broadcaster's accent slip, to reveal his Liverpool roots. Timing is everything in sales: after the Beatles, his accent slippage would have been a plus.

For whatever reasons, Jim's "new friends" the Enochs not only took us to supper at the Empress, they invited us into their house where we stayed as their guests for a month. They lived on Granite Street in Oak Bay, a separate municipality of solid citizenry and well-built houses — and no beer parlours — secure behind what the less well-bred municipal neighbours labelled derisively a Tweed Curtain. The interior of the Enochs' house was almost identical to that of the Margetts, as was most of its construction, but perhaps to match the street's name the exterior sported columns of granite instead of cedar posts holding up its front porch.

The August weather was extremely hot while we were there and my only memory of it is walking to a corner grocery shop, on Foul Bay Road, for my first time buying a cold Orange Crush.

On the subject of drink: the Enochs were the current owners of the Poodle Dog Café, "corner of Government and Yates": a "fine dining" fixture in Victoria since 1904, and possibly longer. The Poodle Dog was in a running battle with the Liquor Control Board — the same governmental organization limiting booze sales in Duncan — because of the café's display sign, which showed an image of the hound sitting upright on its hindquarters, holding a tray with its front paws, and on the tray a bottle. The café management said it was ketchup or vinegar: the LCB said champagne, and that any display advertising liquor in a font more than two inches high was forbidden.

Jim Enoch had his paws in many other businesses, primarily real estate but also, through marriage, lumber and sawmilling. One of the most prominent mills was run by a family called Moore-Whittington, and they also owned summer cabins where they spent holidays outside the city at a place called Glen Lake.

Through a firm called Newstead Realty (owned by an Enoch relative), all these familial components fell into place and my parents were offered one of these Moore-Whittington cabins which had come up for sale. After some dickering over a "lifetime opportunity at a bargain price" — and I shall never know where the collateral came from to provide our "bargain" down payment — for the sum of $7,500, the Gurr family came into possession of two waterfront acres, and its first place to call home.

A Real Steal

Glen Lake wasn't recognized by the post office. The building for that outpost of civilization was part of a shop located at what was still called Captain Langford's Station on the map we were given by the Newstead Realty salesman.

Our address would be simpler: RR 1, Langford, VI, BC. It stayed that way for years. Captain Langford (late of the 73rd Foot Regiment) had arrived from Home almost exactly a century before us to become a gentleman farmer like Jim, but with more adequate resources.

On our first drive out from Victoria, in the Newstead salesman's Packard V8, north on the Island Highway to view our new home, the salesman — wearing a sports jacket and trousers with large plaid squares, and a tie with large flowers — called out various places of interest, then stopped his Packard at the top of a hill and said:

"This is Colwood Corners, which was the name of Langford's farm. That's his dairy over there."

He waved a plaid jacket sleeve at a small stone building in a rough field to our right. The other side of the road was manicured grass. "Royal Colwood Golf Club. The Duke of Windsor played there when he was the Prince of Wales. But the great thing is, folks" (dramatic pause): "Langford, Colwood, Glen Lake — it's all Unorganized Territory. No municipalities, so no taxes. That's what makes your place a real steal."

It also made it a place with no sewers, piped water, streetlights, garbage collection, building inspection, paved roads, or Bobby-on-the-beat. (At least there was a power line from BC Electric.) The BC Provincial Police, wearing Boy Scout hats, took care of speeding tickets and occasional Unorganized Territory logging criminals. The salesman took our minds off these municipal inadequacies by pointing out an attractive house, shaped like a Chinese pagoda, opposite the golf course entrance, and then said, "Van Tilburg's place. Okay, folks, Nimmo's store coming up, Station Road, guess we're in Langford."

The "station" was only an open concrete platform with a bench. The intersection of the E&N railway track and the Island Highway formed a triangle, and that dictated the shape of Nimmo's store. "His place has got pretty much everything you need," the Newstead salesman advised us, "but the old guy's a Welshman, so watch out." (In fact, the name was Scottish. Otherwise, as I would shortly discover, the advice was sound.)

Station Road ran straight, level, and parallel to the railway tracks on our right, past two or three small houses, for half a mile, then came to a stop sign in front of a large building called Public Works.

We stopped. A huge machine with a sort of bulldozer blade underneath it, the Newstead salesman told us, was called "a grader," and this mechanical marvel would keep our road plowed in the almost unheard of event: a snowfall in Greater Victoria.

Another sign said "Jacklin Road." It pointed both ways but the Jacklin Road to our right, across the tracks, was only a narrow footpath winding away between broom bushes and into scrub firs. The salesman gestured at it:

"That way's the school."

We turned the other way, left, at the Public Works grader machine, onto the paved part of Jacklin Road, and past a gate saying Hulls' Farm on our right, then down a steep hill. The Packard had no air conditioning, so the windows were open. A strong smell came in through them. It was hot.

"Lim Bang's pig farm," said the Newstead salesman, "but they're nowhere near you."

Jacklin Road flattened out. We could see the Lim Bang pigs to our left, rooting beyond more of the scraggy firs. To our right, a signpost with its lettering almost gone had enough to show a faint Glen Lake Road. The salesman turned the Packard on to it. Glen Lake Road was unpaved. The Packard began to vibrate a little, and then a lot.

"Washboarding," the salesman said, in a falsely cheerful tone. "Gravel does that. Tell the Works boys and they'll run the grader over it whenever you want."

We learned quickly that this Newstead sales pitch fell short of the truth. Meanwhile, washboarding over more gravel created a small dust storm behind us. We slowed for a bend by a gate with carved lettering, Mortgage Ranch, and the dust began to drift through the Packard's open windows. It was very hot. Angela began to cry.

The salesman flapped his large-checked sports jacket and said, "Yep, she's a scorcher in the bush. Have to watch out for cigarettes in the Fire Season."

Whether or not he mentally capitalized those two words, we certainly did. The Packard slowed for a second bend in Glen Lake Road. Another strong smell followed the dust in through the windows.

"James' mink," the salesman said. "It's a farm, but you won't smell them."

We drove with the dust chasing us up a slight hill, and stopped beside two large Douglas firs and a Newstead Realty "For Sale" piece of cardboard falling off one of them. We could still smell James' mink. It was beyond very hot. Angela cried more loudly.

Because it was the first time I saw them, I must say more about the two large trees. "Large" is not adequate, and the one on the left was no longer an actual tree. Ten feet above the ground it had been cut off. A few feet down from the stump's top, two gashes had been notched by axes. The butt of stump remaining was as wide in diameter as my outstretched arms. About fifty feet beyond it, what was left of it lay on the ground, still at least three feet across, half buried by undergrowth.

The untouched standing fir on the right was not quite so enormous, had a slight bend, and a few jagged branch stubs low to the ground. The "For Sale" sign was attached to it. The salesman nodded, took the sign down, and tapped the tree.

"Old growth. Loggers probably left that one because of the knots. Packard's a little big for the driveway, maybe better if we walk."

What he called the "driveway" in the gap between the two trunks was a rutted track, and at the time it seemed a long walk. It was *too* hot. Angela sobbed quietly. There were several spindly Douglas firs and red cedars growing randomly on either side of the track, with a thick undergrowth of the native salal twined with a mass of wild blackberry between more stumps.

"This will be great for a meadow when it's cleared, folks," the salesman said to cheer us up. The rutted track became a small hill, sloping down. Our new house was at the bottom; because I could see a glimpse of water, I ran past it. The dust was gone. The mink smell was gone. The air was cooler and there it was.

The Lake.

A House Facing Backwards

Glen Lake is small, almost rectangular, about half a mile long, three hundred yards wide; and although the Newstead salesman told us that the locals told him it was bottomless, the maximum depth is only about fifty feet. Its geographic long axis lies northwest to southeast, and gaps between hills at the southern end mean that winds can be fierce when they come through from that direction.

By the time we arrived, in August 1948, the surrounding land had been subdivided into building lots, most of them two acres, except for a marsh to the north, and a very small creek to the south providing an overflow exit at times of flood conditions. Only two properties — the first was three lots to the north of ours; the other was at the top end, beyond it — had any flat arable land. All the rest were still tree-covered by second growth after being "logged off," like ours, and most sloped fairly steeply to the water's edge.

The houses had all been built to serve only as summer cottages: consequently they had no insulation to help in winter. Their septic tank systems for sewage were primitive, but seepage so far had been minimal. The water colour was dulled by mineral content from the adjacent hills, but the water quality of the lake was good, though most houses had shallow wells instead. About a third of the buildings were still only used for holidays and so remained empty for three-quarters of the year.

A few properties were old enough to have started as true cabins, clad with thick rough-cedar siding that showed the wavy edge of the log, and a heavy split-cedar shake roof. Our "new" house (then twenty years old) was typical of the rest, which meant it was placed backwards on its lot because it had been designed to present its best side to passers-by on a city street.

Consequently the front porch, with the front door and broad steps leading down to the ground, faced the lake — from which direction visitors almost never arrived. For practical purposes, the back of the house was therefore our front.

What I saw — when I came back from admiring the lake — was mostly a one-and-a-half-storey gable end, covered by white-painted siding that was beginning to peel. The roof had faded asphalt shingles, not cedar, and one side was half covered with dry moss. A door that was too low for an adult went into a "crawlspace" basement with a partial rough cement floor. The front half of the crawlspace was fine for me, but still too low for an adult to stand up.

The back half of the crawlspace was bone-dry dusty gravel, ideal for poisonous Black Widow spiders, and could only be negotiated by crawling on hands and knees, trying to ignore a mass of spiders' webs overhead. Outside the basement door a set of eight utilitarian wooden steps went up to another door, which opened into the kitchen: so the kitchen door became our front door.

THE INTERIOR WAS LARGER than Margetts' cottage, just. The kitchen had a "nook" with a fixed shelf for a table (Arborite, with a screwed-on chrome edge) where we ate our meals. Again, as in Duncan, there was a cooking stove and no other appliances. The stove used wood to burn, which at first seemed an improvement over the coal that poisoned us with monoxide — until we realized that we had to provide such wood.

A miniature hall connected a miniature inside bathroom (barely big enough for a toilet with a chain, wall- hung washbasin and primitive shower) with our new sleeping and living arrangements. Angela and I now each had a room, although one of them was more like a small sun porch with glass panes like a greenhouse for two of its walls, and it opened from the larger room — which wasn't really large at all. But that space was given to Angela, so that if my mother needed to visit her at night it wouldn't disturb me. It didn't seem to me a valid reason for my getting the short end of the accommodation stick.

Another door from the miniature hall opened into the living room, the largest in the house, about ten feet wide by fifteen feet long. There was a small brick fireplace, and a smaller brick hearth, both of them heavily blackened by soot. To the left of the living room, and a bit smaller, was our parents' bedroom, with its twin beds and two windows.

The end wall of the living room, opposite the fireplace, had the original city design's front door opening to the porch and the lake. The porch was as broad as the house, and five feet deep. Its front right corner had been glassed in — and for the next forty years Jim said he would "do the rest" to make it an enclosed room.

No Seismic Mitigation

That first visit to the lake remains vivid. The subsequent details of our moving in — transportation, furnishings, parental employment, the timing of it all — those are gone. So was summer, which (for the seventh time in seven years) once again meant another school.

Langford Elementary, Grades 1 to 6, was under the care and tutelage of its principal, Miss King. The building was new and the front wall, south-facing the Island Highway, was concrete-block. The back wall faced nothing but bush and was wood-frame. The roof was flat, tar and gravel.

There certainly weren't six rooms for the six grades, but how many were shared, and how many other teachers and children there were, I can't say. All I retain from a year at Langford Elementary is my correcting Miss King's English usage (when she insisted on saying "drownded" instead of drowned) and her never-to-be-forgotten announcement over a PA system: "Will all the male teachers bring their pink balls to the office?"

And the earthquake.

It struck when I was feeling drowsy from the September afternoon sun streaming through the south-facing front windows, unobstructed by Venetian blinds. It was frightening, and I think there was some kind of rumbling noise, and a thump, and the desks moved, and the concrete-block wall between the front windows cracked from top to bottom, and then it was over.

When it was over, I think we went outside.

Vancouver Island schools have now been reinforced for seismic mitigation, and conduct earthquake drills. In 1948 the *Daily*

Colonist newspaper reported it, but said its 5.3 level on the Richter scale couldn't compare with the Big One of 7.0 in 1946, and the school janitor patched the crack. Miss King continued to say "drownded."

The distance to Langford Elementary was a mile and a half from our Glen Lake house. For the first week I walked it, reversing the route we had taken on our visit with the Newstead salesman: washboard gravel along Glen Lake Road to the paved part of Jacklin Road, up the steep hill to the Public Works building with the grader, across the E&N railway track, then following the narrow dirt path the salesman had waved his plaid sleeve at, through Scotch broom bushes and scraggy firs, past one or two half-hidden, tar-papered shacks, until the path came out onto the Island Highway opposite the school. There might have been a painted crosswalk for pedestrians. There certainly was no such fancy city thing as a crossing guard.

There was no such thing as a lot of things. Summer was over, rainy winter was coming; my school headmistress was called a principal and knew nothing; I knew nobody except my little sister, and the children in class beside me seemed to know nothing either.

After Monmouth Grammar and Sherborne and UCS, what I had thought of as "maths" included trigonometry and algebra, even if I loathed them. In grade six at Langford Elementary, mathematics was basic arithmetic, scarcely able to make a common fraction. Forget Latin and Greek and Aunt Dorothea's *Pilgrim's Progress;* English literature at Langford Elementary was "drownded."

My feelings of contempt for Miss King and her teaching were clearly a young boy's mask for depression at being uprooted, unexpectedly and abruptly, once too far and once too often. Stuck in "the sticks," there wasn't even a movie theatre like Duncan's to go to — and when I had to trudge to school, the hazard on my walk was the dog.

Big and black, it lived in one of the tar-papered houses and at first I thought it was a friend. But then I rode my CCM bicycle and the first time I pedalled by, it bit me on the leg.

The bite from the collie in West Bay hadn't punctured the skin: this one did. I think my mother complained to the owner. If so, that person didn't chain the dog, which meant that every school day, twice a day, I had to get off the bike, walk past the again friendly dog, get back on the CCM bike and continue to boredom at school.

And there was no Aunt Nan to talk to.

Boredom and unhappiness couldn't last: I was too busy with "chores," and there was another unexpected change at home. I got back one day in mid-September to find that Jim had used his Hygrade Lingerie sales-management gift of the gab plus Jim Enoch's business connections, and had metamorphosed from a dairy farmer to a Newstead Realty salesman, described on his new business card as "Realtor."

More excitingly, since he couldn't do one (go to work) without the other (make a sale), we had acquired a new car.

It was an Austin A-40, blue-grey, made in England, and I don't have a photo to confirm whether it was the two-door Dorset or more convenient four-door Devon model. Whatever the number of car doors, the A-40 made living "out in the sticks" doable.

My depression lifted. There was a way of escape!

BUT OUT IN THE STICKS also brings us back to the subject of wood for the stove — and the fireplace. These were the only sources of heat for cooking, bathing, and warming a house which had no insulation.

Our water for washing and showering grew hot by being passed through a copper coil inside the stove's fuel compartment; then out of the stove through a copper pipe, into a vertical forty-gallon galvanized tank which stood beside it in the kitchen; then up to the ceiling, either over to the kitchen sink or across the adjacent miniature hall ceiling; then down again into the miniature bathroom (during which progress, hard-earned hot water in the uncovered pipe was given a chance to cool off).

The pressure that allowed this hydraulic operation to continue was provided by a cold-water pump in the basement crawlspace. The cold water was drawn by the pump from a shallow well beside the outside kitchen stairs.

The well wasn't like the round ones in Beatrix Potter books, but square, with a heavy plank lid. Lifting the lid revealed a square box, also made of wooden planks, six feet deep with no sealed bottom, which is where the water came in. The water was seepage from the lake and its level changed with the seasons, as did the lake's.

Only fifteen feet away, across the gravel drive, and only five feet above the water table of the well, was what had been described in the Newstead sales pitch as "an approved septic tank system." But when we finally dug it up to replace it, the septic tank was discovered to comprise some broken clay tiles and a decayed wooden tub. Why this illegal, and truly shitty, sewage system didn't poison us all by contaminating the well doesn't matter, because the next summer it saved my sister's life.

Telephonic assistance for emergencies or gossip was provided by a "party line." The actual BC Telephone Company wire was strung from the road, tacked up beside the BC Electric Company power line, fir tree to cedar tree, until both reached the house.

Initially, our BC Tel party line had eight users (it later dropped to four, and finally two), which meant that when we moved in we could listen to pretty much our side of the lake, and vice versa. We had to count the number of "rings" to know if a call was for us. A different number of rings, produced by cranking a handle, engaged the operator.

To RETURN TO OUR FIRST GLEN LAKE WINTER, and the wood we required to survive it. There were two ways of getting hold of wood, we were told: one way was buying it from "the Hindus"; the other was to get it yourself.

"The Hindus" may have been Muslims, but India had only been subdivided to create a new Pakistan in the year we left Britain. And as the sharp businessmen owning the small local mills were nearly all from the subcontinent, and racial prejudice against dark skins was still going strong in British Columbia, the pejorative "Hindus" they remained.

The Gurr family's problem for the winter of 1948-1949 was that, not only was buying wood from "the Hindus" expensive, it was too frequently dumped off after dark so that the purchaser couldn't tell beforehand that it was still soaking wet.

The wood was wet because it was made from the unwanted slabs cut from logs in order to make them square. The logs were kept in log booms, and the booms floated in the sea. When the unwanted slabs, with the wet bark still on them, were cut again into stove lengths, a lot of soaking wet sawdust (and painful wood slivers) stayed with them.

For reasons of cost, Jim decided to take the alternative method to "the Hindus" and the wet wood and "get it" — that is, cut it — ourselves.

Needless to say: woodcutting, neither Jim nor I had ever done.

Clarence and the Weasels

Our property was covered with trees, either "standing," which meant still growing, or "logged-off," which meant that what was left of them was lying in the undergrowth covered by salal and blackberry thorns. The skill required for us to chop down a standing tree was out of the question, and anyway its sap-filled "green" fuel would still have been too wet to burn well.

The previous holiday owners had left a small pile of dry wood which gave us some breathing room, and in early September winter could still — to an optimist — seem a long time off. Jim felt optimistic.

We started with dead branches that didn't have too many thorns covering them and were small enough for him to cut, by hand, into three-foot lengths, using first a new but ordinary carpenter's saw, and as that soon gave up the ghost, a new bow or Swede saw. I then carried the dead branch sections out of the undergrowth to be placed in the arms of an X-shaped sawhorse, where we could cut them again into one-foot lengths to fit the stove. This was not a rapid process.

To heat an uninsulated house through our first winter at Glen Lake would require, we were told, "If you're lucky with the weather, conservatively, three cords." One "true cord" of firewood measures four feet high, by four feet thick, by eight feet long. At the beginning of October, our pile of chopped branches was barely off the ground. Something had to be done. Jim said this time we would "get it," i.e. wood, from one of the logged-off trunks lying in the blackberry vines.

He bought us a new, two-man, crosscut saw. This device for two men was six feet long, with a wooden handle on either end, and on its lower edge it had a row of teeth that could fit a great white shark. The first fir log he decided to "get" had a diameter of about twelve inches.

I pulled the blackberry vines off it, protecting my hands with a pair of sheepskin-lined leather mitts that we had purchased with our sheepskin boots in Montreal. That cleared the log: but now we needed somewhere to stand, which meant clearing more undergrowth for a distance of three feet either side of it. With standing room achieved, we each took one man-handle of the two-man crosscut.

This was not a rapid process either — nor smooth. To operate such a cutting machine, when the holder of one handle pulls, the other has to push: these two operations have to occur in harmony. Ideally, both pusher and puller would be of equal strength and size, to say nothing about the obvious fact of both being used to doing it. Clearly, with Jim on one end and twelve-year-old me on the other, none of these desirable conditions were obtained.

It almost amuses me to write of it now: then, it was torture. And even though we worked very hard, after my school and his work, and by way of weekends, it wasn't enough. At which point a merciful God and the bush telegraph (an amalgam of party-line and general-store gossip by which neighbours kept an ear and eye on each other) sent us Clarence Woodruffe and the Weasels:

"To save your bacon, eh?"

Clarence was a logger on Kangaroo Road. His unexpected use of "eh?" — in 1948, on southern Vancouver Island, it wasn't yet part of everyday speech — made every routine instruction or comment into a philosophical question. The Weasels were his young sons (my age, plus or minus), who assisted him with miscellaneous logging tasks such as inserting and removing splitting wedges to stop logs from jamming the saw as they were cut.

My six-year-old sister gave them their collective name (they did have ordinary ones) because Angela said that their scurrying movement reminded her of the *Wind in the Willows* weasels attacking Toad Hall.

Clarence "saved our bacon" with a chainsaw. Nowadays, in TV commercials and horror movies, people wave them around with one hand. They wouldn't wave Clarence's. It was a Stihl, two-man, and weighed 120 pounds. As that brute size was out of the Weasels' league, Clarence brought another adult logger with him, "the helper."

The first thing Clarence and the helper tackled with this Stihl beast was the monster remains of the fallen tree, with its three-foot diameter, lying at the entrance to our drive.

Clarence and the helper lifted the Stihl on top of the great log, and started the saw's gas engine. In the time it required to chew, and spit out, its way through the three-foot diameter log, Jim and I, with our crosscut, would not have been through the bark on top.

Each round they cut off still weighed a ton. Using a wedge and a sledgehammer, the Weasels began to split them. If the split began to jam, Clarence or the helper would "give it a tap" with the sledge. The Weasels then stacked the split wood into our first true cord; two more followed from that one great log. Our fuel supply for the winter was solved. As he was departing, Clarence left us with a strange warning:

"Watch out for them widow-makers, eh?"

When our expressions showed Clarence that we had no clue about "widow-makers," he pointed at a dead limb, high up on an otherwise healthy Douglas fir, next door on the Seymours' property, and addressed Jim directly.

"Tree looks good — but one of them dead buggers can come down any time, wind or no wind, so always keep an eye on 'em. Otherwise, they're gonna make the lady wife real unhappy — unless she gets an early pension."

He ended this foreboding homily with a cheery laugh.

Clarence and the two-man Stihl had cut our wood, the scurrying Weasels had split and stacked it, but now we had to burn it. My main chore for the day, every winter day, for three years (after which our kitchen stove was converted to burn oil) was to provide a supply of wood and kindling split small enough to start, then feed the stove and fireplace throughout the day and night. After the winter it was easier because I only had to feed the stove.

Adding the *Star Weekly* delivery route to my labours wasn't my idea. The daily wood chore seemed arduous enough. The most charitable motive I can come up with for my parents' decision was that they felt I needed pocket money which they couldn't provide.

By the time I became its employee, the *Star Weekly* had dropped *The Toronto* from its name, but gained a ton of weight. Every issue was made up of five separate glossy sections, each of them the size of a regular magazine, and before I even began my route, all the sections had to be assembled in the correct order into a single enormous thing. At the peak of my *Star* earnings power I had twenty-eight customers, which means I had to load twenty-eight enormous things into a delivery bag hung around my neck. When my twelve-year-old neck said it couldn't hack it, I added a huge metal basket to the front of my CCM bike.

The *Star Weekly* route earned me a small amount of pocket money. Its main benefit was introducing me to some colourful local characters and showing me the local geography.

The customer I knew best was Old Clarkie. A bachelor Scot, unkempt, he lived on a corner two acres in an old cabin, not a house, with a small orchard of apple trees. He carved objects from their dried wood and also made leather bellows, with brass studs, for getting fires started with a *whoosh*.

He was considered mad and terrible by local children, who would shout at him from a safe distance. Of course my mother got to know him, and claimed to like him, and bought a pair of bellows from him.

In retrospect, I admire him. At the time I did think he was a bit of a grumpy old bugger, but the interior of his cabin full of objects from his past — stuffed animal heads, brass miner's lamps — was fascinating. Besides what he got from selling the bellows to my mother and a handful of other customers, he had a small pension.

At the end of a long life he was ripped off and cheated of a fair price for his two acres after untrue rumours about pedophilia were spread by early developers of the new Langford.

A Magic Sonic Moment

My *Star Weekly* route was mundane drudgery that I was glad to quit. The imprint of the landscape of Unorganized Territory through which I rode, despite what has happened to it since then, has never let me go.

At the time we arrived, beyond the Sooke Hills to the west and the Malahat to the north, all the way out to the Pacific was still free from human encroachment. Even the first inhabitants, the Cowichans, lived close to the sea. If I walked off Glen Lake Road, into the bush, I knew I was in wilderness, and felt free.

And yet …

What sealed the bond between me and my new country was an amalgam of nature *and* human technology. On the opposite side of the lake, at its eastern end, was a Canadian National Railway track. The CNR rails were laid so close to the lake at this point that any small landslide would have dipped them into the water. This squeezed spot was designated a public beach, and in summer might have as many as a dozen local kids sliding down its gravel slope before splashing into shallow water. The public beach was important to me as well: it was the only spot where I could actually see the train from our house.

The CNR track was now a logging line, and ran only early in the morning, up to Sooke, and back late in the evening. The engine was antique steam, with a cowcatcher and a spark catcher (to minimize bushfires) and a bell, which rang when it approached the crossing at Glen Lake Corner.

One evening in our first September I was waiting for the train's return journey when I saw a large bird land in the lake. It had a graceful neck, with a white ring-collar, and a long, white-speckled, black body, low in the water. And now I recognized it. My best birthday present in Duncan — mailed from Nan in London — had been the latest Arthur Ransome book, *Great Northern?* Pictures in the book matched what I was looking at. This beautiful bird was a Great Northern Diver.

(Until Clarence subsequently advised me: "That's a loon.")

I heard the returning whistle sounding for the corner: it echoed across the lake. The train arrived at the public beach and went by, leaving its trail of filtered smoke from the spark catcher; the whistle sounded again for the Jacklin Road crossing, and faded. And as it disappeared, the Diver — the loon — made a laughing cry.

That twinned sound of the train's whistle and the loon's cry seemed (though I couldn't yet have used the word) metaphysically Canadian. Whenever I listen to Gordon Lightfoot's *Canadian Railroad Trilogy*, that magic sonic moment at Glen Lake, seven decades ago, comes back to me.

An Introduction to Glacial Gravel

THE LAND BENEATH GLEN LAKE, Colwood and Langford is gravel, the moraine left by the retreat of a glacier. The gravel under our property made any idea my mother had for "proper vegetable gardening" a non-starter. Eventually, with her green thumb and lifelong effort, she did work small floral miracles, using native plants and more exotic others — and occasionally, tomatoes — in pots.

My introduction to the glacial gravel was a fencepost hole.

Old Clarkie was partially protected from the jeers of local children becoming physical attacks by a barricade of most attractive split-cedar rails, criss-crossed in a "snake fence." None of the other immediate properties around us had any fences at all.

The first post hole I had to dig was for keeping in our dozen newly acquired hens. If I tried to use a spade — now to be told by Clarence, "That's a shovel, eh" — it immediately hit nothing but rocks of different sizes. To get the hole started, I had to use a pick or a crowbar, then a trowel or my hands to clear it out. As with our woodcutting, post-holing was not a rapid process.

The Boundary War

WITH DUE ACKNOWLEDGEMENT to the skill of Robert Frost, a good fence can't stop a neighbour who wants war. His name was Walter Wohlers, married to Mrs. Wohlers, parents of three little Wohlers (Tina, Heidi and Conrad), who were approximately our ages. Walter was tall, bald and Austrian.

Our emerging boundary dispute wasn't helped because "Austrian," to Jim in 1948, meant German. German still meant the war. That Walter Wohlers' war had ended in 1918, after which he too was Canadian, didn't change matters.

The Wohlers already had bantams, coloured gloss-black, used to roaming as they pleased across invisible property lines. Our birds were a rich mix of gold, copper and white, with super fluffy feet. A bantam cockerel itching for a fight is not something you would want to meet if it were your size. Ours, and theirs, went at it for the first time on our side of the invisible line. The noise brought out all members of both families for a council of peace.

As we were the new arrivals at the battlefield, to keep the combatants separated Jim offered to put up some temporary chicken wire for the boundary line portion between the two houses, and a few yards further up the hill, to the point at which the salal and blackberries seemed to be impenetrable.

To a bantam, nothing is impenetrable. Inevitably, the glossy-black next door (who still thought the undefined territory belonged to him anyway) would make his way across the line and bloody battle would recommence. To save poultry lives, we extended the fence another yard: the black marauder went around it.

The only solution to this war of attrition was to extend the fence for the full property line. When Jim and I ran a string to do that, Walter Wohlers disputed it. In the meantime, a cold Fence War was brewing up on our other side.

I NEVER DISCOVERED ANY FACTUAL REASON for even low-level animosity with Major Seymour: my hunch says that it was partly ex-military snobbery — Jim had only been a corporal in the Marines — and the other part religion.

The Seymours were Roman Catholics; their children went to St. Louis College in Victoria (another private educational wing of the Sisters of St. Ann). My hitchhiking experience with the Catholic priest in Langford laid bare the religious differences.

I had wanted to go to Nimmo's store for something, but my bike had a flat tire. Walking usually meant I would be able to hitch a ride, and someone did stop for me on my way there. I bought my latest Superman comic, or whatever it was from Mrs. Nimmo, and began to thumb my way back along Station Road.

A car braked almost at once. From his collar and a cross — and my brief time at the St. Ann's in Duncan — I saw that the driver was a priest. He asked my name. I told him. What follows is verbatim.

He said: "Are you the little heretic?"

I said: "I'm Church of England."

He said: "You're going to be a proper little roasted English ass."

The priest said it conversationally, but not pleasantly. Then we stopped at the Seymours' gate, not ours, where he let me out to burn in hell.

Log-Rolling to a Leper Colony

EXCEPT FOR THIS BOUNDARY WAR on two fronts, we settled in peacefully with people around the lake. When we arrived, in houses to the east beyond the Seymours, there were no other families with young children.

To the west, beyond the Wohlers, the first property was the Shaylers'. They had a girl my age, called Gail, and two younger kids, but it didn't seem a happy home. You could hear arguments, and adults would make a certain kind of face when talking about Jim Shayler, and his drinking.

Beyond the Shaylers were the Williams clan: Johnny and Phyl, plus five kids — my friend Keith, and his four younger siblings. Big and burly Johnny Williams had been in the Navy, drank rum and Coke — or, lacking Coke, rum and ginger — and had what I thought at first was an exciting job: driving a former motor torpedo boat at high speed across Esquimalt harbour.

More routinely, I discovered that it was only a harbour craft doing ferry duty as a "Blue Boat," chugging dockyard workers back and forth from Colwood at the beginning and end of the workday. The journey saved some of them a long drive, but it was a necessity for many because fewer working people had cars. (Johnny ended his long transportation career at Esquimalt by becoming boss of all its movements, as the Queen's Harbourmaster.)

The Williamses were all born in Canada, not from Home, like the Enochs. They had a double lot of five acres with a flat area beside the lake which, when it dried out in summer, allowed them to grow vegetables. Beyond the Williamses was marsh that began to flood when the November rains fell non-stop, and as a result, miraculously, filled with migrating wildfowl.

On the other side of the marsh were the couple with the last name that, if you only saw the spelling on their mailbox, was impossible to pronounce: Colclough, pronounced Coke-Lee. Pat and Mary were originally (by way of the prairies) from Home. The local rumour was that Pat Colclough had once been what people called a remittance man.

"Remittance man" sounded exciting to me, and certainly featured in the opening of the colonial Northwest. The typical specimen was a younger son of a peer, who therefore couldn't inherit an estate and had few prospects in England; his aristocratic family exiled him to the colonies with an annual allowance, thus "remittance," to keep him out of trouble, and their hair. Whether he was one or not, even more excitingly to me, Pat Colclough was now a log roller, who did "birling" by walking in spiked boots along the logs floating in booms, and promised to take me with him to watch him do it out at Sooke.

Except for the economically fortunate few who owned prized waterfront properties in Metchosin or the Saanich Peninsula, people like us, living out in the sticks but needing to work "in town," did so mainly because it was cheaper. A minority had jobs here in the unorganized districts, and living closer to work made travel easier.

One of these was called "That's *Doctor* Artlett, please" (after I had begun to address him politely as Mister). The Artletts lived two houses past the Seymours — the cottage in between was empty, except for the summer. Adults called Dr. Artlett "Frank," and he had a wife whose name I don't remember, and a teenage son I called Roy who felt himself too old to play or explore with me. Frank Artlett was short, pompous and dull, but it seemed that his work might make up for it because, Clarence told me:

"Snooty Frank. He works in the leper colony."

Leper colony. The dread words produced images in my twelve-year-old mind of horrors previously associated with an episode of *Dick Barton — Special Agent,* or with gallant Allan Quatermain — on screen once more, my hero Stewart Granger — confronting the hag witch, Gagool, in Rider Haggard's *King Solomon's Mines*. I saw this, my first "movie-going" in Victoria, at the brand new Odeon Theatre, which had just opened on Yates Street.

Clarence was almost correct about Artlett. Snooty, yes, and though it may seem hard to imagine now, in 1948 there was still a leper colony, with three afflicted and imprisoned inhabitants (the solitary last one died in 1957) on Bentinck Island, near East Sooke. But Doctor Artlett didn't work there. His position was chief chemist at the adjacent William Head Quarantine Station, beside the black-and-white-striped Race Rocks lighthouse.

The quarantine station was run by the government of Canada, not BC. Perhaps because of his position as a federal civil servant, Frank Artlett regularly got films from the National Film Board of Canada which he showed, using a 16mm projector and screen in his basement, on Sunday evenings, to invited lake residents only.

Mrs. Artlett served coffee, and people brought cakes.

Although many invitees quickly tired of Frank Artlett's personality, a lot of the NFB films he got for us weren't as dull as they seemed in the catalogue. They could be coloured cartoons, soundtracked with music by Oscar Peterson, or a backstage look at the Toronto Maple Leafs getting ready for a playoff game, or wartime documentaries. They were welcome in a world of home entertainment on its cusp before the arrival of TV.

Chief chemist Frank Artlett did take me out to his William Head Laboratory several times — in a mood-mix of relief and disappointment, I didn't get to actually *see* a leper. When he found out that I was interested in his microscope and what it revealed (plus all the other brass and glass tubes and retorts, supported on mahogany cabinetry with cubbyholes, and multiple drawers all of which looked like something from the lab in my *Illustrated Sherlock Holmes*), he became not stuffy at all.

My interest in his slides of germs was genuine. It was the first time I had used a microscope. Artlett also deeply regretted the unpleasant necessity of quarantine to prevent the transmission of dangerous diseases, and the unhappiness it caused the lepers who were separated for a lifetime from their families.

My Own Submarine

Jim's mercurial moods ruined our first Glen Lake Christmas. It began normally, with a church service conducted by a man my parents still described as "Our new vicar" — most Canadians said "minister" — whose name was Hywel Jones. When our paths first crossed, he served Anglican parishes in Langford, Colwood and

Metchosin, each with its own small church. Mr. Jones (for anyone brought up by the Aunts, a vicar was never addressed as Reverend), although a native of Great Britain, wasn't considered to be from Home because by his name and his accent he was clearly Welsh.

He conducted my confirmation and first marriage, and until he died at a rank the Aunts could relate to (the ninth Anglican Bishop of British Columbia), Hywel Jones was the only cleric I have been able both to admire and like. An occasional naval chaplain came close.

THAT FIRST CHRISTMAS SEASON at the lake began on a high note for everyone but me, who had to sing *Gloria in Excelsis Deo* for my supper on the night before Christmas Eve. I sang it without accompaniment in front of all the Williamses who had invited us, as well as their brother-in- law's tribe, the Birtwhistles. Ralph, pronounced Ralf — not Rayfe — Birtwhistle was a plumber.

Going solo in St. Paul's Cathedral couldn't have increased my embarrassment. Jim followed me with a medley of other carols played on Phyllis Williams' upright, and as a finale, his own composition from his Singer & Keyes days, words and music credit only to himself as Mr. Keyes:

When the birdies get together …

The next line by Jim-as-Mr. Keyes was *It's the time for love.* This positive sentiment got us through Christmas Eve. I used my kindling hatchet with its leather handle to cut down a fir Christmas tree from our own property, and my mother made Angela and me each a stocking out of heavy brown butcher's paper with images cut from old Christmas cards, then glued on.

For presents, we each had Lifesavers story books again, and Angela got her own replacement copy of *Squirrel Nutkin* (because she had torn two pages out of her original copy — given to her at the mad professor's house in Sherborne — and had marked up the rest so much with crayons that they couldn't be read). Posted from Nan in London, I got *Doctor Doolittle and the Secret Lake.* Just published, it had cannibals and human sacrifice, but it wasn't very funny, so I didn't like it as much as I had hoped.

What I loved was a submarine. It was given to me by both parents and made of painted blue-grey metal, about a foot long, with a conning tower and shark's teeth decorating the front. It also had a propeller attached to a rubber band inside it which, when wound tight (the instructions assured me), would propel it underwater.

I put it in the lake, and it didn't.

My temporary disappointment — the sub worked adequately for short patrols in the kitchen sink — was understandable; Jim's changed mood on Boxing Day wasn't. His "Mr. Keyes" song-and-dance at Phyllis Williams' piano was exchanged for saying to us that he "had malaria"— and going back to bed.

He stayed there for two days, with his face to the wall, ignoring any attempt by any of us to cheer him up. My mother took him turkey soup she had made from the remains of Christmas dinner, but that didn't help either.

This first of too many subsequent "Jim's Silent Nights" lasted all through the Christmas season, and meant that I had to "do" all the firewood for the stove *and* the fireplace, and "do" the chickens as well — letting them out in the morning, feeding them, collecting the eggs, locking them up at night. His "malaria" got better in time for them both to go back to the Williamses for an "adults only" New Year's Eve.

It was only after the psychoanalysis of my own middle-aged feelings about inexplicable abandonment that I began to grasp at a gut level what Jim must have felt he had left behind him on that New Year's Eve. A man who used to be the life of the party in white tie and tails in London's West End, now "tinkling the ivories" for Ralph Birtwhistle *et al*: almost broke, nearing fifty, and "out in the sticks" at Glen Lake.

Harsh Lessons in the Laws of Probability

For my thirteenth birthday (Angela had turned seven the week before, and still didn't go to school), my best present was a fishing rod. It had a fixed reel and no bend or flexibility, but as Clarence had told me "them bass and sunfish buggers only go for worms," and by looking under any rock at our shoreline I could find worms to stick on a hook, lack of sophistication in my piscatorial equipment wasn't a problem at first. By late April I could catch sufficient sunfish to find one that was big enough to clean and eat. I could do the eating by myself. My mother refused to do the cleaning. That meant another on-the-job experience.

Keith Williams provided it.

Keith was a little older, an inch taller, a few pounds heavier, and the only boy of my age that I had to play with. To get to each other's houses by going up our driveways and along the road was too time-consuming and dull. Instead, we made what we called our Indian Trail (childishly unaware that Indigenous feet had actually made a trail here first), cutting it through the Wohlers' and Shaylers' logged-over properties.

Before I chopped any branch off a standing tree, I made sure to heed Clarence's warning about "widow-makers," and look up to make sure there wasn't a dead one waiting to come down on our heads. Once we had the trail safely cut, we needed a fort, which we decided to build in a tree.

Keith provided the lumber and climbed the tree. I stood on the solid ground at the bottom and passed the lumber up to him. His perch in the tree was not solid. I gave him one end of a fir two-by-four, six feet long. He hoisted it about four feet in the air above my head ...

At which point his feet slipped, and his hand holding onto a branch slipped, and so he switched the hand holding the two-by-four — and from a clear blue sky, a sawmilled widow-maker fell on my head, and I passed out.

Irony happens: luckily my skull wasn't fractured. When my parents asked about the bruise, I told them I tripped and fell accidentally against a tree. How much worse things might have been "by accident" was proved starkly by something I did the next day. Why I did it, I don't know, and it should have been impossible.

After the completion of our tree fort, I saw a brown creeper — a very small and inconspicuous bird — creeping in its distinctive fashion up a tree. From ten feet away I picked up a stone, not much more than a pebble, and threw it. The pebble struck the brown creeper's tiny head and killed it stone dead. You already know I love birds. Given my mediocre performance as a bowler in cricket, for me to hit such a target at that distance, I repeat, was impossible. Yet it happened. And that it happened is something I cannot explain, forgive or forget.

Gold Panning in Suicide Canyon

Our mining adventure took place on the 24th of May, Queen Victoria's birthday (and still celebrated on the actual date). While the adults took the smaller children to watch Johnny Williams driving a dockyard float past city hall in the parade downtown, Keith and I went prospecting for gold.

The logical starting point was the Goldstream River (which got its name from an actual gold rush), but to get there required a five-mile hike via the E&N track. Keith suggested that as we were using the railbed anyway, we should take a look at the trestle bridge over what he called Suicide Canyon. The name was scary, but also exciting. To get there before the train made its morning up-island run, we left right after breakfast.

It was a nice sunny day but we didn't get too hot. I had my Boy Scout canteen with water to drink, and my empty metal mess kit, which we intended to use when we panned for the gold. We reached the trestle by nine-thirty, and the height *was* scary — about five times higher than the cliffs at Burton Bradstock. We began to walk cautiously across the bridge, stepping on the creosoted wooden sleeper-ties between the rails, and trying not to look down to eternity at the gaps between them.

Halfway across, we heard the train whistle. We had to decide whether to go on or turn back. Neither choice seemed attractive. At the midpoint of the trestle, cantilevered off to the uphill side, a very small platform had a handrail around it, and a sign reading "Save Your Bacon." The purpose of the bacon-saving platform was to solve precisely our problem if it was happening to a railway maintenance crew.

The train sounded its whistle again. We moved onto the tiny platform — the distance straight down was prodigious. The train slowed to go over the trestle. As it went past us, almost touching us, we waved at the driver, who waved back and grinned.

After the train had passed, Keith said, "Let's start the panning at Niagara Falls."

I thought he was joking, but apparently there was a local waterfall with the same name behind us, around a corner of the canyon. We clambered down from the suicide trestle and followed the streambed, and there it was. Not as big as the real Niagara, but just as high. Unfortunately, when we gold-panned the pool at the bottom we didn't find any nuggets in my Scout's mess kit. We tried again in the Goldstream River itself, but that wasn't any better.

I was ready to call our prospecting quits, but Keith said that as we were out here anyway, we might as well switch from gold, and explore the old copper mine on Mount Finlayson instead.

Today the thought of the effort required makes me want to lie down, but thirteen-year-old boys are the origin for the cliché of boundless energy. To get to the old copper mine we only had to walk back along the Goldstream, climbing over dead logs and hopping between mossy rocks for half a mile; then the same again, overland around the base of Mount Finlayson; then upward in a curve, climbing for five hundred feet through heavy salal undergrowth — at which point Keith said the mine entrance wasn't where he thought it would be.

Weaker souls with even a single neuron of common sense would have given up. We sidled sideways along a rock face and found purple-and-rust-coloured mine tailings spilling from a hole in the wall. Now that we had discovered the El Dorado we were looking for, we had to go into it, and although we had no flashlight, it didn't matter because I had a waterproof box of "Be prepared" Boy Scout matches.

A short distance inside the hole in the wall we found some bits of old rotting wood blocking our way. I lit a match and we pushed the old wood bits aside. The air was colder and the match went out. Keith was three feet in front of me. I suggested that he should stop while I lit another match, and wait until I caught up to him, so that we could see where we were going. He did stop. My suggestion was sound: the next flare of a "Be prepared" match revealed a black void dropping away and below.

Those copper mining playgrounds of ours are now blocked off.

To retrieve some scrap of value from all our hard work, we took a couple of pieces of the purple rock tailings home and tried to smelt them with Johnny Williams' blowtorch, but that didn't get any copper either.

A Garden Tea Party for Prestige

SUMMER ARRIVED and my penal servitude with Miss King and her "drownded" in Grade 6 at Langford Elementary ended, leaving me no wiser — the curriculum hadn't covered anything I hadn't learned before.

By this time I think my parents had realized that my education wasn't following a smooth trajectory. But how, or whether, that course needed correcting had to be postponed because they had more important things to think about.

Jobs and money.

Jim concluded that the shortfall in cash from Newstead was a result, not of a shortage of realty customers or his inadequate knowledge of how business cycles always affected the Victoria housing market — after a short peak which had coincided with our family's arrival, it was in a characteristic slump — but a lack of prestige.

The guardian angel of salesmen flapped its wings and led him to a fortuitous lunch at the prestigious Union Club. Jews and women weren't wanted there in 1949 but everybody else who was anybody in Victoria was. Jim met someone "who knew someone," and came home in May with a new business card, embossed:

Pemberton Holmes Ltd.
Established 1887
James H.C. Gurr, Sales Associate

Pemberton Holmes overflowed with prestige. The Pemberton half, a founding father of Victoria who worked for the ubiquitous Hudson's Bay Company, had long gone to his reward. H. Cuthbert Holmes (Major, Indian Army, Retired) now presided over the firm, which prided itself for having the oldest telephone number in Canada, 8124, as also embossed on Jim's new card.

At the firm's summer garden party I was introduced to the Major (as H. Cuthbert professed to not-needing-to-be-called, but felt annoyed if he wasn't), who wore a white linen suit, thin, metal-rimmed specs, and a trimmed military moustache. He carried an ebony cane for added support. The Major's trim, Indian Army moustache was like Jim's — who had purchased a new, double-breasted, dark blue blazer from British Importers Men's Wear on Government Street especially for the occasion.

The blazer had Royal Marines gold-plated buttons, and on the breast pocket had the Royal Marines gold-threaded crest, with the

British lion on top of Gibraltar and the motto *Per Mare Per Terram* underneath. Strictly speaking, the gold-threaded version was for officers only, not corporals, but British Importers, being tailors, not officers, were just happy to take a badge-buyer's cash, whether on sea or on land, like the motto.

Escorting the Major was "my son Pip," who was an officer (or had been, as an RCAF bomber pilot) and had genuine hero medals and a magnificent fly-boy moustache to prove it. "My son Pip" (aka Phillip) Holmes, heir-apparent to Pemberton Holmes, was extremely tall and when he bent to shake my hand we looked like Mutt and Jeff.

The heir apparent said in a grave tone: "Hello, David."

As he did so, he winked at my mother beside me, who touched her hair and smiled back at him, as she used to with Nanki-Poo and Dickie Baer at Barton Olivers, and so I said, "Hello Sir Pip." I had only meant to say "sir": adding the "Pip" was from nervousness, but the fly boy recipient was delighted, and everyone else laughed. And when Victoria was small, people remembered little things like that.

My mother was in a summer dress, and had her hair down like Veronica Lake's, and was wearing a hat like Ingrid Bergman's in *Casablanca*. She and Sir Pip and the rest of us were at a sales associates' garden party ("for good leads," meaning names of potential buyers) in the Uplands neighbourhood: a capitalized Pemberton Holmes brochure described it as "The Most Prestigious Residential Area in Victoria." It was laid out by Frederick Olmsted, the landscape genius behind New York's Central Park as well as Mount Royal in Montreal (and, in 1949, strictly off limits to any "good leads" who looked like the Hindus or had names like Lim Bang).

Angela wasn't with us. I can only suppose that I was taken along by Jim so that D.H.C. Gurr could be shown off as similarly triple-initialled prestige proof of J.H.C.'s masculinity to the Major and Sir Pip and the rest of Pemberton Holmes Ltd., in the same way my three-year-old self had been shown off to the prewar tailors and barbers of Bond Street.

Having my hand shaken by Sir Pip and the Major impressed Jim, but as the previous important person to shake it, Field Marshal Earl Alexander of Tunis, was now the Governor General, it didn't impress me quite as much.

Nor did going to the Pemberton Holmes Uplands tea party produce sufficient good leads, and thus sales, to keep the financial wolf any further away from 3975 Glen Lake Road. (We had acquired a street number, but it still wasn't needed by the post office who kept delivering to Gurr, RR1, Langford.)

After the garden party, and my mother's Veronica Lake smile at Sir Pip, she said she was going to get a job too — but it wouldn't be until the end of the summer, once Angela was going to school. When I asked who would look after us after school, before either working parent returned at the end of the workday, her face took on its cold expression. She said in her "this one" tone:

"*You* will, of course, until I can think of something else."

The "something else" became Kythe — but the Aunts' visit came first.

The Flushing Situation

The summer of '49 was baking hot. When the Aunts arrived for a "big surprise" visit in mid-July, the temperature on the thermometer I had hung outside the kitchen larder (we still had no refrigerator), in the shade, read ninety-three degrees Fahrenheit.

The dry spell and evaporation had made the lake level drop by two feet, and our shallow well had dropped with it to rock bottom — in our case, gravel.

We could still wash in the lake so we didn't need the shower, but for dishes in the kitchen sink, or to use the toilet, the only solution was to carry up a bucket of water from the shoreline to the house, either to heat in pans on the stove or to refill the toilet tank after each flush. I carried two buckets for balance, and the distance was short, but the slope was steep and it was hard work. I didn't want to do more of it than I had to.

This part has to be blunt: our family members already knew about the "flushing situation." Somehow our visitors were also gently advised to the effect, "Don't flush every time — unless you really must!" To lessen my workload, whenever possible I let more than one person use the toilet to pee.

This meant not so many flushes. It also meant less climbing onto the seat, lifting off the overhead tank lid, refilling the overhead tank from the bucket (balanced with me on the seat), and finally replacing the overhead lid. With visitors on such extra-sensitive occasions I monitored the bathroom flushing situation by waiting out of sight around the corner of the tiny hall, before doing my bucket duty.

The first day of the Aunts' visit passed "flush-wise" with no hitch. They had both worked as skilled nurses during the Boer War, coping with vastly greater military gastrointestinal unpleasantness than our plumbing.

The next day was equally hot. We don't need to know now which adult "went first," and I didn't keep track. The second user this time was my sister who still, at barely six, didn't run on autopilot when it came to "pulling the chain." I let her leave, went to pull the chain for her, and saw a dark rust stain in the bowl.

At first I thought that it had to be sediment which one of my buckets had collected from the lake: then I realized it was blood. Because I did "flush on autopilot," even as I was shocked by what I saw in the bowl, my hand automatically reached for the chain's handle — but then I stopped, and went to tell my mother.

She didn't panic. The first practical problem was identifying the source of the blood — it might not be my sister's; there were several adult women in the house. That was quickly discounted. The internal bleeding *was* from Angela, but how long had it been going on?

I couldn't answer that. I not only didn't study the contents of the toilet bowl each time I flushed it or refilled the tank; I tried to avoid it.

Angela was asked gently: "How long?" She couldn't say.

Then more urgently: "More than a day?" She began to cry.

My mother's best guess was perhaps two or three days.

Elspie diagnosed it as "acute nephritis," inflammation of the kidneys, demanding immediate hospitalization. My parents took Angela to the only general hospital in Victoria: the Royal Jubilee, where the severity of her condition was confirmed. My sister was there for almost a month before she got better; my mother visited her every day.

"No More Worms!"

THIS FISHING COMMANDMENT had been written on a postcard John Sandys-Wunsch sent me after the Aunts left, and we adhered to it as if it had been carved in stone. His father, the retired second-in-command of the RCMP, when he hadn't been tracking and killing Mad Trappers, was a fly-fishing fanatic who caught monstrous trout in the far north back-and-beyond. Their photos hung on the walls of his study between Lawrence of Arabia and the King of Siam.

He also had multiple fly rods, creels and hip waders, so equipment for our trip wasn't a problem, but as the height of John's father was over six feet, the hip waders I put on came up to my neck.

I had gone to Duncan on the train, arriving at Quamichan Lake in time for lunch; as it was unexpectedly raining, we ate in John's pup tent on the lawn. Our fly-fishing expedition to the Cowichan River wasn't until the next day: I suggested a Monopoly marathon to fill the gap. John said he had something way more exciting to show me:

A *letter about our island!*

The CPR had finally replied to our offer to buy it from them for one dollar. The letter said that they weren't quibbling over our price, but "Our Office of Indian Land Holdings and Rights of Way" (I may not have the wording of all this exactly) "are still reviewing whether or not terms of our agreement per Esquimalt and Nanaimo track bed, circa 1883, might be infringed."

(To past and current Indigenous dwellers on Vancouver Island this track bed gobbledegook is always known as the Great Land Grab, because it grabbed 800,000 acres from the natives and gave it to a coal baron called Robert Dunsmuir.)

Instead of waiting for the CPR's lawyers, we went out to look at our one-dollar property in John's new inflatable rubber boat. It was new, but also purchased from Army & Navy War Surplus. That meant at least five years had passed since the date of manufacture, and various bits of it were beginning to perish.

An observant adult might have been concerned: the only downside for us was how long it took, using a foot pump, to blow it up. Going out to "our island" in a canoe would have been much quicker and less effort, but John said we needed the practice with the War Surplus inflatable today, because we would be using it for our fly-fishing tomorrow on the Cowichan River.

The following morning his father drove us, and our inflatable, out to a part of the river that he recommended "for beginners," and waited until our amateur preparations were completed. Then he left us "for a proper fishing spot," presumably for experts, further along the river bank.

The Cowichan is not a stream to be taken lightly. Even in summer, when the flow is reduced, there are still fallen logs and branches hidden below the surface which can rip open a rubber tube — or, in our case, boat — more quickly than an occupant could gut a fish.

John Sandys-Wunsch was cautious and methodical in everything he did. He watched where we went — and where my hooks went while I was learning to cast a fly — and all would have been well until Peter Margetts arrived on a bank above us and began to hurl down rocks.

He was not alone. He had some other boys with him, whom he encouraged to start hurling rocks and abuse at us as well. Why he did that, and why his animosity was so visceral — why he was even there — I never found out because our paths never crossed again. Probably my father and his father and the empty LCB Rye bottles in the milking parlour had something to do with it. And probably my squeaky "la-di-da" Limey accent didn't help.

At that moment, neither Sandys-Wunsch nor I were looking for reasons, or anything else. Our attention was momentarily distracted by the thrown rocks, and our inflatable ran into an underwater tree. The boat was primitive war construction, made to save costs, and only had two separate air chambers, one to each side. The side nearest the bank began to fill with water, and the boat to tip.

At a different stretch of the river, it could have been very bad. Fortunately our tipping point occurred where the current was mild, with a smooth rock bottom just below the log that snagged us. John's father heard the shouting and returned. Peter Margetts wasn't prepared to have a faceoff with a Mad Trapper-killing Assistant Commissioner of the RCMP, and buggered off instead.

In a farcical conclusion to my fly-fishing initiation, I survived the sinking inflatable only to come near to drowning when the commissioner's borrowed hip waders filled with water up to my neck. That hazard was emptied in time for me, at long last, to actually learn to swim.

No Logs Needed

It was so simple. After so many attempts, over a span of eight years, beginning with Aunt Nan's lesson in a pool of the River Wye near the Luftwaffe's bomb craters; then naked with Miss Snow and canvas water-wings in the rain at Sherborne's pool; to Jim's "hollow buttock" fixation in the Duncan creek at the bottom of the farm last year … This year, and this time, it took only five minutes with Mrs. McRae at Glen Lake.

The McRaes owned the cottage between the Seymours and the Artletts, the one that was empty for ten months in the year because they lived in Vancouver and only came over to the island for their summer holiday. For that reason, we hadn't got to know them, but after the prestige party my mother met Mrs. McRae, discovered she was a physical fitness teacher who had taught her own two children to swim, and told me to row over in the dinghy and say hello.

The McRaes' shoreline had no beach: the steep bank was uncleared, and covered with thick salal to the water's edge. The only way through it was by walking down along a fallen, huge dead fir, left behind because of knots, like the one at the top of our drive. The remains of this one had dropped from the top of the bank into deep water.

I knew about the tree. A large bass liked to hide under it, and I used to tie the dinghy to a dead branch and (in those crude angling days before I converted to a fly fisher) drop a worm for it. When I arrived this time, there wasn't a bass or even a sunfish under the log; the McRae kids were swimming around it instead. The person who must be Mrs. McRae was standing on top of the log, wearing a flowery swimsuit which had a short skirt like something my mother wore for playing tennis.

I tied up the dinghy to the log.

Mrs. McRae beckoned me to walk down the log with her. She held out a hand, and said in a pleasant conversational tone reminding me of Aunt Nan something along the lines of, "Hi, you must be David. I know you can't swim but come in anyway."

So, holding Mrs. McRae's hand, I walked down the log with her to a spot at which I realized that my feet were not in fact on the log ... nor had they been on the log for some time. At which point Mrs. McRae let go of my hand and said in her cheerful manner, like Aunt Nan's:

"You don't need the log anymore because you can swim."

Adolescence in a Perfect Eden
or
Act One: "Tragedy and Comedy"

Sir James Douglas, Chief Factor of the Hudson's Bay Company, Chief Magistrate of the Crown Colony of Vancouver Island, looked upon its majestic mountains, its crystal lakes, its flora of Easter lilies and shooting stars blossoming beneath the dogwoods and Garry oaks, and declared it paradise.

A perfect Eden ...

To me it was. To those responsible for my welfare, not so much.

Kythe and cash: in Glen Lake's Eden, the constant presence in our house of the former, and absence of the latter, were an insoluble equation for my parents. My great aunt Kythe Mackenzie was supposed to be its solution. She arrived to start her babysitting just as Angela went to school, and therefore allowed our mother to go to work.

"Please, Sir. I Want Some Credit."

Exchange controls were introduced by the Labour government in Great Britain when the Second World War ended, because said government had run out of pounds sterling, and even more so US dollars.

Very roughly: each adult leaving England on holiday could take one hundred pounds, and each child fifty; if they were skipping town completely, as we did in 1947, a parent could take one thousand pounds. Even doubling that (for two parents) to two thousand — which was then able to buy four times its value in Canadian dollars — we had to pay the cost of sea and rail passage. Our cash cushion was nowhere near enough to live on.

Which is why my mother got a job as a sales assistant at Scurrah's Ltd. — quality dresses and assorted ladies' wear — on Yates Street, two doors down from the Odeon Theatre. Percy Scurrah was its proprietor, and a future mayor of Victoria, keenly overseen by his wife, Mrs. Scurrah (even more keen as a Christian Scientist), employing their daughter, Mrs. Jennings, wife of the sales manager, Gordon Jennings. My parents became friends with this younger couple, comforting Mrs. Jennings when her mother, Mrs. Scurrah, dismissed her daughter's migraine headaches as "all in her head."

I DIDN'T HAVE A NEW JOB to replace the *Star Weekly*'s. I made some pocket money on a dime commission from the occasional sale of our eggs, at fifty cents a dozen, to neighbours without chickens of their own.

One day in August I was at Nimmo's store in Langford, hoping to buy the new *Superman* and *Captain Marvel*, but after getting a cold Orange Crush from the cooler I realized I had no cash in my pocket, and made Mr. Nimmo a business proposition:

If he would grant me fifty cents' credit, I would redeem it with a dozen eggs.

"Credit?"

He said the word with an endless Scots burr to the "r" and a freezing look colder than my Orange Crush; and then — as a summons, not a question — addressed his wife, Mrs. Nimmo, at the back of the store:

"Edna, will ye no come here please."

She came.

He said: "Edna, this boy wants credit."

If you are a Dickens fan, or have seen any version of Oliver Twist making his starved request for "more" from the brutal workhouse master, let me assure you that nothing in print or on film matches the frozen disbelief of the two Nimmos.

He said: "What is your last name, and where do ye live?"

I said: "Gurr, on Glen Lake Road."

He said: "Edna, look that up in the book. Wee Gurr, ye'll stay put."

He pronounced it *boook* and *poot*. Edna Nimmo *loooked*. I stayed *poot*. My parents were phoned from the back of the store. Some agreement was reached.

Mr. Nimmo opened his cash register vault, removed two twenty-five cent pieces, and placed them on the counter in front of me. He rang in the value of my comics and Orange Crush.

With arctic frost on every "r," he said:

"Edna, ye'll be writing this all down."

He pronounced it *doon* as in *doom*.

"Thirrrrrty cents is the total of Wee Gurr's purchased goods. I'll now be deducting that from the loaned amount. His credit remaining is twenty cents. I'll now be pooting the balance back in the till."

He took the two quarters from the counter, put them back in the cash register and said:

"Wee Gurr, ye can be going now."

I don't know if his ledger ever showed, "Balance owing: nil."

Old Trout

Back to Kythe: She had been brought across the world at the age of sixty-five to solve the problem of looking after two young children while their parents were at work. But the children were at school, and their parents were employed, five days a week.

This meant that she was stuck alone in the bush, knowing no-one, and with no vehicular means of escape, for most of the hours of each working day. When my parents returned from civilization, tired no doubt from their labours, Kythe would use that moment to open a discussion with Jim about, if not the futility of her existence, at least the immediate difficulty of her isolated situation. In rebuttal, to her increasing fury, he christened her "Old Trout."

They drove each other mad.

The argument would end with Kythe threatening to leave for Home, before being halted by "having an attack of my angina."

She always recovered promptly (living on to eighty-four) but to me at thirteen the angina attacks looked convincing and frightening. After the worst one she managed to get from the house into the Austin A-40's passenger seat, where I discovered her, apparently unconscious, with her lower false teeth falling out.

Kythe was given the front, small compartment with the greenhouse windows as its two outside walls. Angela and I had the larger interior part, which had space for two beds in it. This meant that Kythe had to go through our room to get to hers. Our bedtime was still early; she was a night owl.

When we got up in the morning to have breakfast, we ate it at the Arborite counter in the kitchen nook. With only four people, the nook was an uncomfortable squeeze. With five people, one of them had to perch on a stool at the end of the counter, blocking the door. In Kythe's considerable favour — and in marked contrast to my mother — she was an excellent cook, which at least made the actual eating more pleasant.

To make sitting down for supper seem normal, Jim acquired an unfinished plywood worktable that he made suitable for a dining room by varnishing it twice and then putting it in the living room — but, because of the other living room furniture, there was no space left for proper dining-room chairs. He got metal fold-ups instead.

After supper, and its dishes, we folded the tin chairs and all sat squeezed on a sofa and a single overstuffed armchair, listening to Jack Benny, or Red Skelton, or Ted Mack's *Amateur Hour* on the radio. Most memorable for me was the CBC's special concert for the victims of the Red River flood in Manitoba. Kate Smith, a huge American singer with an even bigger voice, took our minds off our trivial living difficulties by belting out "You'll Never Walk Alone" and made everybody cry.

Before this natural disaster in Manitoba — but without Kate Smith's (or anyone else's) emotional support — I did have to walk alone: into the five army huts called Belmont High School.

A Truth Universally Refuted

THERE WAS NO ROMANCE about our meeting. Belmont got saddled with its name from our local BC Tel Exchange, and its five huts had been taken out of war surplus storage at Colwood, and transported to their new gravel patch on Jacklin Road, only a year before I got there.

That year students and teachers alike had been required to use an outhouse. By the time of my arrival in Grade 7 (my eighth school in eight years), there were almost two hundred children in Grades 7 to 12. Inside toilets had been installed, but the furnace didn't work.

One separated hut was divided between home economics (housekeeping) for girls and industrial arts ("shop") for boys. The other huts had been stitched together, but roughly, and the joints showed in the floor and the walls. I have no memory of anything academic in that year, which leaves us with my first impressions of the staff:

Mr. A.H. (Archie) Stephenson, principal.

Also Mr. Parrott, social studies (with a clubfoot).

Also Mr. Cook, industrial arts (with a walleye).

And Mrs. Maughan — who had been the mother hen of a tiny school at Albert Head and had brought over her flock to Belmont, with her ample self. She taught English, which is why she made more of an impression on me (as did the intriguing rumour that she lived on a turkey ranch).

There were a handful of others whose personalities gradually emerged, such as Mr. Palsson. He began with chemistry and went on to coach the girls' softball team until, after I had graduated, coaching girls too thoroughly led to his being asked to stop doing both. While still in favour, Mr. Palsson's star turn at Christmas concerts was reciting Tennyson's poem "The Charge of the Light Brigade."

Mr. Cook kept his one good eye on me while I hammered out "Assignment One: A wrought-iron tent peg," very crudely, in his blacksmith class. Then I moved on to "Assignment Two: Fine carpentry, carve or saw a mortise and tenon joint out of red cedar," both bits carved and/or sawn, very badly. I still have the rusted tent peg: now, like its smith, a genuine antique.

Mr. Parrott's unfamiliar "social studies," I discovered, were just what everybody else (in my seven previous schools) had called history and geography. Although — Great Aunt Hetty's at Swyre excepted — I have always liked parrots, I didn't like this one, and still resent him. The social study he applied to me affected the rest of my life. It unfolded as follows:

By some unfathomable process, at the end of the Grade 7 school year a Belmont staff meeting concluded that my previous worthy institutes of schooling had stuffed me so full of knowledge that, in the following September, I should be skipped two years ahead, into Grade 10.

From at least the time of Jane Austen, "This is for your own good" is a truth universally refuted by children to whom it is addressed. Invariably the phrase furthers some adults-only agenda.

Harold Parrott disputed the Terman theory (which said, roughly, that bright kids should be skipped ahead in school regardless of their physical, social and emotional development). He claimed that if I leapfrogged my peers, it would affect their development by making them "feel bad." And he half-won his argument: I would be skipped ahead, but only a single year, into Grade 9.

It's certainly true that academic achievement was a sensitive area in the Unorganized Territory of Langford, Colwood, Metchosin and Glen Lake. Our combined classes were very small: a majority of students would leave Grade 10 to find the work for which they had been trained in home economics and shop. The final roll call of my graduating class had only thirteen names. Ten of these took the commercial program; only three, university entrance.

As I have the last word on the subject: in adult life, I never found evidence that any of the children in the Grade 8 class that I skipped ever felt any better because of it — or worse, for that matter. Right or wrong, that one additional year of missed advancement would have completely changed my future naval — and even my marital — career. The Royal Canadian Navy would have sent me to be trained in the Royal Naval College at Greenwich, designed by Sir Christopher Wren, instead of in army prefabs in Esquimalt; and once back in England, who knows what questions might have been asked, and whom I might have met, or married?

Myrna's Beauty Parlour and the Colour Thing

THE RAWNESS OF BELMONT in its first years meant that from my point of view, in several ways minuses were pluses. There was no gymnasium, so no gym practice. No playing fields, so no organized sports — and no "cavalier and roundhead" tournaments of budding masculinity in the showers, because there were no showers.

The only thing organized for the physical activity hour was picking up rocks to make a diamond for the junior girls' softball team and Mr. Palsson. As Belmont was built on the gravel bed left behind from a glacial river, the rocks returned to the surface every time it rained, which it did almost every second day of the months between October and May of every school year I was there.

In the absence of a cafeteria, the staff and the students from further away brought lunches in lunch pails. But as I lived nearby I frequently went home, usually for egg sandwiches because we had free eggs. If the gravel on Glen Lake Road had been smoothed by the Public Works grader, I rode my CCM bike.

When the corduroy ripples and potholes were too bad, I could walk through a shortcut in the bush that took me past James' mink farm and Shafoval's store. I felt sorry for the mink and tried not to look at them when they stood up to look at me through the wire of their cages. Nobody at Belmont felt sorry for Mr. Shafoval, because he and Mrs. Shafoval with their thick Russian accents thought all of us were thieves.

(Some bottles of pop and bars of chocolate were undoubtedly purloined by students, but the principal thief was in-house: their twenty-one-year-old son. He could not have found the irascible Shafovals to be easy parents. Falling afoul of the law, he went to prison for drug offences.)

Keeping up appearances, for me, meant new clothes for high school from the Eaton's fall and winter catalogue. I was proudest of my bomber jacket, silver-grey satin with a black fur collar.

My US Army and Air Force patches from Dickie Baier had somehow come with me to their starting point in North America (sadly, not the "Big Red 1"), and I got Kythe to sew them onto the bomber jacket sleeves. Despite Kythe's antique Highland aristocratic background, and an upper-class English accent that could shatter glass, she was often surprising in her practical knowledge. As we had no fridge, she showed us how to wrap wet muslin around a clay flowerpot to keep a pound of butter from melting in the summer. And once we got the goats, she knew how to make cheese by wrapping milk curds in the same kind of muslin and hanging them up to drip in the basement.

I also got my first blue jeans to wear instead of the corduroy knickerbockers and knee socks. These jeans were dark blue, but the material seemed more suitable for a canvas sail on our dinghy than flapping around my skinny legs — and flap they did: they had no fitted cut and the cuffs were a foot wide. I felt proud of my clothed appearance nonetheless, but dubious about my first Langford haircut.

There had been a barber in Duncan, and of course there were barbers in Victoria, but that would have meant a half-day trip to town. Instead I was told that I had a special ten-minute appointment at Myrna's Beauty Parlour, two doors away from Nimmo's store at Langford. I approached it with acute misgivings, double-checking in both directions at the Island Highway and Station Road corner to make sure that no other pre-adolescent male was looking back at me as I went in.

Myrna's was a one-woman business with two chairs: one for the person being "done," the second for whoever was either "setting" or, in my case, waiting with embarrassment while one of her regulars, like Mrs. Shayler or Phyllis Williams, had their perm or colouring begun or ended. It was never Mrs. Seymour, who only went to be "done properly" in town.

I DIDN'T FEEL EMBARASSED only about other boys seeing me go into her parlour. Once I was seated in her chair, ready to be "done,"

Myrna ran her hand lightly over the top of my head and down my neck, in a way that made me shiver unexpectedly.

Then she leaned forward, to adjust the smock which would catch my hair, and as she did so her own hair fell across my cheek and something soft pressed against my shoulder. Nothing else happened, but it seemed to be the beginning of something that I couldn't yet describe.

Describing Myrna is straightforward, because she was: perhaps late thirties, blonde, blue-eyed, with curvature that explained what was pressing on my shoulder. Sitting in my waiting chair, I overheard a lot of gossip.

Myrna's love life, or "romance" as her regular ladies called it, had been "on the rocks" but was now again "on fire." The current conflagration had been ignited by the handsome owner of a sawmill on Mill Stream Road, but people weren't supposed to know that because he was one of the Hindus. On my next visit, when the first regular had left and before another one came in, I asked Myrna how it could be a secret if all the ladies knew about it.

"Honey," she said, "if I was peddling life insurance the colour thing might be a problem. But as long as it gives my blue-rinse crowd something to talk about, it's just great for business."

The Recordio Arrives

JIM HAD CHANGED *HIS* BUSINESS. I got back from my haircut with Myrna to be told by my mother that in spite of the maximum prestige at Pemberton Holmes Ltd., established 1887, there hadn't been enough good leads from the Uplands garden party to make ends meet. She said to me, in her cold voice:

"He's made another switch."

"To what?"

"Ask him."

At which point him-Jim came into the kitchen to confront our inquisition — as did Kythe. He was carrying a large box. He put it down on the Arborite table in the nook, and produced another new business card. This one was not embossed:

Hudson's Bay Company
Manager, Major Appliances
(Tell the Lift Operator, Third Floor)

He said: "I told the printers to add the 'Third Floor Lift' bit."

Angela (now in Grade 1) said half cautiously, half proudly:

"Daddy, shouldn't that lift be elevator instead?"

Our mother said: "You've never sold an appliance."

Our male parent didn't usually take her correction lightly. There was a pause, and then he replied to Angela with a patience that surprised all of us:

"You might say an 'elevator' at Eaton's, perhaps. They only started in Toronto. The Hudson's Bay is very old and was started at Home. People in Victoria like 'Olde England.' When customers see me using an English word for their elevator, they will think it gives my *new* business card a little extra class."

For a true salesman, hope springs 24/7 before it's denied. Shortly afterwards, The Bay did a renovation which installed escalators. They kept the elevators but removed their human operators, leaving no-one to talk to.

When our expressions showed less support for the new business card than expected, Jim switched our attention to the large box. A label on the side said "Wilcox-Gay." He opened the cardboard flaps on the top to reveal a plastic lid of something mechanical. This play on words followed:

Jim (pleasedly): "It's for entertainment. Make a guess."

Me (interrogatively): "A new radio?"

Our mother (sharply): "We don't need one."

Angela (excitedly): "A gramophone?" Then (correctly): "I mean phonograph?"

Jim (lifting machine out of box): "You're all wrong. It's something much better." A pause, then (triumphantly): "A Recordio!"

Angela (self-satisfiedly): "I was right. It *is* a phonograph after all."

Great Aunt Kythe (pedantically): "There is no horn. It should be called a radiogram."

Our mother (eye-rollingly): "How much did it cost?"

Jim (mimickingly): "Let's have a worry!" Then (even more pleasedly): "My manager's discount. I get ten percent off."

Me (sensibly): "We don't have any records for it."

Jim (conclusively): "That's the beauty! The Recordio's new technology lets us make them ourselves. We can use it at Christmas when we go to the Williams. I'll do my 'Birdies Get Together' and Dai Dai will sing."

Me (internally): *"Oh no I bloody won't!"*

The Wilcox-Gay Recordio, like all such "new tech," was already behind its time: tape recording was just a hair's breadth away. The Recordio needed its own special blank discs, the size of a conventional 45 rpm, made of semi-soft plastic. It also had its own needles to carve tracks in the plastic as the sound was being recorded.

If that sound wasn't correct, the disc had to be thrown away. And as the same needle that did the carving now did the playing, it continued to carve slightly even as it played. The sound quality, gruesome to begin with, didn't improve with age. Jim wanted to begin rehearsals and test recordings the next day but Pat Colclough, the remittance man, arrived instead.

High Rigging

IMMEDIATELY BESIDE THE FRONT WEST CORNER of our house, one large Douglas fir had been left standing because it originally had too many low branches which would have meant knots. The branches had been removed to improve the view of the lake, but the rest of the tree was a hundred feet tall and leaning over us. Pat Colclough was going to climb up it and chop about thirty feet off the leaning part.

He already had on his logger boots with heavy steel studs in the soles. Now he strapped sharp pieces of metal, like daggers, onto the sides of the boots, so that their sharp tips pointed down. Next he swung a safety rope, already snapped at one end to his wide leather belt, around the circumference of the tree; then he snapped a clip on the safety rope's other end to his belt.

Then he began to climb, stabbing the dagger points on his boots into the bark, holding onto the trunk of the tree with his left hand, while the other one flipped the safety rope upwards. Then he would lean back so that the rope took his weight for a moment, before he did the same thing again. And again. And again.

As if that wasn't difficult enough, every time Pat came to a branch he had to unsnap one end of the safety rope, lift it over the branch, swing it around the tree, lock it on again, and go up some more.

We all stood at the bottom holding our breaths. When he got to the point where he wanted to chop, he threw down one end of an "equipment rope" which he had coiled over his shoulder, and asked us to attach a bucksaw to it.

Today, a high rigger would use a lightweight chainsaw. Pat had to do everything by hand, which also meant using a small axe to chop a notch on one side of the trunk before using the bucksaw to cut in from the other side, two inches higher up than the notch. The notch meant two things: that the saw cut wouldn't bind, jamming the blade, and, even more importantly from our perspective, that the top of the tree would fall in the right direction, into the lake, and not on our house.

All logging is dangerous. High rigging is the most dangerous part of logging. The skill and strength required for the task impressed the hell out of me then, and still does.

In October, I helped Jim to fix our broken wharf with new planks that he believed would allow us to walk to the end of it when the lake rose with the winter rainfall. (I had measured it last year and disagreed, but didn't say so.)

I also started more fencepost holes on the Wohlers' side, to limit the bantams' cross-border fighting; and I killed our first chicken, when Jim refused to do it. I didn't think I could either, but Keith Williams said there was nothing to it, he did it all the time, did I have an axe?

I said: "I use my kindling hatchet, but I think it might be a little dull."

Keith said: "Sharpen it first, hold the feet, put the neck over your kindling block, and just chop."

His instructions were straightforward, but they hadn't mentioned the wings. The chicken flapped them. The task eventually got done, and I got better at it, but I never liked it. Chickens made it easier because they were stupid, but in November we got our first ducks: six mallards with iridescent heads; three white Pekins; and one domestic Muscovy, with red wattles that made it seem part turkey.

When I looked a duck in the eye, an intelligence looked back. Or at least an interest in the proceedings. On rare occasions I gave an already injured one the "Keith chop," but I deserve no kudos: my reluctance as an executioner has never stopped me loving roast duck.

In November the wild ones arrived to spend the winter at the swamp. There were teal, and mallard, and widgeon, but also many I had never seen before, like a hooded merganser, and even the wonderfully costumed harlequin.

The almost non-stop rain that brought the ducks to the swamp had raised the level of the lake to flood all the other low ground, including ours — and also the new planks we had added to our wharf, which Jim had thought would still allow us to walk to the end of it. With more difficulty I again resisted the childish urge to say, "I told you so." The rainforest downpours also began to flood our basement and I had to dig a ditch to divert the waters into the lake.

Clarence Saves Our Bacon

In early December, snow fell on the Sooke Hills, and the lake began to freeze. At first it was just around the edge, and I kept my fingers crossed: if it got firm enough it would provide a super shortcut to visit Keith. It didn't. The ice melted, but two weeks later the snow came back.

We had all gone into town for a Christmas shopping expedition. I was too old for Father Christmas who, in any case, had become Santa Claus, a change of name which for some unknown reason upset me.

My sister still believed in any variety as long as he lived at the North Pole, and Jim arranged for her to get a personalized "Ho ho ho, Angela!" from the Hudson's Bay version in the store. The greeting came with a strong whiff of rum through the beard: behind it, Santa was an off-duty chief petty officer in the Royal Canadian Navy.

We had chocolate éclairs for tea at a bakery on Fort Street. Fort was another Victoria street designed to be wide enough for Rhodesian ox-wagons' turning circles, so that although we had to pay a nickel for a metre, finding a parking spot was never a problem.

It was snowing when we left the bakery, and already almost dark. Jim turned on the headlights of our Austin A-40, but we didn't really need them until we got to the old Craigflower Bridge that crossed the Gorge inlet, just before View Royal village where the Island Highway began. A large vertical thermometer beside the single pump at the sea-level Craigflower gas station said thirty-four degrees Fahrenheit.

Around the corner from the Craigflower Bridge gas station was Four Mile Hill. Our Austin A-40, like most vehicles in Victoria, had no snow tires or chains. Halfway up the hill we got stuck outside Four Mile House. (The building began life as a brothel with booze for Royal Navy matelots in the Age of Sail, who were sent ashore in a work party supervised by an officer to get potable drinking water.) Lacking this knowledge, all I saw was a sign saying: Beer Parlour Closed. A single mock lantern above it was still lit by a dim bulb, and there seemed to be a hint of other light through some closed shutters.

My mother had once owned a motorbike, but Jim was the only one of us with a license to drive a car.

He said, "You'll all have to get out and push."

When that didn't work, my mother said: "There's someone in there. I'm going to knock."

She knocked. A voice said: "Can't you see we're closed?"

It was the voice of our bush telegraph god, Clarence.

My mother said the obvious: "Thank God it's you, Clarence. We're stuck with the kids. Can you give us a push?"

Clarence and two other after-hours drinking companions came out and pushed us to the top of the hill, at which point he let go with the inevitable:

"Saved your bacon, eh?"

We drove down the other side of Four Mile Hill and through View Royal without incident, until we got to Six Mile House, where Millstream Creek enters into the head of Esquimalt harbour. We crossed the creek and the snow became heavier and heavier on Six Mile Hill.

The A-40 skidded and slipped. We held our breath and prayed.

The Austin's British Dunlop tires barely made it, but we got to the top at Colwood Corner: from there it was level or slightly downhill to home at the lake. As we swung right, away from Sooke Road onto the Island Highway, a similar vertical thermometer outside the Colwood gas station registered only thirty degrees Fahrenheit.

Beyond the thermometer, the snow got steadily deeper until it finally brought the Austin's tires to a halt on Glen Lake Road, at the gentle slope just before our drive entrance — where we abandoned it until next morning, and walked.

An Argument about Tinsel

My first high-rigging attempt was on Christmas Eve. It wasn't very high — I was just going to cut off the top of a small Douglas fir, to use it as our Christmas tree — and I didn't have any of Pat Colclough's dagger spurs, or his studded boots to strap them to (I wore my running shoes, which I thought would give me a better grip), or his safety rope. There wasn't any proper rigging either.

Instead I used an old leather harness-rein which had been left in our crawlspace, and strapped that around myself and the tree, tying it safely with a Boy Scout reef knot which wouldn't slip. By the Scouts' book, it should have been a "bowline on a bight," but I couldn't remember how to do it.

The diameter of the trunk at the point where I decided to make my starter cut (the point where Pat Colclough would have chopped the notch with his high-rigger's axe) was only four inches thick. It didn't seem much, until the blade of Jim's ordinary carpenter's saw jammed.

The weight of the tree was binding the saw blade. I finally realized *this* was exactly why Pat Colclough chopped his notch in the other side of the trunk. All I could think of to correct the saw-binding situation was to lean against my leather safety rein and push the top of the tree in the other direction with my left hand, while trying to tug the saw blade out with the right hand.

Neither of my hands was strong, and I had almost given up — when the blade came free! I made the cut on the other side, and one inch higher, successfully. The top of the tree dropped with a satisfying *whoosh*, and flopped into the snow. So did I, because my running shoes slipped. They had only been four feet off the ground the whole time — but it had seemed much higher.

After my mother got over being annoyed by my doing something that she thought was dangerous, she said the tree was very nice. Jim said "The bottom cut is crooked," and then made a better cut himself. After his correction, we decorated my tree with the ornaments we had bought last year for our first lake Christmas.

There was an argument over the placing of tinsel.

Jim said: "Not enough."

Our mother said: "Too much."

Kythe said: "I have always preferred Hogmanay."

Angela said: "When can we have our first present?"

Jim said: "Trust Old Trout to ruin it!" and walked off in a huff.

I saw the Recordio in its box, with all its waiting custom needles and apparently endless supply of blank discs. Even if Jim didn't do it, the damn machine would destroy my Christmas Day.

An Oklahoma Valley of Humiliation

Chores don't stop for Christmas. After Angela and I opened our brown-paper stockings, decorated again by our mother with old cards, and before our parents and Kythe were up, I had to feed the stove and fireplace with dry wood from the boxes beside them, before I went out to feed the chickens, before I had breakfast.

That also meant shovelling the snow. It had continued to fall overnight and was now a foot thick. The chickens didn't like it, but our entire property looked magical. Even our old garbage bag was transformed.

In an era before plastic wrap killed oceans with waste that never dies, we had only our empty glass bottles and tin cans that we put in an old jute-burlap sack, originally for feed grain. The grain sack was tied to a cedar tree, high enough above the ground to keep it away from dogs. On that deep-snow morning the garbage bag, with the dark neck of a bottle sticking out of it, managed to look like what Angela described as "a dwarf snowman perched in a tree, smoking his pipe."

After breakfast and presents — and more wood for the fires — we set off for Christmas dinner at the Williamses. Because of the snow (and a nudge, and a sharp look from my mother towards Kythe), Jim actually took Old Trout's arm. Then he asked me to carry the Recordio box, thus adding insult to the inevitable injury by embarrassment I knew for certain I was going to suffer.

It was worse. The Birtwhistles were there as well. Kythe got things moving vocally by addressing Ralph — in her perfect English diction and with added emphasis on her last word:

"How do you do, *Rayfe?*"

Jim said: "Trout, for God's sake, it's Ralph."

Ralph Birtwhistle said: "Either way's fine. Who wants a rum and Coke?"

Kythe said: "James, with your musical talent, surely you know: the pronunciation is Rayfe, like the conductor, Vaughan Williams."

Johnny Williams, trying as host to cool things down, said: "Folks, there's also rye and ginger. I think I heard my name used there. These conductors in the old country — are we talking trains or buses?"

Kythe said: "Vaughan Williams."

Jim said (triumphantly): "He was a *composer.*"

Kythe said: "When I knew V-W — during my time with Lord Haldane — Rayfe conducted as well. It was the premiere of his Fifth Symphony at a Prom concert in the Albert Hall."

This produced a lull in the proceedings: but not long enough. Jim opened the bloody Recordio machine and made me sing *Oklahoma* into it. Piping out "The Surrey with the Fringe on Top" was already horrible. When the combined Williamses and Birtwhistles applauded anyway, Jim forced me into an even worse encore with: "Ah'm jest a gal who cain't say no. Ah'm in a turrable fix."

In this Okie-accented valley of humiliation and vocal distress, nature came to my aid. The "turrable fix" became a croak. My voice had broken. Although this sound may regrettably exist for posterity somewhere on a Recordio disc, in real life I called singing, as a boy soprano, quits.

Jim's malaria came back on Boxing Day, and he went into his second silent night of depression.

Taking Old Trout to Lunch

THE LAKE FROZE FOR REAL on New Year's Day when the temperature dropped to real zero, Fahrenheit. I read it on the thermometer we had installed on the north wall of the house to check summer temperatures for our kitchen larder.

It was just a cupboard with two square holes through the outer wall, protected by mesh to keep insects out. Until we got the fridge, it was our only way of keeping things cool. At real zero they were too cold. To try and keep butter from freezing solid, I had to close wooden flaps on the outside.

Our cross-country Christmas odyssey with the CPR, which had transported us through four thousand Canadian miles of ice and snow, led us to think that this condition we now faced at Glen Lake was actually the norm: that the two previous mild winters in Duncan and Victoria had been an aberration. In fact — and although the lake was to freeze again a few years later — we had the facts of British Columbia's coastal climate backwards.

We were experiencing record cold.

Our house had been built to be a summer cottage. The pump in the basement froze; the line down the well froze; the chickens froze; the Austin A-40 froze; and it was obvious that we would freeze if I didn't feed the stove and the fireplace with wood, around the clock.

That nearly burned the house down.

The small brick chimney had never been swept. The built-up soot, coagulated with resin from green firewood, caught fire. Langford had a small volunteer fire department across the road from Myrna's Beauty Parlour. The slogan painted over the door of their volunteer shed (with a single truck) was: "We never had a foundation we couldn't save." With that track record, even if the volunteers had been able to get through the snow to our wood-frame house, it would have been too late.

The first rule for a chimney fire is to block the fireplace with anything that will stop the supply of air. We were ignorant. All we could do was stand outside in the snow and watch the terrifying flames shoot from either side of the flue at the top. Miraculously, they went out before the old brickwork could crack and let them into the house.

Fire in our chimney was unwanted. All the other frozen things that allowed us to live "out in the sticks," in an uninsulated house, now needed heat. We bought a dozen coal-oil lamps for the purpose. Keeping the lamps filled meant another chore for me.

Through the whole month of January and the first week of February, I lit and placed lamps beside the pump in the basement, down the well (after lifting the planks of its lid), and beside the engine block of the Austin — it could only take a very small lamp with a flame. I also provided two large lamps for any chickens that hadn't frozen to their perch. In the mornings I removed all the lamps. Every few days their wicks had to be trimmed, and their glasses had to be cleaned of soot.

Skating on the lake made it all worthwhile.

That statement isn't completely true, but the Glen Lake winter of 1950 was a wonderland for a young boy. I had never been on ice skates, and my ankles never got strong enough (nor did our subsequent Victorian winters last long enough) to be a strong skater, but once I had wobbled into motion it was exhilarating. Before the lake's surface was completely frozen over, Keith and I played one-ended hockey in the frozen swamp, watched by miserable, fluffed-up ducks who had migrated here to escape winter.

To cap the birdwatching uniqueness of that real zero winter, a pair of extremely rare trumpeter swans had arrived before Christmas. Each day I watched them as the area of open water decreased, thinking that they must be going to fly away, but they remained. Both Victoria's newspapers (the morning *Daily Colonist* and the afternoon *Daily Times*) reported the swans, and other birdwatchers came out from the city to see them — until the birds got frozen in.

I couldn't understand it then, and I never have since. The only thing that migrating birds need to do to keep warm is to keep flying south. Humans can't make them do that, but some men took a considerable risk, and went out on planks to break up the thinner ice trapping the swans. They didn't say "Thank you" but did at last fly away, making their unique trumpeting cry as they left.

The winter wonderland of 1950 ended by nearly ending Kythe.

SINCE HER ARRIVAL, during the hours that she was alone while we were at school, she had gradually walked all the way around the lake to make the acquaintance of households that we hadn't, because there were no children in them.

One of these childless couples lived three properties beyond the Artletts: another one, opposite it, across the lake. On a Sunday morning, when my parents were home, she announced that she was going to visit these two houses, sequentially. By boat. That she would row.

My mother said: "You're mad. The ice has barely melted at that end."

Jim said: "Does the Old Trout even know how to row?"

I said: "Let me do it."

After more adult discourse, nearly producing an angina attack, it was agreed that I could do the rowing, as long as I promised to turn back if the ice was still too thick. Kythe said that she would walk to the first house, and get them to phone us when she was ready for the amphibious leg. I would row the dinghy over to collect her, and then ferry her to the second house.

The call arrived and I set off. There was a narrow stretch of open water along our shoreline where the southern sun shone to it, but the far side, where the trees shaded everything, looked still frozen.

Kythe was already standing on the bank of the first house, wearing her Mackenzie hunting tartan "trews," as she called trousers: she was looking impatiently at her watch. "You're late."

I said something clever about not knowing we were working to a nautical time of departure, and backed up the dinghy so that its stern was pushed against the end of the wharf.

Kythe said: "You can get out now. I'm going to row myself. The Alexanders are expecting me for luncheon at one, sharp."

I had never met the Alexanders, and was in a double bind. If I abandoned her, my parents would blame me for anything going wrong. If I remained in command, Kythe, enraged, would have an angina attack and might die.

How the next bit happened isn't clear. With my oars, I was pushing the dinghy backwards, to keep its transom tight against the wharf. In a red-faced fit of Highland fury, Kythe kicked the top of the transom. A gap opened. She fell in. The lake was ice cold, and deeper than her less-than-five-foot height. At the age of sixty-five, she disappeared. She couldn't swim.

I let go of the oars. The top of her head appeared. I grabbed her hair. She screamed. The couple in the house finally realized that something was disturbing a tranquil Sunday, and rushed down. I managed to hold both of Kythe's shoulders. That made the dinghy start to swing away from the wharf.

The husband saved the day, and Kythe: I don't remember how. He and his wife took Kythe back to their house to dry out in front of a fire. I was left with the unpleasantness of telling my parents what had happened.

My mother said, "Is she all right? Has she had an attack?"

I shook my head. "That was the most surprising thing. She didn't pass out."

Jim said, "Bloody Old Trout. I've told you her attacks aren't real. Her heart is healthier than any of us."

Coprinus Comatus and Sexual Development

My fourteenth birthday was a week after Kythe's not getting hypothermia from near-drowning. I got a new Raleigh three-speed bike to replace my clunky old CCM and its *Star Weekly* carrier basket. The Raleigh was actually slightly used, but I didn't care: its gears let me think that I was riding the wind. And in those carefree days I never had to wear a helmet.

Then spring did its magic. Our two acres were still half-covered by the undergrowth and leftover remains from the earlier logging. I was clearing a depression beneath a fallen rotting cedar when I discovered two new and rare wildflowers: a delicate pink lady slipper, and a strange white grouping that looked like vertical, waxy tubes with furry legs.

A pamphlet from the Provincial Museum — then housed in the east wing of the Parliament Buildings — following on from a bit about poisonous mushrooms, informed me that:

"The Lady Slipper is a wild orchid. In the species Monotropa uniflora, known as 'Indian Pipe Stem,' as reproduction commences the waxy white flower with its seed-bearing fruit enlarges and becomes erect."

Sexual development cannot be avoided. Keith first suggested (in our tree house), and then showed me, how it could happen for him. When I said that there was still no evidence that this could happen for me, he said:

"Maybe try the lingerie pictures in Eaton's catalogue. That should work."

It didn't.

But a picture of Lana Turner, lounging in form-fitting satin, on a cover of *Photoplay* in Myrna's Beauty Parlour got the process started. Myrna — expert in providing feel-good services to her regulars, after the unburdening of their love lives — with a tactful admixture of kindness and amusement allowed me to keep her *Photoplay*, which enabled me to achieve for the first time, secretly and guiltily, beside the water pump, in the privacy of our crawlspace basement, what the Indian Pipes did innocently on their forest floor.

Gone Birling and Booming

I FINALLY GOT TO WATCH PAT COLCLOUGH "birl" his log booms in Sooke. My parents didn't want me to ride my Raleigh all the way out there, so in April Pat drove me in his pickup truck instead. Sooke was still very small in terms of human population, but its "forest products" were very large.

That unpleasant term for trees was trademarked and copyrighted, a couple of years before our family's arrival, by the second largest logging company in the province, BCFP. I leave you to guess the loggers' use of its third initial, but by now it was ubiquitous on BCFP logging trucks and mills.

Pat Colclough didn't work for BCFP.

All the giant timber firms still tried to dodge union labour as much as they could. In doing so, they employed a feeder network of independent operators to cut down and move logs. The assembled booms formed a floating halfway stop between the wilderness points at which their contents had been felled and the "green chains" up which the logs would eventually be hauled to be made into "wood products" — to actually build what ordinary people still called a house.

Pat was an independent operator. He worked for himself, as a log-birler, whenever he got a call from another independent operator who had a subcontract from BCFP to assemble a boom. These were formed from the logs that had been brought by truck from the old-growth forest inland to be dumped into the calm water of East Sooke inlet. The booms had to wait until the weather in the Strait of Juan de Fuca was good enough for them to be towed by tug to Victoria without breaking up before they got to the several mills that were still there, alongside the Gorge inlet beyond the city's inner harbour. Pat's job was to use two tools so that the booms wouldn't do that coming apart.

His first tool was a peavey: a commercial cant hook with a lethal hinged curved spike, needed for dragging a log. A peavey was brute force, not used so often. What Pat called his birling pole he had carved himself from a piece of straight fir: cedar would have been lighter and easier to carve, but not as strong. The birling pole was about eight feet long, with a sharp metal point on one end.

Most of the time Pat used his birling pole for balance, while he stood on a log. Its point was for jabbing into another log — either to make it start rolling, or stop rolling.

This may sound like doing nothing. On a floating boom it required a bloody sharp eye, a hell of a lot of nerve, and amazing balance. Pat made the logs roll so that he could move them sideways through the water, towards another log already in position. When he jabbed that now-rolling log, Newton's third law would make the log he was standing on want to roll in the opposite direction. To stop it doing that, he had only the huge metal cleats on the soles of his boots.

Log rolling could be deadly. A man — this trade was almost universally male — slipping between two logs would, at the least, have a leg crushed. Crushing parts of the male body above the leg we don't need to think about now, and I didn't then. I just wanted to do what Pat did.

Of course he didn't let me. I wasn't allowed anywhere between two moving logs. But if a log was by itself, with open water on either side, now that I could swim he let me run along it using his birling pole for balance, until I either got to the end or fell off. I had considerable incentive to stay dry: the water of East Sooke inlet in April is not warm.

Testicular Descents vs. Hollow Buttocks

The feud between Jim and Old Trout never abated. How my parents managed to have sex without any of us hearing it in such cramped quarters is a mystery that suggests they didn't have much.

If my mother complained about something Jim had charged on credit to our account (at Scott & Peden feed supply and grocery on Pandora Avenue), he would respond in his needling, mock-anxious, whiny voice that never failed to get under her skin, his mantra "Let's have a worry" — then charge something else for the fun of it.

Our acute lack of living space was eased a little for Kythe — much more so for me — by creating a new room in the attic. As it had no insulation, either between the roof rafters above or ceiling joists below, Jim decided to fix that first with a handy-dandy product called vermiculite.

It came highly recommended ("Easy to use, and lightweight") from a mine in Libby, Montana. It looked like chopped-up bits of shiny mica, squished and then expanded into little accordion folds. In an age not yet worried about the asbestos in it, kids found vermiculite fun to play with.

Jim and I installed it by simply opening the bag and pouring the mica bits between the joists of the living room ceiling: he would pour, and I would level by scraping a piece of wood across the top of the joists. The job went well until Jim stepped where there wasn't a joist, which put both his legs into the living room and almost cost what was left of his manhood.

That was his right testicle. The left one had apparently "just drained away through a catheter" while he was on a lingerie sales mission for Hygrade and staying at the Travellers Hotel in Grimsby: "A bacilli something jumped into my colon."

This medical curiosity, and resultant deficiency, never stopped him from flaunting his remaining nudity in front of us, and occasionally visitors. Letting it all hang out, he walked to and from the bathroom next to the kitchen, via the living room, to his bedroom.

When my mother rolled her eyes and Kythe pretended ostentatiously that she saw nothing, he said that it was good for children to see that the body was nothing to be ashamed of — which didn't seem to match his earlier condemnation of my "hollow buttocks."

THE LIVING-ROOM CEILING WAS REPAIRED by a pal of plumber Ralph Birtwhistle, who knew how "to do drywall." Jim and I sheeted the underside of the attic roof overhead, and the side pony walls, with quarter-inch plywood that we left unfinished. The floor was three-quarter-inch ply, which I varnished. Johnny Williams was able to run wire from the basement fuse box for a single electrical circuit, which gave me one switch, one plug and one light.

My new room stretched the length of the house. The way in and out remained the small hatch, which had always been there. In place of the old piece of wood which had previously sealed it, we made a new hinged lid that could be pushed up from below. There was no space for stairs, so we made a wooden vertical ladder, attached to the wall. The hinge of the hatch, above, was immediately against that wall.

To enter, I had to climb the ladder, hold on to the top rung with one hand, lean away so that my back was supported by the opposite wall, flip the lid up with the other hand and push it away as well, holding it there — otherwise it would fall back on my head — and then haul myself, with a kind of flip, over the edge of the hatch.

This landed me hands and knees on the floor, which was tiresome. My first thought for an easier descent had been to install a fireman's brass pole. When that was vetoed by both parents, I used the same principle in reverse at the top.

I attached a piece of three-inch-diameter dowelling vertically, from the edge of the hatch up to the new sloped ceiling. The dowel gave me something to hang onto while I was holding up the lid, and with less chance of breaking my neck I could now enter my attic.

I COULD; FURNITURE COULDN'T. We solved that problem by cutting a hole in the house's gable end that faced the lake. Then we installed a wood-framed window we found at a second-hand store in Langford. The outer dimensions of the frame were five feet wide by two and a half feet high, which was the maximum obtainable in the gable.

The size seemed ample, but after the opening part was in place — hinged along its top wide edge, and propped up with a stick — it was obvious that a single mattress might go through it, but a bed, and anything like a desk, was going to have to be lifted up in pieces and then assembled. By the end of May, they had been.

For the first time in my life I had what Virginia Woolf dreamt of: *A Room of My Own.*

Privacy was mine — but nothing had improved for anyone else. Kythe got the larger room below that my sister and I had shared. Angela was now moved back into the small outer one, with its two glass walls. This meant that I still had to disturb my great aunt whenever I "went aloft" or "came below."

"Non Sine Periculo"

An adult word here about Kythe. Her generation of young, upper-class British women was doomed to spinster-hood by the slaughter of their corresponding generation of eligible young men in the First World War.

If, by some miracle, those eligibles had been spared, that Kythe would actually have married one of them seems unlikely. She had been blessed with a brain, but not beauty; and, as one of three sisters in a subsidiary branch of the Gairloch Mackenzie clan, instead of a dowry all she could have offered to bring with her to a marriage were her virginity and an ancient Highland name.

She had brought photograph albums with her to Canada, and would show us pictures of herself going to other people's weddings in the decade before the Great War started, but there was never a man on her own arm. (There was a snap of her holding Edwina Mountbatten's arm in the 1930s, but that intriguing picture, like her fascinating letters and any other hints at a lesbian connection, was burned by my mother after Kythe's death, to keep hidden her own secret about me.) Kythe made no secret about being broad-minded on the subject of homosexuality in both genders and any "in-betweens." Her acceptance of the "pansy world" behaviours that others mentioned in whispers for names like John Gielgud and Noel Coward, she hooted for all to hear, in the same cut-glass voice with which she addressed Ralph-the-plumber as Rayfe.

As we've seen with their Vaughan Williams exchange at the Christmas concert, Jim couldn't stand what he called "her bloody 'I knew so-and-so' names." As Jim did that himself at the drop of a hat if it was good for sales, his annoyance was an inferiority reaction: when Kythe said she had met someone famous, like Lord Haldane, she really had.

R.B. Haldane had been a brilliant War Minister and Chancellor of the Exchequer, and when he left politics in the 1920s, Kythe was his personal secretary. In that capacity she did meet everybody. She also did go out to India on the staff of the Viceroy, Freeman Freeman-Thomas, the Earl of Willingdon. And on Jim's home turf, music, her "I knew Elgar, Vaughan Williams and Boyd Neel" was genuine as well.

She was equally well-read (unlike my parents) on many subjects, but her favourite book was a first edition of *A Hundred Years in the Highlands* by Osgood Hanbury MacKenzie of Inverewe, published in 1921. "Your triple-great uncle," she advised me. "And the Gairloch

Estate of one hundred and seventy thousand acres was five times greater than Chatsworth and Castle Howard combined!"

Her ongoing attempts to connect me to the land of Robert the Bruce and the Scottish Blood Royal through the Mackenzie of Gairloch family tree were fantasy, although in my early teens I was delighted to believe them. The printed-on-vellum genealogy that started with the bloodthirsty barons of Ross and Cromartie in 900 AD stopped with Kythe herself in 1886: she had added dated entries for Nan's and Jane's births, written in black India ink. My name and Angela's were also in ink, but Jane's marriage to Jim was an afterthought in pencil.

Kythe kept up her efforts to connect me to a different past: on my twenty-first birthday, she gave me a signet ring with the Mackenzie crest of a stag's head, engraved, and its motto: *Non sine periculo.*

I still have her copy of triple-great-uncle Osgood's book, and for all Kythe's exaggeration, "Not without danger" does seem a fair description of my early life.

Great Expectations and Rubber Prophylactics

Grade 7 ended, risk-free, in June. Scholastically, that's all I could say about it. I had one flicker of interest when the English teacher, Mrs. Maughan, assigned us *Great Expectations* to read.

I had seen it recently at the Odeon. I got in for free because my mother had become friends with Vera Scott, also employed at Scurrah's dress wear shop, only two doors away from the Odeon, next to Birks jewellers.

Vera was married to Harry Scott, the theatre's chief engineer. My free ticket was part of a love life that Myrna appreciated when

I told her about it during my next haircut. Fate played a cruel trick on Vera: she had a *Photoplay* shape and hair-do, but her face had an unfortunate twist, reminiscent of Munch's *The Scream*. It made Vera look cross even when she was happy.

She liked to get her own back by letting men wolf-whistle at her from behind, then turning around to watch their expression of lust change to disappointment. She would then say "Serve you right, horny bastard!" and give them a rude gesture with her finger.

Vera offered me this glimpse of adulthood during a chat with my mother while they were sharing a coffee break. I took advantage of it to say that Harry Scott (who had a severe Mr. Nimmo Scottish personality) was objecting to my free entry, courtesy of Vera, to *Great Expectations,* on what he called "a point of principle."

"Just tell Harry," Vera said, "Vera says, 'You don't get into the movie, he doesn't get in either.'"

The message didn't make much sense to me, but it worked with Harry. He let me in to the tradesman's entrance at the back of the Odeon and seated me in the front row, which put my nose practically against the screen, leaving me with the admonition: "Yell too loud and I'll chuck you out."

Returning to Grade 7 and Mrs. Maughan: She had asked me to write what I thought about the two versions of *Great Expectations,* film and book. Like everything else in my schooling, any record has long vanished, but I think the capitalized gist would have been that from my front-row perspective, with my nose squished against the screen, a twenty-foot-high Magwitch, *The Convict in the Graveyard,* was more terrifying on film.

Young hero Pip, like all good guys, seemed dull in either medium;

and both Charles Dickens and David Lean got Miss Havisham right: her romantic life and appearance were like my Great Aunt Kythe's.

At the end of Grade 7, Mrs. Maughan asked, "Have you made any friends during the year?"

I said, "I may have."

His name was Frank Mitchell, and although he was a year younger than I was, he was also going to be skipped one year ahead, into Grade 9. Frank said that he lived out in Metchosin, off William Head Road, somewhere near Taylor Road, in a house called "Sea Bluff," and he invited me to ride over sometime.

I knew all the road names from my visits with Frank Artlett to his leper colony lab. If I used Happy Valley Road, from Glen Lake Corner, the distance was only about five miles. I usually hitchhiked for longer trips — going to a free Odeon matinee in town — but I decided to make this Metchosin trip, to see Frank Mitchell, the first real ride on my new Raleigh three-speed.

In 1950, hitchhiking was normal, and the route through Happy Valley still wound like a snake because it followed precisely the original wagon trail. By now it was mostly paved with asphalt, except for a few rough spots where its exposed aggregate base had been sprayed with tar and then had fresh pea gravel dropped onto it. Once I got past Luxton Road, there weren't more than a dozen mailboxes (most of whose names I recognized from students at Belmont) until I reached Rocky Point Road, which meant I was in Metchosin.

On a bike you notice things that you wouldn't in a car. As I turned onto William Head Road and got to the bottom of the hill, just past Metchosin Hall, I saw something wonderful: a Himalayan blackberry patch!

Now, anyone living on Vancouver Island would think I was out of my adolescent mind: today that invasive species has covered every square foot of open ground. Then, I knew of only one other patch. It was across Glen Lake Road, in a field belonging to Lim Bang. The wild native brambles had a fruit not much larger than a pea; the Himalayan variety was three times bigger, and because it grew up in the air, not scrabbling through undergrowth, its large berries were much easier to pick.

The house called Sea Bluff was easy to spot after I saw the name on its mailbox. It stood alone at the bottom of Taylor Road on the edge of the sea, looking out at the Olympic Mountains in Washington state, across Juan de Fuca Strait.

The building was more like something to be found on Cape Cod. The house design was a plain, two-story rectangle, with a shingled roof and weathered cedar siding that had all gone grey. The interior was more interesting: wood finish throughout, many windows, a gallery landing to the bedrooms and a dropped level for the living room, which held a grand piano.

The house was actually owned by absentee landlords in Switzerland, who had originally kept it as a "summer cottage"; the Mitchell family were only renting it while they waited for a house of their own design to be built nearby. Frank introduced me formally, with handshakes, to his father, his mother and his three siblings, in descending order: Sue, Bob, and "my baby sister Wendy."

We then sized each other up. I thought I would probably like them, and they appeared to accept me — with a touch of condescension from Frank, who decided to call me Pip.

"From *Great Expectations,*" he told his relatives. "We've just been reading it, and he's from England."

I didn't mind becoming a Pip; at least Frank offered reasons for my latest nickname (unlike Jim). And "Pip" carried with it all the Uplands garden party prestige from Pemberton Holmes. Unfortunately, from time to time Frank (aka, formally, Francis, which he disliked) also had the habit of letting some gilt come off the gingerbread name coating, by adding the word "squeak" to it: a little addition that changed things a lot.

I can't remember the first Pipsqueak occasion, but it generally happened after somebody like Frank's mother or his sister Sue had said something complimentary about me, or vice versa. It was easy for me to say, or think, something nice about Sue. She was strikingly attractive, and for years I had a crush on her.

Frank was equally good-looking, and tall. And at fourteen, adolescent sexual attraction is looking in all directions and finding it in odd places. On my second visit to Sea Bluff, Frank suggested that we should look through the chest of drawers in his parents' bedroom, to see something that would amuse me.

When I said that burglarizing their bedroom sounded like fun, but also dangerous, he assured me that Mr. and Mrs. Mitchell (Jacky and Geoff) had gone to town in the pickup to get salt blocks for the sheep from Scott & Peden, and wouldn't be back for at least an hour. My uncertainty about that added a frisson to the already sensual experience of rummaging through his mother's underwear to find something amusing.

"Look!" Frank said. "Here they are!"

"They" was a small, white, rectangular tin, with an outline picture of a cloaked Arab riding a white horse against a red background over the scarlet word *SHEIK*, in giant letters, and under it, in tiny letters, RUBBER PROPHYLACTICS. More tiny words above the mounted Arab said there were THREE of them, and beside that, a big sixty ¢ using the old-fashioned "cents" sign.

The rest of the underwear drawer burglary was an anticlimax. Frank thought he heard the sound of the pickup returning with his parents and the salt blocks from Scott & Peden — it wasn't — and chickened out of his idea to open the *SHEIK* tin to show me its exciting contents.

Disappointed, I rode my Raleigh home instead.

Mixed Messages

SEX AND THE SUMMER HOLIDAYS continued to get mixed up. John Sandys-Wunsch brought our inflatable rubber raft (repaired after its Cowichan River puncture) down with him from Duncan, to use for fly-fishing on the lake. We set up my pup tent and a camp cot so that he would have somewhere to sleep.

The conversion of my new attic room had put no insulation between its roof rafters, which made it a furnace at the end of a summer afternoon: I set up a second camp cot in the tent as well. It promptly rained the next day, and instead of fishing, we had a Monopoly tournament for old time's sake.

Angela came into the tent, wanting to play, which annoyed us, and I told her to leave. She cried and complained to Kythe. Our parents came home. Kythe said something to Jim. An argument started.

To get away from it, John and I decided to fish in the rain anyway, and we paddled the inflatable to the other side of the lake, where

I knew there was a large bass. But I thought he wouldn't catch it on a fly.

He caught it, which annoyed me, but then, happily, said, "The sport is in the catching, not the eating." Unhooking the bass, he dropped it back for me to catch next time. We paddled home. Jim met us at the end of the wharf and said to John Sandys-Wunsch:

"What did you say to my daughter?"

John got red in the face and said: "What?"

Jim said: "Angela says you said something to her."

John Sandys-Wunsch said: "I never said anything. I've never been so insulted in my life. I'm going home at once."

HE DID, AND WE NEVER MET AGAIN UNTIL, on one of my cross-Canada book tours in the 1980s, to our mutual astonishment we bumped into each other in a studio green room, and discovered that one had metamorphosed into a balding man in a brown corduroy suit (me), and the other a bearded Anglican theologian with a pontifical way of speaking (him), who said he had no recollection whatsoever of Glen Lake, let alone an episode involving Angela and a tent.

I told adult John, lightheartedly, that he had been lucky not to have been beaten, as I had, by Jim and his leather belt for exercising free speech. The Reverend Dr. S.-W. wasn't amused, so I changed the subject by asking what had finally happened with the CPR and our one-dollar offer for "our island."

He said, "What island?"

It's still there, undisturbed. I glance at it whenever I drive past Quamichan Lake, to dance the Argentine tango on the edge of the sea at Maple Bay.

"Has Anyone Seen ... ?"

"DON'T GO NEAR THE WATER!" was the mantra that lake parents shouted to warn any little kids who couldn't yet swim. For those who could, the message was *"Never swim alone!"* Usually followed by *"And stay out of the weeds!"*

"The weeds" at Glen Lake were really a species of lily. They grow densely from the shoreline, outwards until the water depth reaches about a fathom (for landlubbers, six feet). The leaves are small, and lie flat on the surface; the blooms are negligible, not much more than small, dark-reddish buds that people don't think of as flowers at all. The parental warnings were about the lily stems. They grow close together, coated with a jelly, and can easily entwine a swimmer's legs.

When it happened to me, I didn't like it, because it felt yucky, but I didn't panic. Mrs. McRae had shown me, in my first swimming lessons with her on the old log, that as long as a swimmer moved slowly, the weed stems would slide off.

"Has anyone seen Gail?"

I didn't hear that first inquiry. My head was underwater while I tested my homemade snorkel apparatus (using an old war-surplus gas mask and corrugated automotive hose). My mother heard it relayed from Tina Wohlers' mother, who heard it from Gail's mother, Mrs. Shayler, next door.

The "Has anyone seen?" question was asked by everyone, from sunrise to sunset, every day of the summer school break. Even an impatient repetition was commonplace among parents gathering children who wanted to stay outside and play as long as they could.

The third time she asked the question, Mrs. Shayler came over herself, to talk to Mrs. Wohlers and my mother — who sensed from the tone in another mother's voice that something dark might have happened.

I came up for fresh air and saw my mother waving to me from our front porch. The gas mask didn't cover my ears. I could hear her call, "Have you seen Gail?"

I shouted, "I think she might have been swimming near her house."

My mother said, "Oh God." And then, before she ran to tell our neighbours, "Don't go over there yourself."

Of course I did. I could see people coming down from the Shaylers' house, but they were on land. The Boy Scouts' motto is *Be prepared*: I was in the lake, and equipped to go under it. Staying clear of the lilies, I towed the cork-float supporting the end of my breathing hose past the Wohlers' house.

The Shaylers' property became flat near the lake, but it had no real beach, only mud, and the lilies grew right up to it. I turned from the open lake and swam slowly through the lilies, between their slippery stems, looking down with my face mask.

I DON'T REMEMBER FEELING SHOCKED. Gail was lying on her back on the bottom of the lake, but only a few feet away from the shore, as though she was doing the holding-her-breath game, as we all did, to see how long it would last before we had to pop to the surface for air.

She was wearing her swimsuit, which was some kind of colour that made the whiteness of her arms and legs stand out in the brown tint of the lake's water. She was only about three feet below my outstretched arm. My hose let me go that deep. I swam down and touched her arm. She didn't move. Her eyes were open. Her hair seemed to float.

I swam back to the surface and waved at the people on the beach. Johnny Williams waded out to where I was. As the water got up to his shoulders, he thought he would need a boat, but he didn't.

He was able to lift Gail, and carry her back to the shore. He placed her down on the grass, and someone tried artificial respiration — not the modern "kiss of life" but the old-fashioned way, with pressing and squeezing. It didn't work. Gail's unshaven father, Jim Shayler, started howling.

That was a shock.

Adolescence in a Perfect Eden
or
Act Two: "The Age of Indiscretion"

THERE WAS NO GRIEF COUNSELLING in our Unorganized Territory. Parents thought *"There but for the grace of God,"* and gave an extra *"Don't swim alone"* caution to their children. Kids observed it to a greater or lesser degree, depending on their sense of responsibility vs. their desire for adventure.

Funny Wings and Agincourt

KEITH WILLIAMS AND I DECIDED TO BUILD a second fort at the south end of the lake, where it was drained by the creek in midwinter. In midsummer it was almost dry, and getting there required forcing our way, with the dinghy under oars, through the thickest possible lily growth for half the length of a football field. Then we had to wade through mud up to our knees.

Building the fort, by cutting alder and scrub willow branches, took us all day. Whenever we got too hot, we would reverse back through the mud and nearly impenetrable lilies, jump from the dinghy to have a swim and cool off. There were no houses then at that end of the lake. This was as far from a parental — or any other adult's — line of sight as a Glen Lake swimmer in distress could be.

Our jumping into the water from the dinghy required no skill; getting back into it, by hauling ourselves in over the side, risked capsizing. To avoid that, we would swim to opposite sides: one of us could climb in, while the other kept the dinghy steady. It worked well — until an unexpected gust of summer wind came through the Sooke Hills and blew the dinghy away.

(As I'm writing about this, you know we survived. I offer it only to demonstrate my ability as a young adolescent to disregard sound advice.)

That lake summer ended by building a stable — Jim and me, with skilled help from Johnny Williams — and getting some geese. The first, because my mother wanted to have a horse: the latter, to be good watchdogs, because Honey Bee wasn't.

Instead our beautiful spaniel was pregnant by "Mr. Trubshaw," an English Golden Cocker with a pedigree as lustrous as her own. Mr. Trubshaw belonged to Jean and Godfrey Holloway, who were from Home, and at least as proud of their Anglo-human heritage as they were of their dog's.

The geese were a pair of grey Toulouse, and quickly demonstrated remarkable intelligence in two ways. To keep out a large Alsatian dog kept by the Shaylers, we had strung barbed wire on the fence posts along the Wohlers' side. There was a patch of grass beyond the wire.

A few days after the geese arrived, I saw the gander put one web foot on the lower strand to press it down, then put his neck below the upper strand and arch it, which raised the wire enough for his wife to walk through the resulting gap. For better or worse, after he let go of the wire, she didn't know how to do the same for him, and I had to walk around, and down the Wohlers' driveway, to get her back.

It was childish of me to appreciate the other thing about the geese: they immediately hated Jim. When they saw any of my female relatives, or me, they only made the gentle sound which meant "food, please." Whenever they saw Jim they went on full intruder alert: first by standing and flapping their wings, plus a full-throated cackle, next by the hissing charge. If Jim turned his back on them, the gander pecked him on the bum.

They were wonderful watchdogs and unsuccessful parents. The goose laid her eggs, but only one hatched, and the gosling didn't grow up properly. It was christened ("Funny Wings") by Angela; killed (very reluctantly) by me; and eaten (guiltily, before Christmas) by all of us.

September of that year saw the completion of the stable, the arrival of a horse, the well going dry again, and the ho-hum start of Grade 9. The horse came for free; it needed a good home after a life of hauling Tally-Ho carriages full of tourists around the Parliament Buildings and Beacon Hill Park in Victoria.

That meant it would be old and large, and not used to being saddled: hardly an ideal mount for someone learning to ride. My mother said the "someone" was me, and she would do the teaching.

Our equine old-age pensioner turned out to be a mare, and she was large: almost eighteen hands (six feet): nearly the size of the Dorset shires I admired when the blacksmith shod them at Burton Bradstock. My mother called her Misty. She proved to be good-natured and didn't mind a saddle — not an American cowboy's but an English cavalry officer's, with no pommel.

My mother quickly got tired of walking in front of Misty, holding a halter, while I did nothing up on her back. Then my mother showed me how to fit a bridle, which put a bit between Misty's teeth, handed me the reins, and we were off — a slow plod at first, which was fine by me. At eighteen hands the ground seemed a long way down, but as we got used to each other, I began to urge her with a few giddy-ups into a clumsy trot. She even began to gallop.

Lawrence Olivier's *Henry V* had recently been shown in a rerun at Harry Scott's Odeon and I thought, romantically, that perhaps Misty was getting a memory from the days of Agincourt when her ancestors carried knights in armour, like me, into battle …

Brasso and Blanco

I BECAME A SEA CADET IN TIME for the start of the Korean War. Both events came out of a blue, last-of-summer sky. It all happened in the same September week that I started Grade 9 at Belmont.

Johnny Williams, with his Esquimalt dockyard connection, had always wanted Keith "to go," and my parents said that as there were no Boy Scouts at Glen Lake, and the Sea Cadets' base was in Victoria West — which meant needing a car — that the two couples could alternate, and thus share the driving load and the cost of gas of ferrying us both, there and back, every Tuesday night. It seemed logical, therefore (they said), that I go to cadets with Keith.

It didn't seem logical to me.

HMCS Rainbow was an old waterfront building at the foot of Robert Street in Victoria West, the outer portion of Victoria Harbour. Colville Island lay just offshore. The building, and our division of the Sea Cadet Corps, were both named after an antiquated Royal Navy cruiser.

It was "donated" by the Admiralty in London for Ottawa to start its own ramshackle Royal Canadian Navy in 1910, to help out the Empire in ruling the waves. From that rusty beginning, astonishingly, the RCN had grown to become the third largest navy on earth during the Second World War.

I don't want to belabour us here with too much "shivering me timbers" material. Suffice to say that in 1950, the RCN and its dockyard in Esquimalt were still second only to the provincial government in the economic and social life of Victoria. At that time also, the Navy (as opposed to parents) unabashedly regarded the Sea Cadets as prime recruiting material. The Corps was "boys only" and anything needed for *Rainbow* to turn boys like me and Keith into sailors — such as uniforms, or boats, or signalling flags, or bayonets and rifles — was readily provided off the shelf by the RCN.

"Enough blue sky to make a pair of sailor's trousers" means a patch of clear weather. My "Romantic Jolly Jack" or "Square Rig" uniform trousers were exactly the same as a grown-up sailor's, and exactly as uncomfortable.

The jumper and bell-bottom trouser material was coarse, navy-blue serge. Both had to be pressed. The trousers' fly was a horizontal flap, with multiple buttons on each side; there were no pockets, so nothing to put wandering hands into.

(RCN "Old Salts" trying to impress girls would iron seven

horizontal accordion pleats — "the Seven Seas" — into their bell-bottoms, but this "fancy waistcoat" practice was out of bounds for cadets. In the regular navy, and then only at a captain's discretion, they might be worn by sailors going ashore on leave.)

Under my serge jumper, in winter I wore a navy blue, coarse wool, long-sleeved sweater which scratched my skin. In summer, it was replaced by a short-sleeved white cotton undershirt, called a "flannel." The regular issue of flannels for Sea Cadets had probably been "in stores" since the Battle of Jutland.

The flannel was made of carded wool, just as abrasive as the winter sweater, but if you were lucky — or had a relative who was an actual sailor, and could smuggle you one — the newer generation of flannel would be made of satin-smooth cotton. Beginners like me never knew this subtle difference, and for my first year, winter or summer, wearing my uniform was unpleasant.

THERE WERE ALSO THE NELSON'S navy trimmings. These started with the traditional sailor's dark blue collar, with its white stripes (which had to be freshly ironed).

Then a black satin ribbon thing called a "silk" which went under it (also ironed), and had to be tied — properly — with a bow; as did another ribbon, called a "tally" (ironed again), to tie around the sailor's flat cap. The tally had the ship's name on it.

We're not finished yet. Next: a white lanyard with a special knot, which had to be tied in the correct way around the silk.

And for parades: white-webbing gaiters around the ankles, and a white-webbing belt (which had to be *kept* white with Blanco, a thick liquid paste that eventually dried). The belt had a brass buckle, and God help you if it wasn't shined (with Brasso).

Also two caps: blue for winter; white for summer (more Blanco).

And talking of shining: the boots.

PUTTING THIS STUFF ON isn't what a Smart Device-clutching teenager with ripped-knee jeans will be inclined to do now. Nor was I, then.

To make sure that we had done it correctly, we had inspections. To encourage us to "Do it bloody better the next time!" we had punishment drill, administered lovingly by the Gunner. His parade square bark was a far cry from Mrs. Seeley's ladylike *dib-dib-dib* Wolf Cub murmur.

The Sea Cadets had their own officer structure, whose uniforms also looked like the real thing except for their gold stripes, which didn't have the traditional "curl." The junior officers were young, and had only just stopped being cadets themselves. The older ones, like the Gunner, had been in the RCN during the war, and a few were still in the Reserve.

The man in charge of *Rainbow* during my time was Lieutenant-Commander Dando: when he wasn't commanding Sea Cadets, Mr. Dando helped to manage the Sydney Reynolds china shop on Government Street.

My juvenile persona regarded a lot of the men who had charge over me with a contempt that I had no right to exercise. Almost every one of those men had been in the wartime armed forces. A majority saw active service in the face of the enemy. Some of them were less than good at their military or civilian jobs, but as I look back, I cut them now a lot of slack.

The Light Bulb and Bobby Socks Connection

A PHOTO OF GRADE 9 at Belmont High shows about twenty absurdly young faces. To me, having just skipped a grade, most of them seemed suddenly older, especially the girls. It was a very small school. I already knew all the girls' names — and Frank Mitchell had skipped with me — but that fall term had the old "new kid on the block" feeling from all my other schools.

I blamed that feeling for the first occurrence of what became an autumn ritual for the next five years. For the first time in my life, a report card was something that my memory recorded, because some of it was bad.

It was bad enough that my parents were asked to come and see my principal, Archie Stephenson (the balding ex-army captain with a military moustache). When Archie said I hadn't been trying, and looked at me through his wire-rimmed glasses, he never raised his voice. His tone was merely disappointed, as though I had personally let him down.

He asked my parents what they thought might account for my lacklustre scholastic achievement. My mother said she had never been good at school. Jim didn't know. Again he took it as a direct reflection on his own performance, got angry, and suggested punishment as the cure.

Archie said (or at least I think this is more or less what he said), in his mild-mannered but disappointed voice: "I don't believe that'll be necessary. I'm sure David knows what he has to do now."

For some reason I decided that I would show *him* — and especially Jim. At the same time (which now seems counterproductive), to show off to everyone else, I decided that I would never take any homework home.

I would do it all at school. Without being seen to be doing it. Which I subsequently did: by ignoring most of what was said at the beginning of one class, and completing the written assignment — given in the previous one — instead. The end result, in June, didn't disappoint Archie.

Occasionally, my homework scheme got thrown off track by sex. The girls in Grade 9 wore 1950s pleated skirts and bobby socks. The skirts came below their knees, but when Maxine Fraser sat at her desk in front of me, one over, to my left, her clothing distribution meant that I could see the exposed back of the calf on her right leg. On magic moments, when she adjusted her position — usually out of boredom — I could even see the bare skin behind her knee.

Philip Roth and Portnoy reached this stage of male adolescent development three years ahead of me: our end results were the same, except that I never daydreamed about aiming for a light bulb while doing it, or making a fortune from writing about it.

From Adult Books to Bedwell Harbour

I spent my fifteenth birthday aboard the Algerine Class minesweeper, *HMCS Sault Ste. Marie*. She was used for reserve training, and as most of those being trained were either still going to school (Sea Cadets), or had civilian jobs (two-thirds of everyone else on board), these training jaunts took place over weekends.

This was my first time setting sail with the navy at sea. I should have a host of salty first impressions for you, but the February weather was immediately rough in the Strait of Juan de Fuca, and despite my sea legs gained on the *Empress of Canada*, I succumbed with the rest of the cadets (and most of the reservists), feeling acutely unwell all the way to Bellingham, USA.

The other one-third — regular navy members of the "Salty Sue's" complement — offered medical advice in the form of swallowing a piece of fat pork tied onto a string, the mere sight of which had an immediate emetic effect on the afflicted. This produced a gale of laughter (added to the weather) from the Good Samaritans.

It was also my first time "across the line" into the United States. The waterfront of Bellingham, in Washington State, looked almost the same as Victoria's, with log booms and fishing boats, but ashore I could see several saloon signs and a gun shop's under an oversized Stars and Stripes.

None of the crew had magical overnight leave, but the regulars and over-twenty-one reservists were free to roam until midnight. Sea Cadets and everyone else underage had to be back on board by 22:00 (ten p.m.). Anticipation of pleasure ashore was heightened by the sight of a large cardboard box on the quartermaster's desk at the head of the gangway:

Prophylactics
For the Use of
Prevention of Disease Only: One Gross

"Fill your boots, boys. It's all free. Don't be shy."

The quartermaster grinned at us. Disregarding the disease warning, knowing that I was blushing the same scarlet as the lettering on the *SHEIK* tin hidden at the bottom of Frank Mitchell's parents' drawer, I still let my hand reach forward.

Inside the Gross box there were smaller packets saying "Prophylactics 6."

At no cost. To buy three *SHEIKS* from a pharmacist — I would never have had the courage — would have taken two hours of my Pat Colclough gardening wages. These "safes" for sailors appeared to be unlimited in quantity, but I contained myself and took only one package of six.

With nothing to do ashore, we were back on board in an hour. The real tars took pity on our virginal selves and gave us a pack of Adult Books playing cards, of real naked girls, in poses that were completely unobtainable in Victoria.

(On our return we smuggled this treasure trove into *Rainbow*, for future recreational purposes to go with our free prophylactics packets. That was the only name given to these vital objects in the navy. Landlubbers in the 1950s used "safes" or "rubbers"; the now universal "condom" was never heard.)

We had sunshine the next day, for our passage west — after lashing, unslinging and stowing our hammocks — through the San Juan Islands.

Back across the border line dotted on the chart, we entered Haro Strait, then turned north — past aptly named Turn Point — to Ganges Harbour on Salt Spring Island.

The navy had a long link with Salt Spring. The harbour and village are named after *HMS Ganges*, the last wooden battleship in the Royal Navy. We were allowed to go ashore to look at the sights, which consisted of a one-room BC Tel exchange and a "Sale of Jam" in the Mahon Hall.

Returning aboard *Sault Ste. Marie*, my Salt Spring idyll was shattered when, after being assigned to lookout duty on the bridge, I lifted the pair of binoculars hanging around my neck and shattered a second front tooth. The first one had been smashed on the Hampstead asphalt of UCS. When I got home, a dentist in Victoria advised my parents that to prevent an abscess, I shouldn't get this one fixed, either. It wasn't, and the abscess happened anyway, further inhibiting my adolescent willingness to kiss or be kissed.

The last leg of my first RCN voyage took us to the navy's primary West Coast anchorage at Bedwell Harbour, on the western end of South Pender Island. It was called an anchorage, and ships could do that; but there were also two large mooring buoys that ships could "secure" to. Because the "Salty Sue" wasn't being provided by the RCN for a joy ride, but to train us, we did both exercises.

When we were secured (tied up) to our buoy and I stood on top of it, rocking slightly, I had a moment to look at Bedwell Harbour. There was a small wharf with a hut, painted dull red, which served as a customs office in the summer yachting season but was now closed. The sloping hill behind the wharf had the usual dense bush covering of dark green firs and cedars to the water's edge, except for a bare cliff about fifty feet high.

The face of the cliff had been made into a visitor's book of previous ships' names and visiting dates, mainly painted white but some in yellow, and one was red. *Sault Ste. Marie* had been there several times. Two of our crew had now rigged themselves a bosun's chair from the top of the cliff, and were adding our new date. Before they left, they touched up some others whose paintwork was fading.

Salary or Commission

JIM CHANGED JOBS AGAIN. He was still in sales, but this time of cars, on commission, for Thomas Plimley Ltd., "Distributors of Quality Transportation, Est. 1893," on Yates Street.

My mother's job change was a night-and-day switch: she stopped selling Scurrah's quality dresses and became a social worker at the Family and Children's Society in Spencer House, working with unmarried mothers.

(The interesting thing about *that,* in 1951, compared with today: someone with no "Social Worker" academic qualification, or any professional training, thus getting his directorial seal of approval for a lifetime's career.)

I thought that my mother probably got her job because we gave the Spencer House director one of Honey Bee's puppies, by way of Mr. Trubshaw — a litter that were born before Christmas.

Never Name a Turkey

MARCH WINDS AND APRIL SHOWERS found me digging new fencepost holes on the Seymours' side. I also built a desk for my new attic room: because it would have to go up-and-in through the new window, I made it in pieces during shop classes, under Mr. Cook's good eye's supervision.

When it was reassembled, I painted it with scarlet enamel, and was pleased. Jim looked at it and found some small part to be crooked. I think that was the first time I said to him, directly, that he was never satisfied with anything I did.

May found me blowing my own trumpet, actually a bugle, in

the Sea Cadet band, marching in a parade along Douglas Street on the twenty-fourth day of that floral month to celebrate Queen Victoria's birthday — which everywhere else that was still coloured red on the globe called Empire Day.

I had wanted to be a drummer, not a bugler. Had I known then how the military mind always works in reverse, I would have changed the order of my request. I never did learn how to blow the damn thing properly, and so used to pretend, by puffing out my cheeks at the right moments.

Bugling was less hard work than shouldering a rifle while marching for an hour. The May 24th holiday was still being held on the actual day of the week, rather than being tacked onto the closest weekend, and on this day it rained.

After the parade my helpful English teacher, Mrs. Maughan, told me that if I wanted it, I could have a Saturday job helping her husband Stan on their turkey ranch, at fifty cents an hour.

It meant a long bike ride out to Rocky Point Road, but the pay was double the amount I earned with Pat Colclough, and as a bonus Stan promised us a free turkey next Christmas. I thanked him, but said that wasn't necessary; we were raising one ourselves, and calling it Henry.

Stan Maughan, a stocky, cheerful man, said: "That's a mistake. Turkeys are stupid, but give 'em a name, you'll never eat 'em."

The turkeys were cannibals. When contained in a large flock, the mass would pick on an already ailing bird and then peck it to death, devouring the pieces they pulled out of the hole made in its back while it was alive.

Stan Maughan said: "That's because they're basically vultures. Let me show you how to kill them — but I don't want to waste one now. We'll use a chicken."

He selected a passing Rhode Island Red, flipped it upside down, grasped its legs with one hand, wrapped some string around the legs with the other, and hung it on a hook. Then he reached over to a shelf and picked up an object that looked like one of the old straight pens, with a nib, that I had dipped in an inkwell long ago on the desk at Monmouth Grammar. The "nib" part was a flat, curved blade, razor sharp, with a pointed tip.

Stan Maughan put the pen called a stabber in my hand, and opened the beak of the Rhode Island Red. "This is the stabber. Here, you do it. Make sure she's open wide, and stick it straight up through the roof. Do it right, and it'll come out by the crest on the top, and the feathers will hardly need plucking."

Stan said all this in such a cheerfully straightforward manner that I hardly realized I had done what he said until it was over. The Rhode Island's wings flapped for a moment, and then stopped.

"Now use the blade to slit the throat and it will bleed out into the bucket."

I did, and it did. His advisory about the subsequent plucking proved accurate as well. If the tip of the stabber severs an exact point of the cortex in the chicken's brain, the follicles holding the feathers relax. When I left at the end of the day, Stan gave me a stabber of my own, reminding me to keep it sharp.

I got home from killing turkeys to discover that we were keeping one of the puppies and getting another horse. We had also just acquired goats, which we were to collect and bring home in Jim's new Thames truck from Plimley's.

The Age of Indiscretion

The Thames truck was the worst of these spontaneous acquisitions. If there was one thing that North America did well, it was pickup trucks. The Fordson Thames ET was a made-in-England Ford, which meant that it was too small, too underpowered and too uncomfortable. Jim had traded in the Austin A-40 because Horace Plimley gave him "a special-for-you deal." The Thames was special, all right: if there was another one in Victoria, I never saw it.

My sister chose the "puppy bitch, out of Honey Bee and Mr. Trubshaw" that we were keeping from the litter and called her Winnie the Pooh. After the name was registered with the Canadian Kennel Club for breeding purposes, "Winnie" and her definite article were dropped. In conversation, or when calling them, mother and daughter became just Honey and Pooh, which vaguely made sense.

The goats were two nannies from a farm on the east side of Flatty Hill, off Humpback Road behind Fisher's abattoir. Getting there provided the first evidence that the Fordson made-in-Dagenham Thames was unsuited for Vancouver Island's Unorganized Territory.

After we had loaded the nannies into the truck, I had to sit with them all the way home to stop them from jumping out. I didn't like it at the time but, as with many other things in my life, the experience would prove to be useful. The nannies had to get pregnant to keep producing milk, so we made several return trips in the Thames to Flatty Hill in order for them "to meet a Billy." Sitting next to the nannies he "met," once that euphemism had been performed, made me stink as badly as their Capricorn donor.

The second horse was the reason I had been digging fencepost holes along the Seymours' boundary. The new nag's name was Lady Griselda — and nag, or bite, or kick, is what she did whenever she felt like it. Our new mare was a bitch that we had to fence in. Her colour was roan, similar to Misty's, but more grey than white. Because of that and her bad nature, we shortened her name to Grizzle. She was part Arab and so had a finer line than Misty's shire horse background. Although almost as high, she was younger: when she broke into a gallop, I felt the earth move.

On several occasions she tried to kill me.

When she wasn't doing that, it meant that my mother and I could now ride together. We usually went up the Pipeline Trail to the Humpback reservoir, which allowed us to stay off paved roads. Less often we rode along the tarmac of Sooke Road, and then again on gravel to the top of what people called Triangle Mountain (real name Triangular Hill, elevation 738 feet). In 1951 there wasn't a single house built on it; just a concrete gun-emplacement at the summit, left over from the war — like the one at West Bay in Dorset.

When we tethered our horses and, with no other human near us, stood on the moss-covered concrete, it commanded a panoramic and unforgettable view of Esquimalt Harbour (which the gun had been supposed to protect). We could see the Strait of Juan de Fuca, from Mount Baker to the east, the entire Olympic Range to the south, and beyond Race Rocks to the west.

After we finished staring at the view we rode down the other side of Triangle Mountain through West Coast old growth which hadn't yet been logged off, across a tiny creek out onto Happy Valley Road, and thence home.

THOSE RIDES ON HORSEBACK with my mother formed a bond between us that lasted to the end of her life. When we rode together up Triangle Mountain and the Pipeline Trail, through territory not yet organized into subdivisions and box-store malls; that landscape still with its rare sections of massive trees; the moss beneath them; a scarlet-crested pileated woodpecker hammering in otherwise total silence above the flowers; those panoramic views ... the brittle artificial tension in conversation that was ever present in the house with Jim and Kythe dropped away. We were mother and son; that was enough.

And when her remarkable long life was ending, and I returned to share those last few years with her, she frequently went back in memory to our rides. After her death I took some of her ashes and scattered them on a far reach of the Pipeline Trail that still survives.

Carpe Diem

GRADE 9 ENDED with my getting something called the Commander Beard Proficiency Trophy for Junior High School.

A photo shows the blushing award-winner holding the silver trophy cup, standing on the Glen Lake porch with his Myrna haircut, wearing a knitted Hudson's Bay sweater with an embroidered elk on it. Honey Bee sits on a ledge beside him. I look no older than twelve.

I made no psychological connection between winning the trophy and the autumn meetings in Archie Stephenson's Principal's office to discuss my disappointing report card. I thought the award had been given under false pretences.

I didn't play sports. And I wasn't a member of the student council.

Yet the fading, type-written, and poorly punctuated citation has words like "By exhibiting qualities of leadership, cooperation and fair play in co-curricular activities and by showing some excellence academically can be considered an outstanding citizen of the school."

Carpe diem was Belmont's motto.

I SEIZED THE MOMENT to take off for the summer. That July, the Pipeline Trail was closed to horse-riders. The Victoria water board had decided to replace the pipe. Massive Caterpillar drillers and diggers arrived to blast a trench; another huge machine lowered thirty-foot lengths of pipe into it. Each section was then wrapped and sealed with a special tar at the joint.

The diameter of the pipes was almost four feet, and although the entrance to the latest section was blocked off by the workers at the end of their day, the blocking was only a piece of tape with a sign saying "Keep Out." Keith Williams and I were still nowhere near the age of discretion. The sign might as well have said "Get In."

The work crew conveniently provided transport in the form of a dolly, like the one mechanics use to go under a car. Keith and I used it to ride down the tunnel of the pipe. This meant first pushing the trolley far *up* the pipeline from the current start of it, to the crest of the first hill. If we had gone over that crest, it would have been difficult (putting it mildly) to get back.

The first time we tried this trolley ride it was moderately thrilling. But as each new length of pipe was added, the light grew dimmer until, for the last few workdays, it was pitch-black and made the trip terrifying enough for us to want to do it twice.

To our regret, once the pipeline got to Glen Lake Road, the work crew sealed it off completely at the end of each day.

Skinning the Muskrat

From macro to micro: Our well went dry again. Jim decided that the only solution was to run our own half-inch copper pipeline down to the lake from the house, and get our domestic water from the lake instead of the well.

I found the muskrat the morning after Ralph the plumber installed the new line's electrical connection. The muskrat's bare tail was draped across the copper line where it went into the water. The rest of its dead body lay stiff on the bank. I bent down to pick it up and received only half as much voltage as I had from the faulty switch outside the bathroom at Barton Olivers Two, but more than enough to say *"Shit!"* out loud.

This latest Gurr family theatre of the absurd got more so. Jim decided that the way to prevent human beings from getting electrocuted was simply another sign, hand-painted by him and placed near the water, with the warning:

"When you swim don't touch the pipe."

Most people observed this advice, unless it was at one of the summer parties which began to be held for my mother's new social worker friends, or Jim's car sales pals, who all drank enough to ignore the sign and get a considerable shock of surprise, which made everyone else roar with laughter. At other odd times an electrified sunfish could be found floating, belly up.

I kept the muskrat and, after reading an article on tanning fresh hides in the *Encyclopaedia Britannica* at Belmont, I skinned it and dried it, rubbing it frequently with coarse salt and linseed oil. The only thing wrong at the end of this process was an extra earhole, but I overlooked that and kept the muskrat's sleek pelt on my dressing table for almost fifty years until odd bits began to fall out and I consigned it, sadly, to where it should have gone so long ago.

One other note for naturalists:

The previous winter, my mother and Angela had found a feral male kitten in the hedge beside Lim Bang's pig farm. They brought him home, had him "fixed" and called what was left "Smoky," for the colour of its fur. Smoky had been deprived of his balls, but the wilderness never left him.

The day after discovering the electrocuted muskrat, I found Smoky crouched halfway along the wharf, hidden against a vertical board where the planks changed height with a four-inch rise.

The end of the wharf had small, wooden square pillars on each side of it that I could use as diving platforms. Two wide steps went down between the pillars to the water. Smoky was watching barn swallows swoop over the lake. After a few minutes he changed position to one of the front steps and lay down on it so that I couldn't see him.

Nor, apparently, could the swallows. As one zoomed by at its usual super-high speed, a grey paw flashed up even more swiftly and clawed its prey from the sky. He repeated this process until I couldn't stand the avian agony any longer and chased him away. The step below the one he had been hiding on had eight feathered bodies lying side by side like dead mice.

From micro-killings it was only one short leap to a macro death. One week later, Smoky did exactly that: leaping from the bank onto a full-grown mallard drake, he crunched his pearly feral teeth around the beautiful iridescence of the mallard's neck and half-swam, half-dragged a whole duck ashore — which, I'm ashamed to say, we ate.

From nature to nurture: the next day TV came into our lives.

Disobeying the Prime Law of Thermodynamics

Television arrived with old Rob Kitching.

The Kitching family (also from Home) — father, mother, and two teenage sons — had recently bought the empty house beside the one that belonged to the people with the wharf from which Kythe fell off. Their newly purchased property had a sloping bank and no wharf. The father, Rob Kitching, was very tall and mostly bald: any hair that remained straggled over his collar in an abandoned ponytail experiment. That "appearances deceive" held true in his case: Rob Kitching was an electronics genius who had worked at W.G. Pye & Co. Ltd. in Cambridge, and in 1937 Pye had made one of the first television sets.

Astonishingly, Rob Kitching told us that he had brought not one but two of these fabulous devices with him from Home. He was keeping a set for himself, but would be pleased to install the spare unit for us, if we wanted it, in exchange for using our house for changing, and wharf for swimming, until they built a new wharf of their own.

The only shadow across a brave new world of viewing pleasure — which, he promised us, we would be able to get from television stations in Seattle — was that in order to receive it, we would first need to build a special rhombic antenna.

Building the rhombic antenna meant stringing copper wire in a diamond shape, with each of the four legs supported by attaching the antenna to a tree, as high off the ground as possible.

"Ideally, as David could probably tell you already from school" — Rob Kitching told Jim — "to accommodate the VHF wavelengths, each rhombic leg should be approximately two hundred feet. But if you're willing to accept a little ghosting in the signal, we can make do between thirty and fifty feet per leg. Not much more than the footprint of your house."

From my limited knowledge of science absorbed so far from Mr. Palsson at Belmont, I absolutely could not have told him anything about VHF wavelengths. We did have the trees for supports, but with only one good eye, Rob Kitching couldn't climb them.

Although I offered to do it, my parents wouldn't allow it, which meant asking Pat Colclough to come over and high-rig each leg. Pat said he would, but couldn't until early September.

A Pye-Eyed View of the World

Monday, September 3rd, 1951: the day that infamously brought us the fouling and cheating world of all-in wrestling at the end of it, because Pat Colclough had high-rigged the rhombic antenna during the long weekend for Labour Day.

With considerable difficulty he had managed to string the single strand of copper wire making up the first four legs of the required rhombic diamond shape, at the same time ensuring that once it was in place, no "widow-makers" could damage the wire in a future autumn gale.

Pat climbed down the last tree and walked with the connecting wire over to our house, at which point old Rob Kitching said that he had changed his mind about "ghosting," and a triple-strung array would be better. Would our logger friend please go back and do that stringing twice more?

Pat Colclough just gave his quiet smile, took off his spurs and said, "No."

The Box of Delights, by John Masefield, wasn't in the handful of precious boyhood possessions I was able to bring to Canada, and I certainly wasn't thinking about its title while we watched Rob Kitching produce an object from a cardboard packing crate in our Glen Lake living room.

The box had the distinctive circular PYE logo stamped on its top flap. The top branches of the Y in the centre extended over each of the other two letters. Rob Kitching said that design had been meant "to echo radiating rays from the sun."

The small brown Bakelite plastic box that he plugged in to our single living-room wall socket, and then connected to Pat Colclough's hand-strung rhombic antenna, gave us three elves — singing and selling "Ajax, the Foaming Cleanser" — and the logo of Channel 5, KING-TV, in Seattle. (The KING logo was designed by Walt Disney. It had a grinning microphone wearing a crown, and an ermine scarf.)

"Small" was the operative word for the Pye set's picture. The screen was only a nine-inch diagonal — a minuscule five, horizontal — and its background was green. Until that first day, we had heard the Ajax commercial on the radio but had no idea about the other content Rob Kitching's tiny PYE box suddenly presented to us.

We had never heard of all-in wrestling, or its stars: like villainous Gorgeous George who had golden ringlets and who, after climbing into the ring, while the crowd booed and hissed him, cleaned his hands with Chanel No. 5.

George's famous (but equally unknown to us) opponent was a

pure innocent named Nature Boy. Innocently, with his back turned, bowing humbly to the crowd, he would immediately be kicked, gouged and otherwise fouled below the belt by Gorgeous George.

The process would then reverse.

The greater problem for us was that on Rob's tiny PYE screen we could hardly see any of it. Thus George's gorgeous golden locks were green, and when the referee didn't see Nature Boy being cheated, we didn't either.

The image constantly wobbled, or faded, or had another image from an adjacent channel superimposed on it — the dread "ghosting" — but, like all the other virgin viewers at the dawn of Newton Minow's "vast wasteland": the Gurr family loved every minute of it.

Couldn't get enough of it.

And tried to see more of it, by putting a plastic "magnifier" over their new PYE-eyed world.

Henry Meets Smoky and a Sad End

As TV SLITHERED INTO our Glen Lake Eden, Kythe was banished from it. She was replaced by an "unmarried mother" who had a suitably biblical name but whom, for privacy's sake, we will refer to by another, as Mary.

I don't remember whether Angela and I were given any advance warning of this latest seismic shift in the Gurr family's underlying plates, where, from the day of my birth, everything that caused significant movements on the surface remained hidden. There was a row: Kythe left. She went to become a live-in housekeeper and companion for a retired widower, twenty miles north of Victoria, in his waterfront house at Cherry Point.

Unmarried mother Mary came to us from somewhere on the mainland, by way of Spencer House. She was cheerful, and could cook better than our actual mother, but not as well as Kythe. Highly visible pregnancy became part of my daily life for the next three years as "unwed mothers" came and went.

Our small house wasn't made any larger to accommodate pregnancy. Unwed Mary got Kythe's room at the foot of my attic ladder, which meant the same inconvenience for both parties whenever I used it. Our supply of hot water didn't get larger, either, but it was a little more reliable because we had converted the kitchen stove from only my split wood to oil.

For no single reason, doing unwed laundry seemed more of a headache. We still had no machines for washing and drying. In fair weather, things got hung outside; in foul, they were placed on a rack suspended with pulleys from the kitchen ceiling. When the rack was down, it filled the space between the sink and the stove; you couldn't walk past it, and had to wait until it was up. When it *was* up, because the ceiling was only eight feet high, anything larger than a handkerchief meant we had to duck. (Probably because of the cost, we were still using — and reusing, which meant boiling — linen handkerchiefs, rather than the miracle of disposable tissues like Kleenex.)

Fuelling the stove with oil, rather than wood, produced a steadier heat, but it didn't work any faster. Taking showers in the evening was done by a roster, and if someone seemed to be enjoying it for too long, someone else would bang on the door to make them stop. This process decreed that after ten o'clock at night, for several hours, the hot water tank was full of cold water.

Anyone taking a late shower was out of luck.

ON CHRISTMAS EVE, A LIFE-AND-DEATH decision had to be made about Henry, our turkey. You may recall Stan Maughan's warning (which we had ignored) about giving Henry his name.

I had my killing knife but I couldn't use it. Carrying Henry over to Johnny Williams for the execution was almost as painful as doing the deed. I asked Johnny if he would ask Keith to pluck Henry for me as well. When the dismal task was completed by the male Williamses, I carried the now-plucked and cleaned corpse of ex-Henry back to our house and hung him up by his feet in the basement, on Christmas Eve.

I was able to tell my conscience that Henry's feathered self had flown away, and the roast turkey that remained would be delicious the next morning. After our stockings and first presents — including a first one for unmarried Mary — beneath my latest, high-rigged, now-decorated tree I went out of the kitchen, down the outside stairs and into the basement.

Smoky, our feral killer of swallows and ducks, had somehow got there before me. As he couldn't kill Henry, he had done the next best thing and torn his plucked breast into tattered shreds hanging down towards the basement floor.

We laughed, we cried, we damn near died of rage; and my mother did her best to stitch the pieces together and roast them. What was left of Henry, after Smoky, made a Christmas dinner that actually tasted pretty good, but Jim got depressed anyway.

Adolescence in a Perfect Eden
or
Act Three: "Curtain Up"

A LIFE ON THE STAGE was not my aim in the New Year of 1952. I would be sixteen in February and thus eligible for a BC learner's license which would allow me to drive a car, or the Thames truck, under the guidance of an adult.

Jim showed me the Thames Ford clutch and three primitive gears, then let me drive alone up to our gate, turn around and come back. The first couple of runs were exciting for a novice; an adolescent thrill-seeker in possession of the wheel immediately wanted more.

I began to go a short distance along the bumpy gravel of Glen Lake Road: first to the Artlett's entrance, then, as nobody asked where I had been for so long, to James' mink farm, and finally, triumphantly to Old Clarkie's corner at Station Road — where I did a U-turn and collided with Mr. Bing's vegetable and flower truck.

Mr. Bing was a pleasant Chinese man with a pigtail, who gave his delivery customers a flowering lily bulb in a pot every Christmas. He wasn't pleasant now.

"Stupid kid. You coulda kill me."

That could not have happened, I explained. I showed him, with gestures, that I was only making a slow loop to go back into Glen Lake Road and, although the connection between the left front fender of the Thames and the right front fender of Mr. Bing's ancient Chev pickup did seem to have pushed each other inwards, and some vegetable crates had fallen off the back —

"Stupid kid. I don't wanna hear. You tell your parents you fix."

I told them.

Jim was justifiably enraged. I had to hammer out the dents on both vehicles, and was told there would be no more truck driving without my learner's. And that wasn't going to happen until school was finished at the end of June.

Dickie Proudfoot bought a beat-up Baby Austin 7. The Baby Austin overloads with four people; we always made it carry at least eight. Dickie Proudfoot (licensed) drove us all to AYPA (Anglican Young People's Association) evening meetings in St. John the Baptist church hall at Colwood. After AYPA, we (unlicensed) took turns hot-rodding the Baby Austin, without lights, between the graves and Easter lilies in St. John the Baptist's graveyard while I tried to pretend that I wasn't aware of what my thigh pressing against Maxine Fraser's was doing to another pressing matter.

Item: Frank Mitchell, only fifteen, at Halloween helped me to remove a farmer's gate on Rocky Point Road before we went back to Glen Lake to stuff a firecracker into the keyhole of the antique lock on the front door of the old Sooke School District frame-construction office building next to Belmont on Station Road, and light the firecracker; and when the glowing remains wouldn't extinguish themselves, in panic I urinated into the keyhole and felt relief in two ways.

Returning to where we left off with Mr. Bing. Although, thanks to my collision with his vegetable and flower truck, the Lord had taken away my first opportunity to get a learner's license for a car, sometimes the Book of Job is proved wrong: The Lord, disguised as a sales whiz called Stew, at Plimley's dealership where Jim was working, found me a motorbike instead.

And in 1952, if I lived and owned a bike in Unorganized Territory, the Government of British Columbia didn't require me to take *any* test to drive it. I was no longer like Badger, grounded under his *Wind in the Willows* sheet of leaves at Sherborne:

I was Toad at the wheel, on the open road.

In less carried-away terms, the bike wasn't free; it cost a hundred dollars. And it wasn't new: it was a 1939 James Cadet 125cc that had been through many mills. Stew (leaving his surname tactfully aside) said it was a steal. I was to discover that it had in fact been stolen more than once, and its engine could never puff sufficiently to get me over the Malahat without repairs en route.

Stew was one of the happy band of eternally optimistic car salesmen whom Jim met on Plimley's car lot. He had drifted from the prairies to peddle Studebakers — not Austins — and to "do it up brown" (his favourite phrase), he wore the same kind of checked plaid sports jacket as *Mad Men's* Don Draper, but with louder colours and less taste. The same applied to Stew's ties. His wardrobe sold a lot of "Stewdies" (as punned on his business card), and must have attracted his wife, Mickey, who had stood with him — she told my mother after a couple of warm-up rye-and-gingers — "through a pile of thick and thin shit in Alberta."

COMMISSIONS FROM THE STEWDIES allowed Mickey and Stew to become possessors of a real television set: the new twenty-one-inch Admiral TV home theatre, with "Dynamagic Radio and Triple-Play Phonograph."

This 1952 electronic marvel was housed in "a smart compact cabinet" that had doors to hide its (to us massive) screen when not in use. I didn't think the cabinet was smart — Mickey and Stew's model was an unpleasant blond maple finish — but when its doors were open, the picture of Gorgeous George and his golden ringlets in green-free black-and-white had all of us hooked.

We only saw Gorgeous George in good weather. Mickey and Stew lived on the far eastern edge of Victoria, a district just shy of landing them in the Enochs' more genteel part of Oak Bay.

To get four of us there from Glen Lake meant putting a large seat-cushion from our sofa into the open deck of the Thames truck, upon which Angela and I would sit with our backs to the cab and enjoy the brisk fresh air and rich Thames exhaust for fourteen miles each way — or not enjoy, when it started to rain. On the rare occasion that we caught the eye of a policeman — there were no policewomen in our Unorganized Territory — it was caused by the Thames truck itself, and not by how my ten-year-old sister and I were sitting in the open back of it.

Our evenings with Mickey and Stew and their Dynamagic TV ended on a sad note. A former unpleasantness over the "thick and thin shit in Alberta" caught up to a Victoria police check over a Stewdie speeding offence, and led to a term of imprisonment in BC.

The Acting Bug

It crept up on me slowly, like the Thames truck. Drama arrived via Harold Parrott's new system of dividing the school into "houses" to encourage Belmont students to belong to something collectively, and thus discover and/or "develop their individual self-worth."

This exciting journey of discovery began for all of us with learning which of the four new house names (A, B, C or D) we were in. Mine might have been C, but that doesn't matter.

Belmont also had a drama club, and each house produced a mini-play for the Christmas concert of 1951. A "Dramatics Report" which I wrote about all this for *The Blue and White* school annual says that "Maxine Fraser and Robin Kitching were chosen Best Actress and Actor," and that subsequent to this recognition of excellence the decision was made that the Belmont drama club would enter a play called *Birds of a Feather* in the Victoria schools drama festival in March.

This confluence of two things happening at the same time and affecting each other while they're doing it, without knowing they're doing it, was a neat example of Heisenberg's uncertainty principle at work in human lives — as well as quantum mechanics.

I don't have any memory of the original casting process, but the play was chosen and directed by a new teacher, Miss Gladys Wade. She was a graduate of the Fine Arts School of Montreal and had won awards. The one-act play that Miss Wade picked, *Birds of a Feather* (subtitled *A Welsh Wayside Comedy)* by J.O. Francis, has four "birds."

In order of appearance:

Twm Tinker (Middle-aged, weather-beaten; typical poacher)
Dicky Bach Dwl (A young fellow; not typical, see below)
Jenkins the Keeper (Angry, suspicious; typical gamekeeper)
The Bishop of Mid-Wales (Gaiters, muddled; typical bishop)

Twm, pronounced "Tim" — played by Frank Mitchell — had to look after Dicky Bach Dwl (pronounced "Dool") who was me: "A young fellow dressed in rustic clothing, with a battered soft hat set on his mop of unkempt hair. His facial expression shows a mind a little awry. There is, however, nothing unpleasant about him, but rather something pitiful and appealing."

Before anyone got to meet me as Dicky Bach Dwl, being "a little awry," the stage direction says: "He begins to sing on the road to the L." I have no idea what I sang offstage left (the L) or how I was awry. I do know that I nailed the difficult, lilting but sing-song Welsh accent, because it was the only time in my life that I did something well thanks to Jim's help. Drawing on his own teenage exile to the farm at Mold in Wales, he coached me in the kitchen after supper.

THE PLAY BY J.O. FRANCIS IS SO SLIGHT, the dialogue so simple, the plot so preordained from the start that no audience should be forced to sit through it. Yet if you add "strings of red paper" over a lightbulb to represent a campfire, and sniff strongly enough over an empty frying pan that is said ahead of time to contain "steak and onions" ... Such is the magic of theatre that you can hypnotize that audience, and an adjudicator, into declaring it "Best Performance of the Festival," and Dicky Bach Dwl its best actor.

A girl in a different play — Jennifer Ford, from St. Margaret's —

was awarded best actress, and we each got a scholarship to attend a summer school of the theatre, either at the University of British Columbia or the Banff School of Fine Arts. Whichever we chose, we wouldn't go there until July. After our honour performance, everyone stood up to sing "God Save the Queen."

(Subject to this historical footnote: as George the Sixth had only died the month before, and a majority of our audience had been singing "God Save the King" for their entire lives, most of them couldn't belt out "the Queen" without a stiff nudge. The following year I would march and blow the bugle in Her Majesty's Coronation Day parade.)

The Cougar Queen

I MET HER WITH TWO COUGARS at the Maughans' turkey ranch. It was my first ride out to Metchosin on the James motorbike, and I had gone to tell Stan that I wouldn't be able to kill any turkeys for him that summer: I was going to Vancouver to study theatre instead.

The cougar queen's real name was Joan Milwarde-Yates, a graduate of Saint Margaret's School for young ladies, before she decided to go for the forty-dollar bounties offered by the BC Game Commission for killing big cats. A pedigree like that was too good for my mother and Kythe to resist; they had both met her, but I never had — nor cougars, for that matter.

The cats were draped, one on each side of the hood of Joan's old Ford truck, with their heads staring at me over the headlights. The two hounds that she had used to tree them, before she shot them with her Lee-Enfield .303, were in the cab of the truck, drooling and staring at Stan's turkeys.

I recall the cougar queen's costume as masculine, topped by the bush hat of a big hunter in *King Solomon's Mines.* I'd like to say that she was smoking a pipe, because I think she was, but that may be another false memory from a Stewart Granger movie. True or false, one thing was certain:

Like my hero, Stewart Granger, I was going to be an actor.

The decision to choose the new summer school program at the University of British Columbia, rather than the longer-running and more prestigious Banff School of Fine Arts, was based on cost.

My festival scholarship covered tuition and gave me seventy-five dollars for pocket money. The cash would cover my Canadian Pacific ferry trips to and from the mainland — also riding my James bike — with a bit left over for gas. Room and board in summertime Banff would have been prohibitive.

Mr. Trubshaw's owners came to my rescue. Godfrey and Jean Holloway had recently moved to Vancouver and bought a house there: I could stay in their attic. They would also feed me. Whether that was from the goodness of their cocker spaniel-loving hearts or some backstage arrangement with my parents, I never found out.

Hello, Mrs. Holloway

There was a lot of other stuff going on. Summer holiday travel, for a start. Theatre school at UBC was beginning on July 2nd, a Wednesday: so Tuesday, July 1st, was Dominion Day (not yet known as Canada Day), and the James bike and I barely got squeezed onto the *Princess Kathleen.*

Then I realized I would need a map of Vancouver in order to ride from the CPR ferry terminal at the foot of Granville Street, out to the Holloways' house in West Point Grey. The ferry gift shop only had a cartoon map for tourists, but it showed a picture of the Hotel Vancouver at one end and a thunderbird totem pole marked "UBC Campus" at the other, with a Jericho golf course in between and a Marine Drive connecting them.

After an only slightly hair-raising five-mile ride for my first time alone through a big city, I found the Holloways' home perched on the uphill side of Marine Drive, overlooking the beach at Spanish Banks. The house was a 1930s, three-storey frame construction, both roof and walls encased in cedar shingles, stained dark brown. Cedar trees and an arbutus grew beside it.

Jean Holloway met me at the door. She was an attractive woman with dark brown hair. (Myrna would probably have described it as "her own colour, flat; no perms.") She was wearing a dress — stylish, light summer, without stockings — not shorts.

I put out my hand to shake hers, and said: "Hello, Mrs. Holloway."

Jean Holloway didn't notice my hand, and pecked my cheek with a kiss instead. She said, in her middle-class English voice: "Godfrey's at the office, dear. He's always at the office. The children are resting. I'll show you your room. It's upstairs."

My room was in the attic, and because BC was having a heat wave in July, and the 1930s roof of the attic was uninsulated, it almost felt as if I had never left home.

Jean said, "You may have a bit of trouble opening the window. God knows how many times I've asked Godfrey to fix it. Let me try now."

I was looking at the spectacular, third-floor view over Spanish Banks and across Burrard Inlet to the Twin Lion mountain peaks behind West Vancouver. Jean had to press her chest against my shoulder in order to be helpful.

"I'm afraid it's still stuck." Jean had to brush my shoulder again as she straightened up. "If Godfrey's ever home in time, we'll have supper at six. And you can see I've made up your bed. I hope it's big enough."

The bed was one half of a bunk set. Godfrey did come home in time, and so I held out my hand and said: "Hello, Mr. Holloway."

Godfrey Holloway did see my hand, and shook it, and said pleasantly, in his middle-class English voice: "Call me Godfrey, old chap. I've been walking Mr. Trubshaw."

Jean said: "You said you were going to the office."

To repeat: there was a lot of stuff going on, and my octogenarian head may be reading — and now writing — more into that innocent conversation than I could have detected at the time; but I had lived a child's lifetime of sensing friction between adults locked into a marriage that they shouldn't have entered.

Besides, I would have told you then that all my attention was given to what was going to happen to me the following morning, when I started my Summer School of the Theatre.

A Bastard in Amber

The UBC campus in 1952 struck me as half-a-dozen imposing granite buildings all sited the wrong way for taking advantage of stupendous views. The main theatre building was not faced with stone but white stucco, and a bit of vaguely mock-Tudor woodwork.

There was a tall fly tower at the back. I spent half my Summer School time in it, doing practical things like building and hanging scenery, scrim painting and sizing, rigging lights and changing gels.

Working in the fly tower with the ropes to lift and drop scenery flats was the most fun: a cross between a treehouse and going aloft on *HMS Ganges*. "Sizing" flats was mind-numbingly dull. I had to apply Rosco white primer with a paint roller or brush to an acre of canvas to make it taut as a solid wall, before real colours were applied to it.

Scrims and gels showed me stage magic. Scrims are made of painted mesh; when lights are shone onto them from the house-front, they look to the audience like solid walls of scenery — until the lights in front go off and others behind go on: then the scrims allow you to see through them to another scene, or actor, you had no idea was there.

Gels (short for gelatine) are sheets in a range of colours that fit over the floodlights, or spotlights, to change the mood. The Rosco Company invented gels and gave them names like Amber Bastard and Serendipity. Amber Bastard makes skin tones of aging thespians young again. Purple "does royals," and Brown "does masculine."

Learning to act under the lights took place in two more army huts. Like Belmont's, they had been joined together and, when they weren't still being used as a snack bar, were now called the Frederick Wood Theatre. The huts were in a grassy field that sloped down behind them. My first assignment was to stand at the bottom of the field and recite to Joy Coghill at the top: "Speak the speech, I pray you, as I pronounced it to you, trippingly on the tongue ..."

After being Hamlet in the field, splitting the ears of the groundlings (my fellow students), I did Henry V for Joy: "Once more unto the breach ..."

We returned to it on a daily basis.

Joy Coghill was a short, perky woman, of much patience as well as skill. She directed me as "Curdkin, a Courtier" in *Cinderella:* alas, alackday, my only role on a summer stage.

I thought I had come close to landing a "good one": "Joshua, a crumbling butler," in Christopher Fry's adaptation of Jean Anouilh's *Ring Round the Moon.* But no amount of makeup could make my sixteen-year-old complexion crumble enough, and at the end I was dumped.

Curdkin had to wear a goatee and moustache that makes me look absurd in a photo (I had yet to own a razor). The spirit gum required to keep the false hairs in place made my skin break out in a rash. I didn't care. Making different faces with makeup was pure fun. I loved it all with a naïve but genuine passion.

The third play being mounted for our summer festival of the arts was Lorca's *House of Bernarda Alba,* but it was written for an entirely female cast. Thinking I came close to a "good one" was more stage-struck illusion. Even if I had possessed the talent to play the prince in *Cinderella* or — the characters I really wanted: the Hugo-Frederic brothers' combo in Fry's version of *Ring Round the Moon* — my youth would have kept me locked out of the meatier parts. Everyone else at the summer school was young-adult, a few even young-adult-plus; they weren't going to let a juvenile-minus steal a plum role.

My considerably less than drinking age also locked me out of nearly all the extracurricular summertime life of the theatre. I knew there were Spanish Bank beach parties happening with beer.

On Sundays, when Godfrey Holloway returned from walking Mr. Trubshaw, or from "the office," he would offer me a glass of Dry Sack sherry and call me "old chap." Jean Holloway would appear to resent this and start an argument with him. On other random occasions — which also seemed to coincide with his late evenings at the office — she would appear in my abruptly opened attic doorway saying:

"Sorry, I always seem to forget to knock. Just checking if there's anything you need, dear. Godfrey must fix this damned window. It's always so hot in this room."

Her evening visits to check on things did bring a whiff of lust to West Point Grey, but still, and in retrospect sadly, nothing worth reporting back for Myrna to pass on to her beauty parlour regulars.

One more vignette of a vanished Vancouver way of life. I was eating a Sunday breakfast at the Holloways' when the phone rang. Jean answered it, and then with a tone of considerable surprise as she handed me the receiver:

"It's for you, dear. A woman from Home. Her name is Sheila. She says she knew your Aunt Nan."

With deep regret, I have no way now of recovering Sheila's surname. Her voice said she was a physiotherapist, which was how she knew Nan, because she had been trained by her. She had wanted a holiday in Canada. One thing had led to another (making contact with my mother, and thus finding me over here at the Holloways'). Now she was "taking care of a house on Granville Street" while its owner was away, and would I like to have an early supper with her there?

Of course I would, and did.

The large properties on Granville Street were already beginning to be subdivided into smaller lots, but in 1952 the street was still attractive. Ugly townhouse blocks now squat on them, wall-to-wall, from the airport to downtown.

The real estate where I found myself having supper was the biggest of the big. I rode the James bike up Granville, past Shaughnessy, and then south downhill to 57th where I followed a brick wall for a whole block to find an archway with a solid, closed wooden gate, and over it a sign saying *Shannon*.

The "house" being "taken care of" by Sheila was the mansion home of Austin Taylor, baron of Bralorne Mines, legendary owner of racing-stable winners, old-growth logging companies and everything else in BC, including these ten verdant acres of South Vancouver surrounding the mansion, now going by the name *Shannon* above its gate.

THE WOMAN BEHIND THE VOICE on the phone met me on the other side of the solid gate. Sheila was attractive, vivacious, perhaps thirty, and living in the estate coach house where we ate a delicious supper that she had cooked herself. Before we ate it, she made me my very first G&T which, she assured me, would wear off before I had to ride home.

The drinking age in BC was twenty-one but in a private home it was okay. Over my very first in a lifetime's gin and tonic, I regaled Sheila with my life in the theatre, and felt extremely grown up.

A hint of sex might have hung on the evening air of the Shannon estate, but nothing could have happened: my broken front teeth formed a psychological and physical barrier. The problem that two dentists had identified — "still-growing adolescent teeth may form an abscess if they are capped at this age" — happened anyway because they hadn't fixed them.

(An abscess did form above the tooth on the right — the one that had been diagonally broken on the UCS asphalt in Hampstead. Pus would build up a bubble in the gum above the tooth, becoming painful. By chance, I had discovered that pressing the swollen blister with my index finger would discharge the pus down through the dead nerve of the tooth, into my mouth. The discomfort of pain would be gone; the embarrassment from the taste and smell of decay remained until I could brush my teeth. I should have complained to my parents but I was afraid of having my front teeth "pulled out" and then having to "put in my upper," like Jim.)

This antisocial, *anti-anything-happening with a girl,* now happened again as I was finishing my first-ever Tanqueray gin and Schweppes tonic. Our dining chairs were far enough apart that I didn't think that Sheila would be able to smell my bad breath as we ate.

But when supper was over, and I said with regret that I ought to ride back to Point Grey before it got dark, and put out my hand to shake hers — when Sheila instead went to kiss my lips goodbye, I turned aside and blushed the deepest Rosco gel of red.

The Graveyard Shift

I RODE DOWN THE DRIVE eager to tell everyone at the lake of my theatrical adventures over a leisurely Saturday lunch, but no-one was at home. My mother had left me a note on the Arborite table in the nook. It said that unmarried Mary had delivered her baby, and was being replaced today by unmarried somebody else, whom my mother was collecting, with Angela from Spencer House.

And Jim?

"Is at an IWA Strike Vote Meeting which Please God they will settle. Make yourself lunch."

During my time as Curdkin in Vancouver, Jim ("to make ends meet") had switched roles from the fraternal order of car salesmen, like "Stewdie" Stew, and had become a card-carrying union member of the International Woodworkers of America.

BC Forest Products put him on the graveyard shift.

He was on it from midnight until dawn's early light and beyond, for an eight-hour sentence on a hellish mechanical contraption that was called the green chain, and was the property of BC Forest Products.

This midnight monster was a chain drive armed with giant claw lugs. The claws grabbed and hauled raw (green) logs out of Victoria's Inner Harbour, dripping wet with anti-rot chemicals, to meet ferocious teeth on giant rotary saws. Human beings had to manhandle these anti-rotted logs en route from chain claws to saw teeth — hoping not to get in the way of either one as they did so.

The good news was that the IWA ensured top wages. The bad news was that they were also the most militant union, and thus — as Joy Coghill had bid me bellow to her, as Hamlet, at the bottom of the Freddie Wood Theatre field — to "suit the action to the word," the IWA had just gone on strike.

The strike didn't settle. Jim returned to tell us that "When one man stood up to suggest anything reasonable, another guy knocked him out." The strike went on to be the longest in a long history of BC logging strife.

For old time's sake, I went swimming on Sunday with Keith. We reverted to our early adolescence by diving down below his sister Sally and her friends, so that we could watch them frog-kick above us. Afterwards (I take no pride in this), when they all came over to our house, I showed Keith — in my attic room, with the trapdoor almost but not quite shut — how we could glimpse the girls getting changed out of their wet swimsuits in the unmarried mother's room below us.

On a higher plane: the next day I received a handwritten invitation from Kythe to come and stay for a weekend with her and Colonel Maxwell Dopping-Hepenstal, DSO, CBE, Croix de Guerre, in Duncan.

Conquering the Malahat

It didn't sound like fun, but I had nothing better to do, and it was an excuse to ride my James bike over the Malahat. A journey of thirty miles was three times further than going to town: I imagined myself as a military despatch rider — but for that role I needed proper kit. One of Victoria's long-term street characters gave me the idea.

He was male, of indeterminate age, and for three decades, winter or summer, he would stroll into Eaton's department store or Birks jewellers sporting a bomber jacket with fur collar, carrying a tightly rolled-up umbrella, and on his head wearing a leather crash helmet and goggles, exactly like the fighter-ace ones worn by Biggles when he defied the swastika.

I had a bomber jacket. My Biggles fighter-ace leather helmet was now too small, but I found one like it at the Army and Navy surplus shop on Government Street, where I also got a pair of massive black gauntlets that came almost up to my elbows. For my time in Vancouver, I had already solved the problem of stowing baggage on a motorcycle by attaching one of Mr. Bing's wooden vegetable crates to the back of the James bike, using metal clamps.

Ready for the road, I set off.

THE UP-ISLAND JOURNEY was smooth until Goldstream, after which it was not. Once the James 125cc engine met the Malahat, the carburetor quit. Once I cleaned that out, by blowing through the uncoupled gas line, the spark plug didn't spark. I had to take a piece of emery cloth to scour the carbon off the tip. By the time we reached the top of Tunnel Hill the single piston said it had had enough.

This was major, but I knew how to cope with it. All I had to do was use a socket wrench to remove the four bolts holding down the head of the cylinder cap, take off the cap, rotate the flywheel to bring the piston to the top, scrape off the carbon that had also built up on it, lower the piston, clean more carbon out of the two fuel entry ports on the side of the cylinder, put it all back together, and away we went.

For another five hundred foot ascent, when it happened again. And again. I haven't mentioned that I couldn't simply carry out these repairs wherever we happened to be: most of the Malahat Highway in those days had a cliff on one side and a precipitous drop to Finlayson Arm on the other, leaving almost no verges on which to pull over. If there wasn't space beside me when the bike stalled, I had to push the James, and Mr. Bing's vegetable crateful of my belongings, uphill, hugging the edge of the pavement until I found an open spot.

Other passing traffic was usually broad-minded, and waved — a sawmill flatbed driver even offered to transport me and the bike on his open deck, as far as Cobble Hill. I was too foolishly proud to accept — but a logging truck barrelling towards me downhill around a corner, air brakes hissing, fully loaded, could be alarming.

ONCE PAST THE MALAHAT SUMMIT we were on the mountain's good side and the James could coast the rest of its way into Duncan, where everything was still familiar. I turned off the highway at Trunk Road, and then over the creek on to Lakes Road, where Margetts' farm looked exactly the same.

(Why wouldn't it? Nobody then could imagine the subsequent rate of change to the Vancouver Island landscape. Margetts' farm today is a subdivision, top and bottom, with a school in the middle.)

Lakes Road curved around the west side of Quamichan Lake, taking me past Admiral Mainguy's property and then onto Stamps Road, which was, as another letter from Kythe, with driving instructions, advised me:

"Where our neighbours, the Americans, say I now 'live in sin' with Colonel Max and his Medals for Gallantry. But don't be alarmed by the Americans, or Max's scars. He earned his medals nobly, and he's really very nice."

FOUR YEARS AGO I had only seen his small figure at a distance, under a large Boy Scout hat that he wore to our jamboree for Governor General Alexander. Minus the hat, close up, the scars were terrible.

Burns had destroyed both sides of his face, his scalp and his hands, none of which reconstructive surgery in 1917 had been able to do much about. The surface of the once-burned skin was now shiny, like the shell of a turtle, with patches of similar brown-hued colours mixed with a little that was still human — in his case, white.

He got his burns and Croix de Guerre from rescuing French soldiers and civilians out of a flaming barn. His other military awards, from George V, were for leading Gurkha troops into battle against ridiculous odds.

I've already told you that I thought my weekend visit to this odd and very elderly couple would be dull. To guard against it, I arrived on Saturday afternoon, figuring that I could make it through to saying goodbye to them on Sunday evening.

Their daily routine was so unchanging that it had to be boring ... and yet I stayed for a week, and then returned in two later years. I'm describing it for you now, as a vignette of an Anglo Vancouver Island daily life — and Canadian broadcasting — that briefly was, and now isn't.

Kythe and the Colonel

The house exterior was cream stucco, two-storey, vaguely mock-Tudor, with a cedar shake roof and, surprisingly for this area, a full basement that was half below grade, and used mainly for storing garden fruit and vegetables on wooden racks through the winter.

The vegetables came from a kitchen garden surrounded by a high cedar fence to keep out the deer. The property was one of a series of long rectangular lots that sloped down from Stamps Road to the edge of Quamichan Lake. The colonel's land was thirteen acres, and its driveway length was about a thousand feet from the road to the front door — which was more like a small back door, with a porch protected by a stucco arch — and had cleared grass meadow, not bush, on either side.

The front of the house that faced the lake had a wide porch, with half of it properly enclosed by glass (unlike ours that Jim never managed to complete filling in) and French doors that worked. There was a wharf, but it didn't look as if anyone used it. The house belonging to the people whom Kythe had called "the Americans" was about fifty yards away to the west, half hidden by trees.

The interior of Colonel Max's house was badly done Edwardian (after the style of Samuel Maclure, self-taught designer of the Dunsmuirs' Hatley Castle and BC Government House), with square box beams, wainscots, pocket dividing doors that slid into walls, newel posts and banisters, edge grain fir floors and stairs.

All of this wood was dark-stained and gloss-varnished. The rooms weren't large, nor were the mullioned windows. As with too many kitchens in houses with great views, this one had been placed where the person who spent more time in it than anywhere else in the home, while they washed dishes and peeled potatoes, instead of being cheered along by looking out at the gleaming lake and Mount Tzouhalem, got their eyes dragged down to where the peelings would end up: the compost pile in the vegetable garden.

I had my own bedroom.

That sentence deserves to stand alone. It was only a normal guest bedroom, and to any other normal guest, only what they would normally have expected. It had a normal-sized bed with a normal mattress, a normal chest of drawers, a normal light overhead and two normal lamps, one on the normal bedside table and the other on a small writing desk (perhaps not quite so normal).

It also had writing paper and a pen, with a normal chair to sit down on; and the normal casement diamond-paned window opened in a normal fashion, with a normal latch; and the door was a normal door, with a normal handle — and even a normal lock with a keyhole as part of the handle.

Not one of these normal things was in my attic space at Glen Lake, and most of them were the opposite: my camp-cot bed, in particular, with hardly any spring on its frame and a stiff thin mattress on top, with horsehair bits that stuck out and scratched me.

Nor did I have to go through anyone else's bedroom to enter or leave mine. Revelling in so much spacious normality, I placed my pair of polo pyjamas and shaving kit — containing just my toothbrush because I shaved only about once a week — recovered from Mr. Bing's vegetable box on the bike, carefully into the empty top drawer.

I HAD ARRIVED IN TIME for a five-thirty supper — which Kythe said would be referred to as "dinner," and that we would "dine at seven." But first, we must have what she and Colonel Max called "our chota peg."

This phrase for an alcoholic drink was one of many usages from their time as servants of empire in British India. I expected something with an exotic name like Bombay gin but Kythe said, "We always have a Manhattan at six. It's Max's favourite. Of course you'll wish to join us."

Of course I would.

Kythe did the mixing of my first Manhattan: "We only use Crown Royal for the rye whisky — when we go next door to the Americans, they always insist on their *horrible* bourbon. It *must* be

Italian Martini & Rossi for the red vermouth, and only Angostura bitters. Max prefers a ratio of two-to-one for the whisky. Some people find that a little strong."

Kythe looked at me over her glasses, while she passed Colonel Max his drink. He sipped the Manhattan and nodded. I nodded too.

After that, I wasn't fully conscious of the dinner that followed the cocktail hour. Kythe's Duncan meals held few food surprises — I was already used to her skill as a cook — but the vegetable dish was different at our next day's luncheon. It was never called "lunch," and always preceded by a single glass of Max's favourite Amontillado sherry (slightly chilled): all of this announced by a gong, rung by Kythe at exactly one o'clock. The "veg" consisted of what looked like small cucumbers, sliced in half horizontally, then grilled in the oven. When I asked if they were baby marrows — a vegetable I strongly disliked — she said:

"Courgettes, I haven't had them since the south of France, because they won't ripen at Home — and of course the greengrocers don't sell them *here* — but we can grow courgettes successfully in our garden. Our friends the Americans for some reason *insist* on referring to them as *zucchinis*."

Colonel Max's meal rituals were a bit like going back to Barton Olivers and eating with the Aunts. Breakfast wasn't announced by a gong, but still began on the dot of nine, precisely, because Kythe waited to serve it until the CBC radio in the dining room completed a beep-beep-beep countdown to a final long beep, and then a voice like Noel Coward's said, "This is the BBC, in London. Here is the nine o'clock news for North America."

I may not have the words exactly, but close enough, and they continued to be heard over the Canadian Broadcasting Corporation for another decade or so — at which melting point in the Canadian cultural mosaic, the BBC's Noel Coward announcing was ditched, together with classical music, from the CBC's AM band.

Kythe served fresh coffee, then bacon and eggs and fried tomatoes, and toast with its slices neatly arranged in a silver toast-rack. When the BBC news was finished, I expected her to turn the radio off. Instead, we listened to a soap opera called *Our Gal Sunday*. It followed — and again, I approximate: "The travails of an orphan girl from a small mining town in the West, and can she find happiness as the wife of Lord Brinthorpe, England's richest and most handsome lord?"

Colonel Maxwell Dopping-Hepenstal recited these phrases in time with the announcer, and listened with full concentration for the fifteen melodramatic minutes that followed, until they ended with a cliff-hanger. The CBC's own announcer then urged listeners to do the same thing again every Monday to Friday.

My portrait of an eighty-year-old retired warrior enjoying such maudlin rubbish makes him seem another Colonel Blimp. Something for the brilliant minds behind *Beyond the Fringe*, and wannabes like me, to make into a figure of fun.

If Colonel Max had been that Blimpish sort of man, I wouldn't have wanted more of his company. But I did, and after breakfast he invited me to join him in his study and tell him something about myself. That was a first surprise. Naturally, the ham side of me was delighted to comply. Discovering that he was fluent in Japanese was a second surprise. That he had a black belt in judo made it a clean sweep.

He didn't reveal any of these achievements unless a question of mine led him to one of them. When I asked him about a Japanese scroll hanging on the wall of his study, next to a photograph of someone looking like the Gilbert & Sullivan's *Mikado*, he explained that he had been a British military attaché to the court of the Emperor Yoshihito — father of Hirohito — in 1921. Another photograph of himself taken at the Royal Military College, Sandhurst, produced a casual aside that a classmate next to him was Winston Churchill.

His judo prowess was all the more surprising because he was a very small man, barely five-foot-six, and at "just under nine stone," or 125 pounds, no heavier than my teenage weight. Yet a picture showed him standing upright next to a toppled Sumo colossus. When I asked him how that was possible, he just smiled and offered me an abridged version of Gibbon's *Decline and Fall of the Roman Empire*.

Colonel Max had a small but excellent library of fascinating books and could speak Hindi fluently, as well as Gurkhali — the language of the fierce, short soldiers from Nepal whom, as colonel of their regiment, he had led, and still loved, more than anyone else on earth.

Several *kukris*, the fabled weapons the Gurkhas employed to sever the head of a bullock, or an enemy, with one blow, hung on the study walls. The "everyday" *kukris* had horn handles and buffalo-hide scabbards, and were ornamented with silver. But he kept two special ones, that were partly finished with gold, under a glass sheet on his desk.

Two years later, when I was saying goodbye to him before I joined the navy, he gave me one of the partly gold ones as a going-away present.

Buggers Might Ride

When I wasn't talking to colonel Max, or listening to Kythe tell me more about my Mackenzie of Gairloch links to ancient Highland history, I was enjoying the more typically young male activities that Max's house had equipment to support. These were a Hardy split cane rod and reel from England (only the USA said "split bamboo") for fly-fishing in Quamichan Lake, and a Remington .22 for hunting the rabbits that had suddenly appeared in recently cleared land on the other side of Stamps Road.

In midweek Kythe informed me that we had been invited next door, "to meet *the Americans*, for drinks, with their son 'the author,' and his *friend*, who have just arrived from New York."

Meeting Americans didn't seem unusual enough to warant Kythe's emphasis. The parental couple next door were her age, late sixties, unremarkable — except that I thought perhaps they were from Kentucky originally, because they served us mint juleps, addressed Max as "Colonel," and seemed slightly in awe of him.

They introduced us to their son:

"And this is our dear George, the author — his book has just been published by Appleton-Century-Crofts, in New York. And this is his friend — "

I was impressed by meeting an author for the first time. But I don't remember the friend's name from that visit, because the Americans didn't remember it either. Their Dear George didn't look pleased by his parents' forgetfulness. He said, "You know perfectly well we're both up here because it's also been published in Canada."

The book was called *Beggars Might Ride* and its writer's full name was George Albert Glay. The cover that his parents proudly produced from their coffee table left off the "Albert."

POST-MODERN LIT CRIT decrees that all genres are now equal: a bodice ripper is just as good as *Crime and Punishment*. In 1952 it wasn't. Appleton-Century-Crofts, the publisher that Dear George's parents were so proud of, was a subsidiary of the Meredith Publishing Company. That was a corporate way of hiding in plain sight that in fact an author had actually written something like a Harlequin romance.

What was being hidden in plain sight in the Americans' drawing room, on the edge of Quamichan Lake, was homosexuality. It was hidden to me, but not Kythe.

"Queer as a dog's hind leg, and 'beggars' in his title is a *little* unfortunate, though the young blond *friend* was rather nice. When he laughed, he reminded me of the Prince of Wales when *he* was their age."

Colonel Max said nothing. Stripping Maxwell Dopping-Hepenstal of his illustrious rank and medals leaves us with a small, very old man, referred to in his obituary as a lifelong bachelor. It is probable that he was celibate through his time in the army, and no whiff of scandal attached to his Boy Scout service — but repressed gay, I have no doubt he was.

(I met George and his friend again when they moved to Victoria ten years later and opened a coffee shop on Fort Street's antique row, near the Royal Theatre. Kythe subsequently told me that George Glay's parents accepted reality when, before he visited them the next Christmas and they asked what he would like as a present, he said, "Two pairs of matching satin pyjamas, please, laid out side by side on the bed.")

Mike and the Zephyr: Ave

The Satin Prize Ribbon for rabbits, at the Luxton Fall Fair of 1952, should have been awarded to Hayseed, my beautiful Californian, with her lustrous white fur and shiny black nose and ears that reminded me of my pet toy Panda (before I shaved it), so long ago at Barton Olivers One.

The Luxton fix had been in from the start. The Glen Lake ladies who were the judges all knew each other and rotated the prizes annually between themselves.

On judging day I was able to drive Hayseed to the fair in Mike Gould's brand-new, leather-upholstered Ford Zephyr Six — not the Thames truck — and I could be in his driver's seat because I had just used the Thames to pass my BC driver's license test when I came back from Duncan.

The licensing office then was in Birdcage Walk, an old brick adjunct at the west side of the Parliament Buildings. The written test about road signs was easy, and for the practical part, the instructor was so uncomfortable in the Thames passenger seat, with his knees scrunched up and his head almost banging the windshield, that he kept things to a bare minimum:

Once around the Empress Hotel; back to the Buildings; parallel-park in a triple-empty spot in front of the office; and stop.

I was introduced to Mike Gould and his wonderful Ford Zephyr Six at the first social workers' summer party my parents gave at the lake. Like the fall fair, for a number of years these lake parties became an annual event.

As the social workers let down their hair and took off some

of their clothes, a lot of liquor was consumed, which led to more unrobing, to a point where there was sometimes no more clothing to remove, and a little man called Glenn ran around showing off his red pubic hair. His wife, Marjorie, later left him, and her house and children, for Bhagwan Shree Rajneesh at his commune in Oregon.

MIKE GOULD DRANK A LOT but didn't show it, and he wasn't a social worker. During the war, he had been a lieutenant-commander in the RNVR, or Wavy Navy (because of the zigzag gold stripes on its officers' uniforms), the Voluntary Reserve of the Royal Navy.

He had driven his motor torpedo boat to attack a German cruiser at full-throttle forty knots. Now he was both managing and running the bar at the Maple Bay Yacht Club in Genoa Bay, just below Mount Tzouhalem, at Duncan, where everybody said he was "tailor-made for the job," and how much they loved him, and "how sad it is about Mary."

Mary, his wife, had tuberculosis, and the only treatment in 1952, just before the widespread use of antibiotics, was cold air at a mountain sanatorium, and/or collapsing a lung. The Goulds' family tragedy was dual, because Mike also had TB from his wartime service and had probably transmitted it to her. They had two children. Finding people to look after the children when their parents were hospitalized was how my mother had met Mike.

I hero-worshipped him then for letting me sit in his leather-upholstered driver's seat of his new Zephyr Six. And take it solo for a spin. On the day before going back to the drudgery of school, in Grade 11, I dead-footed the Zephyr to its maximum-rated eighty miles an hour on the barely one-mile-long flat bit of Station Road: fifty yards more and I would have hit the public works grader.

A Date to Remember

Eleventh hour, eleventh day,
Around the world men stop to pray,
Remembering men who died before …

These were the opening lines of my Remembrance Day poem on November 11th, 1952, for which I won a prize from the Prince Edward branch of the Canadian Legion of the British Empire Service League.

The Legion, for short, still named His Majesty the King as patron-in-chief at the top of its letterhead. To be a wee bit fair, the late King's daughter, Elizabeth, had not yet been crowned. A letter with my prize was signed at the bottom by "Geo MacGregor, Secretary," who, in between that and the greeting, typed these kind words: "The enclosed order on Diggons Ltd., Victoria, will enable you to choose any article up to the value of four (4) dollars, and I hope that you will continue to write poetry of such a high order."

The Legion's generosity allowed me to buy my first stapler and a blue leather blotter from Diggon-Hibben's stationery shop. My Remembrance Day flicker of an effort through poesy was followed by the now ritual autumnal Archie-Stephenson-being-disappointed meeting about my dismal midterm academic results, with my parents, in his office.

Things picked up again in mid-December for the Rainbow Sea Cadets Christmas concert and its star turn: the girl contortionist. It was my first date.

I remember the girl I was taking, and the occasion, but not how I got to either one, because I lived out in the sticks and she lived in town. Her name was Jacky (short for Jacqueline) New and she wasn't short, in any dimension. Even without high heels, Jacky was at least four inches taller than I was, and "very well developed" — as people used to say — for her age, seventeen, a year more than mine.

And as she *was* wearing heels, when we walked into *HMCS Rainbow* it didn't take more than a minute before somebody again mentioned a similarity to the long-and-short cartoon characters Mutt and Jeff. (The first time was me and Sir Pip at the Uplands garden party.) Jacky just laughed it off, and — after a small stab of mortification, once I realized that since I was the guy who had the "well-developed girl" on his arm, there was more envy than derision in the jibes — I laughed too.

We knew each other because Art New, her father — for some reason, everybody called him "Paddy" — was another car salesman. Unlike Stew and his Stewdies, Paddy sold top-end British sports cars like Aston Martins and, a year later, the first Austin-Healey 100.

To peddle them, Paddy New wore dapper tweed jackets with leather patches on the elbows, sported a dapper pencil moustache like David Niven's, and smoked cigarettes in an ebony holder. He also spoke rather like David Niven in clipped English sentences but his wife, Jacky's mother, Molly New, had a Cockney accent like Michael Caine's and a raucous, costermonger's laugh.

Two years after our *Rainbow* dance, the New family all moved to Los Angeles, California, where Paddy made a not surprising success of selling sporting roadsters to people like his lookalike, David Niven. What *was* surprising: Molly became the private secretary to the president of the Santa Anita race course, giving complementary passes to bettors like Frank Sinatra. Jacky quit school to marry a policeman.

But now ... back to the real hit of the *Rainbow* show for Christmas, 1952.

The girl contortionist: She was the third part of a three-piece act, after the juggler (oranges and knives, mixed) and the magician (cards, a dove and a rabbit). The contortionist (spangled swimsuit, baton and top hat) could do the most remarkable things, like bending her head back between her legs to come up grinning at all of us hypnotized cadets, staring at her face above a swim-suited crotch.

Which, whenever I look back at it in memory, somewhat disturbs my adult conscience. Her amazing flexibility, and the reason she could be so disturbing to young male adolescents, was possible because our spangled peep-show star was only about eight years old.

(I don't have to rely on faulty memory to prod my conscience. Fifty years later, a fellow cadet called Fred Green sent me a photograph marked "Christmas Concert & Contortionist" which he had discovered in some files that he was cleaning out of his desk — by then, Fred had become an eminent judge.)

Beauregard in Love

Christmas high, Christmas low: Jim's malaria came back for 1952's season of joy, and, because of the chemicals used by BCFP to preserve the logs that he hauled up after midnight on the green chain, the skin-rot condition of his hands was worse than ever.

Treating them meant removing thick bandages wrapped on all his fingers; removing the dead skin; coating or recoating the exposed, raw flesh with special ointment prescribed by Dr. Greenwood, his dermatologist; then rewinding the thick bandages, while trying not to squeeze them tight. Before, during and after this agonizing process, Jim stayed in bed with his face to the wall, day after day, with my mother being alternately solicitous with soup and beside herself with rage at the way in which he spoiled our holidays.

I raged too, at the time. It isn't a male adolescent's place to analyse the psyche of a male parent, or himself, while both are playing out the main roles in their live performance of *Oedipus Rex*. Now I can give a bit more credit to Jim, and the brave face he showed the rest of the world.

He used those same damaged musical hands, which could no longer play a piano, to train his fellow IWA union workers on the green chain to hold waste bits of wood as imaginary instruments, and then conducted them as an imaginary orchestra, backed by the tympani thumps as the logs fell off the chain claws on their way to the massive circular saw teeth that sliced them into lumber.

All mammals need to find relief somehow ... which brings us to my seventeenth birthday and our growing lake menagerie. It had expanded to two English golden cocker spaniels, two horses, three goats, two cats, one rabbit, multiple chickens and bantams, and a new bull calf. The calf was "theoretically" being raised to become veal: after the experience with Henry the turkey, no-one in our family was capable of seeing an adorable baby calf actually go to Fisher's abattoir.

The last thing we needed was another dog, but he arrived anyway. Because of his size we nicknamed him sometimes Jumbo, other times Beau — his full pedigree name was "Beauregard, out of" some other, high-falutin' canine moniker — and he was the largest Boxer the breed had ever produced. Nor, because of his valuable pedigree, had he been neutered.

For my birthday treat I took Jumbo, via the Thames truck, into town to the vet, to be given a rabies shot. When Beau saw a Chihuahua bitch sitting on a white towel on a little old lady's lap on the other side of the vet's waiting room, the result became at the same time pornographically hilarious and one of the most embarrassing moments in my life.

The Chihuahua wasn't much bigger than Beauregard's noble Boxer's head. She was also, obviously even to a human eye, sitting on her towel because of a female condition that would make her receptive to an amorous canine advance. Beau was sitting on his haunches at my side, facing the animals and owners on the other side of the waiting room. Consequently they saw first what I could not.

Beau was becoming aroused — increasingly, and extendedly, and crimsonly — until finally, drippingly, onto the waiting-room floor — by which time I realized what was happening.

My face was in a richer crimson state than Beau was. The more that the other humans in the room tried to ignore what was going on, the more hilarious some of them found it until, as the cliché has it, "the room rocked with laughter." Except for the little old lady hanging on for grim life to her Chihuahua bitch, who was attempting to leap out of her owner's ancient arms and off the towel to meet Beauregard halfway to paradise.

Their love hadn't been consummated, and I tried not to dwell on the horrible visit to the vet, but Beauregard's passion, coming as it did on the heels of my first date, left an awkward yet fascinating question hanging:

If nature could allow such a Mutt and Jeff consummation, devoutly to be avoided, to happen between canines … what about me and Jacky New?

Here Comes the Blackball Ferry

"Still developing." That was the verdict of the medical specialist who examined me when I was fourteen, because Jim thought I was "too small for his age." He meant that only one of my testicles had descended with puberty. The specialist concluded that my legs were already long enough, but my torso had been held back by wartime rationing. The missing bit of me, in the middle of these two halves, would descend in its own good time.

Now, at sixteen, Keith Williams had decided to quit Sea Cadets. But because of parental pressure, I hung on reluctantly — while they no longer had the inconvenience of driving me back and forth to Victoria West on Tuesday nights. The RCN now provided a navy-blue GM bus, with a streamlined front, to pick us up and take us home. There were so few cadets in our Unorganized Territory that the bus stopped pretty much wherever we lived. It did so for me, at the corner of Glen Lake Road and Jacklin Road. That convenient bus ride was to teach me harshly the most important lesson in my military life.

The New Year of 1953 was fine at *Rainbow* until Lieutenant-Commander Dando decided for no good reason that I should be the uncomfortable messenger of authority on the new bus. This turned into a problem when, in late January, prior to our return trip home, a No Smoking sign suddenly appeared on the inner panel of the bus door, at the front, beside the driver.

The Gunner, in his usual terrifying manner, pointed the No Smoking sign out to us: "Obey that, and don't ask bloody questions, or I'll have your bloody guts for bloody garters. Gurr, the C.O. says you're in bloody charge."

Fear of the bloody Gunner was sufficient to keep the bus smoke-free without any help from me for two Tuesdays, but on the third run a cadet called Gavin, who lived on Station Road, took out a forbidden cigarette and lit up. I said something mealy-mouthed like, "Gavin, the Gunner said we aren't supposed to do that," which produced a laugh all round, and a second cigarette.

Keeping quiet was easier than being laughed at. On the fourth Tuesday, after I arrived at *Rainbow* and stepped off the bus, the Gunner greeted me with his worst glower.

"The bloody driver says there's bloody smoking on his bloody bus and you're doing bloody nothing about it. Next bloody time you bloody take their bloody names and give them to me and I'll be among you and them with a bloody rope's end. Do I bloody make myself clear?"

His message could have been stronger — if we hadn't been cadets, he would have used "fucking" as an adjective — but not clearer. On the ride home Gavin was smoking again, and I said, "Gavin, please put that out." After the rest giggled and lit up, I followed up with, "Gavin and you others, you're warned. If you don't put them out, I'm taking names."

They didn't obey. The Gunner was away on leave but I did as he had ordered me to, and told some other substitute disciplinarian at *Rainbow* the miscreant smokers' names. The substitute assigned them only an easy-going twenty minutes' worth of polishing brass. Indoors. That the Gunner would have had them all changing targets at shooting practice out at the range for two hours in foul weather didn't make the recipients any less annoyed.

But on the next bus ride home, nobody lit up. Despite leniency in its application, I thought the Gunner's punishment threat must have worked. The bus stopped at my Glen Lake Road corner and I got off.

Without streetlights, it was pitch-dark. I think I must have realized that the bus door hadn't made its usual hissing sound to indicate that it had closed behind me, but by then a number of arms had grabbed me — at which critical juncture the door did slide shut, and the bus drove away.

I COULDN'T SEE THEIR FACES but I knew them from their voices. There were three grabbers, and Gavin. The grabbers sounded nervous. Gavin was excited.

He said: "His pants, take them off."

The grabbers didn't really want to, and I certainly didn't, but I thought it was only going to be the schoolboy "debagging" pants-off that used to go on routinely at Sherborne and UCS.

Gavin said: "And his underpants."

As nobody would be able to see me, I still thought this meant nothing more unpleasant than having to walk home half-naked, getting cold. Then Gavin said:

"Hang onto him. I've got the Kiwi. Here comes the Blackball Ferry."

BLACK KIWI SHOE POLISH roughly applied to my genitals was more than unpleasant. The grabbers let go of me and ran. Gavin said something juvenile about crime and punishment, and no hard feelings, and ran after them. I pulled up my white Jockey shorts and Jolly Jack bell-bottomed trousers, but didn't bother doing up all the fly buttons of the flap. I walked through the darkness for the third of a mile it took to get home, dreading the embarrassment of explaining things to Jim.

I don't know why I thought about him rather than my mother. In the event, I was spared that final degree of humiliation, because he had gone to bed early. My mother was alone in the kitchen, and when I saw her, I cried.

And here comes the kicker: Because of the change in our heating system, we now had a roster for taking showers … And when I needed it most, there was no hot water.

Removing black shoe polish from sensitive skin with only cold water is neither easy nor effective. Eventually it was done, and although my humiliation was a steep price to pay for it, I had, as previously stated, been taught a vital lesson:

Never give an order without the force to back it up.

There was one other good thing from my descent into Kiwi hell: I now had a second dropped ball to be blackened.

"A Midsummer Night's Dream in Tobacco Road"

PROFESSIONAL THEATRE ARRIVED on stage in Victoria, and in my life. They called themselves the York Theatre Company, and set up shop in the original Pantages Theatre building (now the McPherson Playhouse) on Government Street.

The glory days of the Victoria Pantages had witnessed performing lions leaping through burning hoops, and Jack Benny and Gracie Fields doing their shticks and singing their songs.

Then it fell into being a cinema for bad B movies, followed by a darkened interval of years ... but now, in March 1953, triumphantly and appropriately ("Attended and applauded by Premier W.A.C. Bennett, and wife, May"), it was brought back to life with a production of *Curtain Up*.

The York's second production was *French Without Tears* followed by *Harvey,* in which I did not get the role I dreamed of: a talking rabbit. This was followed by *Mr. Roberts,* a recent Broadway hit about the US Navy in World War Two, which a wag described as "a *Caine Mutiny* with laughs."

Third time lucky. I got the role of Lindstrom, the American sailor who gets to see the birthmark on Nurse Girard's naked bum as she takes a shower on the island of Elysium. Unfortunately, neither I nor the audience got to see any part of actual naked nurses in a shower. I pretended to see mine through a telescope.

I wish I could say that I got the part of Lindstrom because of my acting ability. The truth is, I got it because Frank Mitchell, in a wily move — he had the part of Sailor Wiley — told our ambitious director, Ian Thorne, that I knew how to handle goats. Worse, he told Thorne I had a truck that could *transport* a goat.

There are no goats in either the novel or the play version of *Mr. Roberts.* There is a palm tree, which becomes the dramatic centre of attention prior to its being thrown overboard. The palm tree is the pride and joy of the captain. Going by the US Navy rulebook, tossing it overboard would be mutiny. Ian Thorne decided that, for a Victorian audience, this mutinous act would be funnier if a goat watched it unfold.

The goat was not one of ours. The thespian nanny lived on Glanford Avenue, which — Frank Mitchell again helpfully told

Ian Thorne — would make it a breeze for me to pick up and return on my way in and out of town. It wasn't a breeze. The nanny didn't like to get into the Thames truck any more than I did, and tried immediately to get out of it, butting me with her horns as she did so. She repeated this sequence twice a night for the first five nights of the play's projected one-week run.

When we got to the theatre for the first dress rehearsal with a live goat, Ian Thorne realized that somebody would have to look after her when she wasn't onstage. I suggested wily Frank Mitchell, but *he* pointed out that, as Wiley, he was only offstage when the goat was on, and vice versa. Whereas my part, as Lindstrom ... you can guess the rest.

What no-one had guessed — although I could have told them if I'd been asked — was that on opening night the nanny would eat the palm tree. This act, which could have brought the house down, happened, alas, backstage. There wasn't an understudy for the palm. So what the opening night audience got to see being dumped overboard by Mr. Roberts was a bare stick in a pot, with some green bits of paper stuck onto it.

In spite of, or because of, the goat, the first five nights of the run of *Mr. Roberts* were a box-office smash, and Ian Thorne offered me a reward for my nanny-ferrying. After our current play closed, the next York production was going to be his own interpretation of *A Midsummer Night's Dream*, and I would be his Puck.

He gave me the script. Dreams of stardom filled my head as I drove nanny home to Glanford Avenue. Once at my own home, I read Puck's lines until my head fell down on the pillow at two in the morning, and then again when I woke up.

Up and down, up and down ...

PUCK'S WORDS OF WARNING could not have prepared me. On the sixth night, I collected nanny and arrived with her at the stage door to find that our play about mutiny had mutinied. Or as the *Daily Colonist* headlined it:

Marquee Darkened by Disagreement

All seats for the play had sold out. Under the darkened marquee in front, eight hundred disappointed patrons of live theatre in Victoria were milling around on Government Street trying to read a scrawled note on the locked doors:

There will be no show tonight.
Please keep your tickets.
They will be honored later.

Meetings between the York Company's mutineering stars and their fiscal management went nowhere, followed by the York itself, and my first crack at a professional theatrical career.

FOR NOW, THE YORK WAS EXTINGUISHED. That didn't dim the brightness of the footlights I could still see shining on my future life in the theatre. The smell of the makeup, the glimpses of company stars like Diana Ricardo and Michael Rothery — said to be "in an affair" — moving unconcernedly undressed between dressing rooms ... Nubile Diana, wearing only bra and panties: my first occasion for seeing such a vision in the flesh.

My overheated, stage-struck dreams instantly got cold water dashed on them, by Jim.

It was part of a pattern that I didn't yet see: one which, even when I did begin to see it, I couldn't understand. I didn't know what drove him, whenever my name came up for any small success, to need to undercut it. A trivial example was a misspelling of my name, as reported in a *Daily Colonist* clipping about *Birds of a Feather:*

> NAME'S GURR, PLEASE, SIR
>
> "His name appeared on the program incorrectly spelled as 'Turr.' It might have gone unnoticed except that David gave such a 'Fine Performance' that Adjudicator Jack Thorne used the play, and David's acting, as a good example to the rest of the young actors and actresses."

Jim ignored the "Fine Performance" puffery. Instead, he dumped the misspelling on *my* head.

As for any career in the theatre — according to his years as one half of Singer and Keyes, trying to be Noel Coward in rundown British music halls — the chances of my success were almost impossible. And even if they happened, for me it would be only "cold days in cold rooms on the road," and "too much drinking with too many wrong people," and "too much sex with too much buggering ..."

This cold-shower litany from Jim should have cooled my theatrical ardour, but it was reignited in late May:

Tobacco Road hit town.

THE PLAY WAS A BOX-OFFICE DREAM and a last-ditch chance for the York to make a fiscal comeback. The newspapers were full of "Adult Entertainment Only" warnings, and titillating titbits about "dirty language" and "a too revealing, scarlet dress on Ellie May."

The opening production in Vancouver, by Sidney Risk and his Everyman Theatre, had been raided by the police. Its director, Dorothy Davies, was charged, convicted, and sentenced to "a maximum fine of twenty dollars, or ten days in prison."

The convictions were all overturned on appeal. One of its stars, Bruno Gerussi (playing the lead, Jeeter, a foul-mouthed share-cropper patriarch), then made a joint venture with the York and brought the play, with its crimson reputation, to Victoria.

I had met both Dorothy Davies and Gerussi — who said I had "it," whatever "it" was, and told me to call him Bruno — last year at summer school. When he arrived at the York stage door, I told Bruno that I wasn't allowed to buy a ticket because of my age, and begged him to give me any kind of job that would let me watch the show from the wings.

The whole idea of "Adults Only" censorship amused and outraged him. Bruno let me move some props and, to satisfy morality in Victoria, changed some of Jeeter's "by Jesus'" to "by Judas'" and the "dirty old whores" to "sluts." He also added a safety pin to stop Ellie May's slutty scarlet dress from showing so much forbidden thigh. And the York Theatre Company, through Gerussi, had itself one last hit. Bruno would become famous, as Nick, in the CBC TV series *The Beachcombers*.

Another company, the Totem Theatre, arose in Victoria from the York's ashes. After Ellie May's slutty thigh, and the previous dressing-room vision of Diana Ricardo in her bra and panties, this was more than enough to keep the flame of having "it" as an actor (whatever that was) alive in my head for the next two years at least.

Everest Conquered but Prizes Denied

My Grade 11 school year ended with two anticlimaxes. The first was the successful capture of the Kiwi-balling ringleader Gavin. In the daylight following his shoe-polished attack on my genitals, he lost his nighttime bravado. Whenever he emerged from his Grade 10 class he began to look furtively over his shoulder to see if he saw Frank Mitchell, or me, anywhere near him.

We let that happen for a week. On the next Monday afternoon, we notched things up. Frank borrowed his father's GM pickup and drove it in first gear behind Gavin as he walked up the hill from Belmont to his house on Station Road.

We did it again on Tuesday. By Wednesday, when we pulled in front of him, blocking his front door, and stopped the truck, he was shaking. When we opened the tailgate of the pickup, he began to cry, and said "It won't happen again."

Then, as we had no idea what we were going to do with him anyway, I said fatuously, as if I were the Gunner, "It bloody well bloody better bloody not." It sounded as absurd as it looks, and we let Gavin go.

The second downer was academic. I had once more taken Archie Stephenson's autumnal disappointment in my academic prowess to heart, and as a result I came first in a number of subjects.

On the first of June, a day when I would otherwise have been enjoying a Sea Cadet celebration of a glorious date in Royal Naval history — the Fourth Battle of Ushant, in 1794 — Mr. Parrott once again consulted his burgeoning theory of teenage social development. He decided that the social development of everybody else would be adversely affected if I received most of the prizes usually awarded for such achievements, and so there wouldn't be any, for anyone, for anything at Belmont this year — except sports, which meant only softball for the girls coached by Mr. Palsson.

On June 2nd, 1953, I thought then (and still do now) that Harold Parrott and his development theories were grossly unfair. But I didn't have time to mope because, at the crack of dawn, I had to ride into town on the James bike to march, and blow my bugle, in the coronation parade for Queen Elizabeth the Second.

There had been a similar early start for a parade rehearsal on May 29th, which had begun and ended in front of the Parliament Buildings. This time, as I arrived and parked my bike there for the final, a *Daily Colonist* delivery truck was just dropping off a bound bundle outside the doors of the provincial museum. A vending machine beside it displayed the largest headline ever seen in Victoria:

EVEREST CONQUERED

Riding on Shanks' Pony

All sorts and conditions of men, as well as women, pray to be blessed with the birth of a child. If that doesn't work through the usual channels, they ask somebody like my mother to help them adopt one.

In my teenage world, all the word "adoption" meant to me was that she very quickly got to know a lot of very different people, which gave me a foot in the door for possible summer jobs.

The starter was helping to create the city of Victoria's very first beer parlour, in the Drake Hotel. The significance of this event cannot be overstated. Prohibition had been repealed for more than thirty years, and booze by the bottle was sold by the government monopoly Liquor Control Board stores, but beer by the glass in downtown Victoria was still unobtainable.

Change had to be gradual; the new premises, spotless. Farmer Construction won the bid to renovate the Drake, and my mother got me the opportunity to assist the Farmers in this historic task.

Prohibition aside, there had been some kind of pub for sailors at the corner of Johnson and Store Streets near the Inner Harbour since Victoria began ninety years earlier, but all had run downhill since then. The last death-of-hope place was called the Rex Hotel, a dive I never went into. Farmer's had the job of removing all trace of the Rex's interior, on all three floors and the basement cellars, and replacing them with polished mahogany and gleaming glass.

I didn't get to polish and gleam: I was given digging-out-the-cellar, which extended in front of the building below the sidewalk of Johnson Street. Some small squares of thick, frosted glass set into the sidewalk overhead allowed a dingy light. A large, hinged steel plate in the cellar roof, beside the glass, had originally been designed to open to allow beer barrels to be rolled down from the street.

As no barrels had rolled since prohibition began in BC, on October 1st, 1917, the hinged steel plate allowed anyone passing by to drop anything they wanted into the cellar below. Thirty years had allowed them to drop a lot, which could have been archaeologically interesting, and when I began to dig, I had the enthusiasm of Howard Carter in Egypt, unearthing young Tut's tomb in the Valley of the Kings.

Unfortunately, what I found under Johnson Street was ninety-nine percent earth. The balance was mixed with (mostly dried) cat and human shit and some vintage bottles. It had been used as a long-time base of operations for thankfully now-dead rats.

When the Drake eventually had its grand opening the next year, I was invited to the ribbon-cutting for the new mahogany bar. But I still wasn't old enough to buy a drink at it and, in the presence of all the city worthies, the barman didn't feel free to "bend my elbow" by bending the law.

I LEFT THE DRAKE HOTEL BASEMENT DIG to do the same thing: this time, digging in the open air of Mrs. Molliet's garden on Admirals Road, overlooking Esquimalt Harbour, for an occasional hour or two. The James bike's mobility let me drop in on my way from Glen Lake to somewhere else, and Mrs. Molliet (also originally from Home) supplied all the tools, and cups of tea and Cadbury's chocolate biscuits.

I mention the small gardening job because of the Indigenous graves. As I said about my friendship with Jack (the boy by the creek in Duncan) in the 1940s: no settler that I met ever described the original inhabitants of the Pacific Northwest Coast — like Jack's people, the Cowichans — as "First Nations."

Those humans, who, for millennia, had occupied all the land from the *Rainbow* headquarters to the whole of Esquimalt, and Mrs. Molliet's garden, were the Songhees people. Now they lived on a fraction of it, in a reserve near Craigflower Bridge. Mrs. Molliet's property was an adjacent five acres, sloping down from Admirals Road almost to the water of the harbour and the RCN's sailing club. Only a third of the land was a cultivated English garden, with the usual rhodos and roses; the balance was covered by the usual West Coast cedar, and Douglas fir, and salal undergrowth.

While I was routinely clearing up fallen brush in that wooded area, I tugged on some branches and found a pile of moss-covered rocks underneath. A couple of rocks began to roll free, and I thought I might as well tidy the rest of them — at which point Mrs. Molliet arrived with her tea tray, and shouted, *"Stop."*

She explained that the "rock pile" was an Indigenous gravesite, and showed me others like it in the wooded portion of her garden, of which she had advised the Provincial Museum. They had told descendant leaders of the Songhees who, she said, came over twice a year to perform a Drum Ceremony for their ancestors.

An office job at my mother's agency, Spencer House — before a mouse-click was invented — required transcribing names and addresses from a list of several hundred held in a Rolodex and writing them out, by hand, with an ink fountain pen onto something else.

For what purpose, I don't remember. It went on for seven sultry summer working days, with no fan. A kind secretary, very tall, called Miss Couchman, or, more affectionately, "Couch" (pronounced confusingly as Kooch), brought me glasses of her homemade lemonade. But a note she handed me from my mother about "possibility repairing motorbikes for Old Pop Shanks?" was much more my cup of tea.

"Old Pop" was Richard Shanks, ancient patriarch of Reg and Bob, and founder of Brooklands Motorcycles Ltd. at the corner of Fort and Quadra, adjacent to the Anglican cathedral, which was convenient for the grieving relatives of riders recently lost to the joys of the open road — more of which, anon.

In 1953, Old Pop (from Home: born in Chertsey, Surrey, in 1876) wasn't as ancient as I am now, but he seemed like it to me then. His Brooklands' showroom windows showed off the dealership's bread-and-butter: most-lusted-after 1200cc Harley-Davidsons and, to celebrate the coronation (from the Birmingham Small Arms Company), Gold Star 500cc BSAs with the newest "swing-arm rear suspension."

The new machines faced onto Fort Street, but bikes brought in to be fixed were taken to the rear of the building — on Meares Street, next to the gravestones in the cathedral's cemetery — and then down a ramp for two levels of repair work. The biggest chunk of this came from the Victoria Police Department's fleet of "Indians." The VPD still had quite a large motorcycle squad, several of whom, on the "Indian Chiefs," had just escorted me and my bugle in that Coronation parade. (Indian Chiefs were super-powerful 1200cc bikes, and Old Pop's special love, but the year I met him, and them, was the last year they were made.)

"YOUNG REG" WAS THE WORKING MANAGER of the Shanks' Fort Street operation. He took one look at my James 125cc and said, "My God. That's still around? We sold it ten times over." He was joking, slightly, and the veteran mechanics made fun of the James because of its dwarf size — yet they also respected it, as a slice of bike history, for its role of despatch riding in war. Reg only assigned trivial cleanup jobs to me, but I was able to observe quite a bit as these powerful beasts were taken apart and, to increase profit and reduce cost, put back together with as few new pieces as possible.

Bob Shanks sold occasional new bikes as well as saddlery. The usual Harleys and Indians, but Nortons and Royal Enfields too — all still proudly labelled, "Made in England." No hint yet of the Asian tidal wave about to engulf their legendary names.

The most lucrative repair jobs were for machines that had been badly damaged in a fatal crash. They were excellent for business because the relatives of the departed never wanted to see any repaired, or original, part of them ever again, as long as they lived. Bob could sorrowfully buy them back for, as he said, "a gravedigger's song," and then sell them on again, for considerable profit, to the next over-confident young male.

The success of this truly "re-cycling" operation was on the wall of the workshop for all to see. Each time a fatal-accident machine arrived, its name — in red, plus a black skull and bones — got painted on the whitewashed wall above it. During my month of rag-wiping oil leaks off the lino floor, finding two wall-skulls was not uncommon. One record-breaking Golgotha machine's name had three skulls beside it.

The Bantam War

The last battle of the Bantams (between ours and the Wohlers') was launched with the driving of a copper pin by the Surveyor General of British Columbia to mark our property line on the Wohlers' side.

For the sake of accuracy: when I first met Ernie McMinn, he hadn't yet scaled to his eventually impressive titular height. He was then merely a government surveyor who had already driven similar copper spikes into mountain peaks of the most remote parts of the province, like the Nahanni River, establishing the BC–Alberta provincial boundary all the way down from the Yukon.

Jim was able to enlist Ernie's professional skills and equipment to mark our property line — as he had done in the Rockies — because of Jean, Ernie's wife, another of the Spencer House social workers who came to the 1953 end-of-summer social workers' party at the lake.

Jean McMinn was a horse-mad equestrian; she despised the parties and the drinking (and, most of all, Glen Hamilton doing his party trick of running around showing off his red pubic hair). Ernie enjoyed a good drink, and the first time he saw Glen Hamilton's naked parts, said, "H-h-he only n-n-eeds a S-s-sergeant Major's b-b-b-oot up his arse to s-s-s-quare him off."

Which is to say, Ernie stuttered. He blamed the disability on his frontline infantry-fighting against Kurt Meyer's armoured 12th SS Panzer Division Hitlerjugend in Normandy. Ernie's stutter lessened when he knew people. I got to know, respect, and like him a great deal.

(Meyer and his Panzer Hitler jugends were convicted as war criminals and sentenced to death for shooting Canadian prisoners from Ernie McMinn's regiment; later, and controversially, Meyer's sentence was commuted.)

Jim described to Ernie our need for a proper boundary between us and the Wohlers: not just to keep the bantam combatants apart, we finally needed to put in a proper fence for all our burgeoning livestock.

Ernie set up his theodolite at the top of our property on Glen Lake Road and began working his way down the line, placing Rocky Mountain bronze pins at corners also marked by white-painted identification stakes for easy future reference.

We didn't have to wait for the future. Walter Wohlers attacked at once. He couldn't do anything to the bronze pins, but immediately pulled out the first white stake.

Ernie said: "Hey. W-w-what the h-h-hell do you t-t-think you're d-d-doing?"

Walter Wohlers said: "Zis sticks means nussing."

Ernie said: "Are you a f-f-fucking K-k-kraut?"

My mother said: "It's all right, Ernie, they're Austrian."

Ernie said: "I'm g-g-government. He d-d-does it again, I'll s-s-shoot the f-f-fucker."

This governmental message appeared to sink in. Walter Wohlers went back to his house. Ernie finished marking the line and, after a stiff drink to calm down, went home to Jean and their twenty gentle acres of horse meadows and stables in peaceful Cordova Bay.

That night, my mother heard a loud tapping noise. Jim was away on his midnight green chain shift at BCFP. I got a flashlight, and went outside to find Walter Wohlers knocking the first white marker stake between our two houses out of the ground. Moving steadily through the night, carrying an oil lamp to guide him, ignoring my adolescent shouts and yells, he knocked out another, and so on, up to the road.

This pattern — with an increasingly perturbed Ernie McMinn casting racial aspersions that placed Walter Wohlers' behaviour and fate closer and closer to Kurt Meyer's — happened twice more.

On the third occasion, Ernie returned with a sergeant from the Provincial Police detachment in Langford, after which, Walter Wohlers sold his Glen Lake property and moved his bantams, and family, up to the Cowichan Valley, to live in peace and harmony with his presumably un-demarcated neighbours as a dairy farmer like Captain Margetts.

A Dynamite Last Act

The start of Grade 12 in September still seemed far enough away from the ending of school in June that I could postpone making what Harold Parrott called "career choices," and what most of the baker's dozen Belmont grads called "getting a job."

I wanted to be an actor. I don't know why I stayed in Sea Cadets. It never occurred to me that the two activities could be related: that a Jolly Jack's bell-bottomed uniform was a costume, or that marching in a Coronation Day Parade was being on a large-as-life stage.

On the last day of June I got a certificate of proficiency stating that I had "qualified by examination as leading cadet," but the Blackball Ferry experience — from trying to enforce "No Smoking" on the bus — had shown me that rank meant nothing if authority wasn't behind it.

Inertia is a powerful drug, and the minor promotion let me choose a specialization of naval trade to go on with. I picked communications: it allowed me to sit through the winter in a warm room, tapping out Morse code instead of marching, rowing, sailing or shooting in wind and rain. I had done enough of all that anyway. Four years as a *Rainbow* Cadet had given me as much naval knowledge as an able seaman in the regular force RCN.

Professional theatre was staging one more "last gasp" in Victoria. Another pair of "Never say die" actors, Stuart Baker and Thor Arngrim, whom I had also met the previous summer in Vancouver, had transmuted the York Theatre Company into a new company called "Totem." I arrived back from a placid Quamichan

Lake week with Kythe and Max to find that this Totem bunch would be putting on *Gigi* as their opening production.

I rushed to the stage door to be told by the lighting guy that Thor was having "an actual affair" with a talented actress called Norma MacMillan, who was Gigi. (Norma also wrote the last play that Totem put on in Victoria, *A Crowded Affair,* which sold out.) After their staged *Affair,* Thor and Norma got married, and then quit the West Coast for the brighter lights of "Big T.O.," stage-speak for Toronto.

I hung around the Totem whenever I had spare time, and Thor Arngrim found backstage odds and ends for me to "keep my hand in" with scrims and gels; but despite all my pleadings there was nothing nearer the footlights.

THE DAMP SQUIB applied to my "name-in-lights" dreams for the theatre nearly got things off to a headline-making bang in Mr. Palsson's chemistry lab at Belmont. The lab was set up in the converted back half of Army Hut 4, which made its un-opening windows face south, and the Grade 12 chemistry lab class was the first after the lunch hour.

It was a sunny mid-September day. The lab was hot and everyone was drowsy, already fed up with being back at school. My partner for whatever dull experiment had been assigned by Mr. Palsson was Robbie Robertson.

When Mr. Palsson with his little Hitler moustache wasn't coaching the girls' softball team or reciting "The Charge of the Light Brigade" with its "Cannon to right of them, / Cannon to left of them," complete with sound effects at the Christmas concert, he tried to inculcate chemistry and mathematics.

Now he stopped beside Robbie and began to say something which began as a normal, after-lunch, couldn't-really-care-less, "How is it going with you two ..."

Then, as he saw the beakers on our bench, his question changed to an almost strangulated "What the hell are you doing?"

Robbie said in the language of science: "Mixing acids with stuff."

Mr. Palsson pointed at our beakers, labelled "HNO_3" and "H_2SO_4," and said in an even quieter, almost strangulated voice:

"Nitric *and* sulphuric — you morons mixed *those* acids?"

I would usually have just nodded, sardonically. Because his tone was beginning to smarten me up, I said: "Yes."

"Mixed them," Mr. Palsson said in the now barely audible, strangulated voice. "With *what?*"

Robbie said: "That beaker over there. It didn't have a label. Just some oil, I think."

Mr. Palsson initially whispered: "Good God." Then, "Glycerine." Followed by, a fraction louder, "*Where is your resultant?*"

I produced the test tube of yellowish liquid that for some reason I was holding behind my back, and said: "Here ..."

Mr. Palsson bellowed: **"GIVE THAT TO ME. EVERYBODY ELSE, GET OUT."**

Having a Graduation Ball

I TOOK CAROLINE FUTCHER TO IT in the Thames truck — and that statement doesn't begin to reflect either my embarrassment or Caroline's discomfort: the Thames had never been designed to carry even one passenger in any kind of comfort.

To accommodate an extra person, Jim had taken out the passenger's original tiny bucket seat and replaced it with a wooden bench. This was only a two-by-six-inch plank, with stubs nailed underneath at each end to make it level and a bit of plaid cloth on the top for pretence at upholstery. It stretched across the gap from the closed passenger door to the edge of the driver's bucket seat.

This allowed the physical placement of someone the size of a small child (my sister) to be squeezed between driver and squashed-adult passenger. The gearshift column on the cab floor extended upwards, guaranteed to hit body parts of anyone seated on the plank with the knob on top of the gear-handle, and *ipso facto,* by the driver's right hand on top of said gear-handle.

Caroline's father, Mr. Futcher, was the name that stood behind her reputation, and behind Futcher's Fencing Installations (which would have saved me from a lot of post-hole digging if we could have afforded his services). Caroline's two brothers liked making old cars feel better. Their current patient was a 1947 something-V8 from Detroit, now up on blocks.

When I arrived in the Thames to pick up my attractive, intelligent, kind, but ultimately reluctant date for the graduation ball, the myriad component pieces of a complete engine block and transmission lay on the ground around the chassis. I had to step between and over the V8 bits, in an automotive-playground hopscotch, trying not to get oil on my shoes.

So far we've only surveyed the dating scene at Belmont High from the juvenile male's point of view. It was bleak enough. During each year of frustration after I reached puberty, the few girls of my age at Belmont only wanted to date grown-up loggers of eighteen. One notorious teenage nubile — now a respectable great-grandmother — while still in Grade 10 taunted my overheated imagination with rumours that she danced naked for these "mature" young loggers on a tabletop in Langford, chugging Labatt's beers as they cheered her on, while at the same time getting ready to cut off the table legs with their chainsaws.

For an intelligent girl like Caroline to find any kind of date with a flicker of amorous sophistication from the full selection of adolescent males at hand in Colwood, where she lived behind a solidly constructed, Futcher Installations chain-link fence, was a tough nut to be cracked.

In our graduating class of thirteen students, she was the only female in the quartet of us who had taken university entrance courses. The conventions of high-school graduation ceremonies in 1954 ignored any backwoods supply-side difficulties and dictated the terms: Caroline had to have a date, plus a corsage.

She was stuck with a wilting white gardenia, and with being squashed beside me on the wooden bench of my Thames truck while I blushed uncontrollably. The blushing started when I had to help her into the Thames in front of her brothers, who took one look at Jim's homemade seat and guffawed.

Caroline was wearing her graduation gown, specially purchased for the occasion and typical of its period: wasp waist, bare shoulders and voluminous amounts of layered skirt, cut just below the knee. I don't remember the colour of the dress and I don't have any pictures of us, thank God.

Helping Caroline to get the skirt into the Thames was difficult enough. The bouffant mass of fabric filled the lower half of the windscreen. The fronts of Caroline's nylon-stockinged knees hit the dashboard. The nyloned tops of Caroline's garter-belted thighs were scrunched against her breasts. I finally managed to close the passenger door without trapping more of the skirt, and we set off.

My blushing got out of control because of the gear stick. Every time I moved it, I had to stroke Caroline's nyloned left leg. Every time I stroked it, Caroline gave a tiny shudder, gritted her jaw, and stared out of the passenger window to her right.

Belmont's graduation ceremony was an anticlimax with no climax. To spare any feeling of awkwardness about academic accomplishment, or otherwise, Harold Parrott convinced Archie Stephenson to present each of the thirteen graduates a co-equally printed piece of paper saying, beneath Belmont's motto, *Carpe Diem*: "Member of the Grade 12 Class."

In 1954, the entity known as Belmont High transmuted itself from the dross of five army huts into a new three-story building. A photo album shows a trio of idiots — Robbie Robertson, Frank Mitchell, and me — wearing our boulevardier berets and puffing our Woolworth's cigarette holders and peashooters in front of the construction site, with a new tar-and-gravel roof being finished off. In keeping with the spirit of the times, the playing fields of Belmont also got upgraded, as reported in our yearbook *Keenyaai Yuens*:

> So far the work accomplished by the school board has been leveling off the ground and applying topsoil. The PTA furnished the lime which was put on the soil last fall. Several student work parties were formed to remove rocks. The successful labourers were rewarded with refreshments supplied by the school board. The girls were present to boost the morale of the stronger sex.

Frank signed my *Keenyaai Yuens* — above the headshot of himself — as "Francis Harris Mitchell," with the notation "Dave and I are <u>bosom</u> pals."

Under the *Keenyaai Yuens* entry "What do they want to do

next?" other students predicted: "Go to Naval College." (Perhaps ... but by no means certain. Despite Jim's tossing cold water on it, I still harboured the acting dream — although the reality of finding my way from Glen Lake to the Royal Academy of Dramatic Art in London seemed impossible. As for naval college, I wish now that I could define clearly what pressures or steps sent me towards it then, and wonder today how much the drive might have been genetic inheritance.)

Before closing the book on Belmont, I have to go back to that new name for its 1953-1954 Jr. Sr. H.S. Annual, previously titled *Blue & White* from the school colours on its covers. The new *Keenyaai Yuens* cover had a red-and-black silkscreen image of a thunderbird mask from a Haida totem pole.

Back in 1954, the students' reasoning for the Belmont annual's name change, using words from the Haida language, was stated in a foreword above a picture of a smiling Archie Stephenson holding the first proof copy:

> *Keenyaai Yuens* is not a greeting. It is as far as the Haida Indian is concerned, a statement of fact. "The Bearer of Good News." To the editorial staff of the annual it is an expression of policy. The annual has become one of our major co-curricular efforts and there is reason for its staff to feel that *Keenyaai Yuens* is a fitting name for it. From the front cover to the final advertisement it has been designed to be representative of Belmont and the community in which the school is situated.

With allowance for the "Indian" — and the budgetary need to thank advertisers — the Belmont students, by showing such awareness of the original owners of the land on which they went to school, were way ahead of their time.

A Giant Leap with Grizzle

PROCRASTINATION IS THE GIFT OF SUMMER. As with the fable of the grasshopper and the ant: swimming in the lake, or sunbathing beside it, or haying in the meadows ... all these lazy pleasures provided my grasshopper pretext for postponing the most significant decision I had so far had to make about my life.

The first misleading part of that statement: haying was anything but lazy. The gravel soil of our property could grow almost none of it, and bales were expensive. This meant that, like the ant, we had to toil for it: first cutting, then gathering, and then bringing it home from anywhere else that we had been able to find someone willing to let us have it: preferably, for free.

Free hay wasn't easy to find. Jim worked his midnight shift on the green chain and had to catch up on sleep during the day: consequently, my mother often went with me to sweet-talk reluctant hay meadow owners into parting with it. This was often as far afield from Glen Lake as the tip of the Saanich Peninsula, twenty-four miles to the east, or Metchosin, only seven miles to the west.

That point of the compass was where my mother, Jane, and Frank Mitchell's father, Geoff, found common cause, and chatted about it. The nature of the Geoff-and-Jane chatting was closed to me — but it was close enough, and frequent enough, to make Frank's mother, Jacqueline, outspokenly jealous.

MAKING HAY WHILE THE SUN SHONE meant that I actually learned to use a scythe and a sickle: instruments of torture for the back, and peril for the arms and legs of the user — and anyone else who, accidentally or foolishly, found themselves within the arc of the blade sweeping through the grass.

Bringing cut hay home in the underpowered Thames truck was equally life-threatening. The vehicle's centre of gravity was another of its multitude of weak parts. To carry hay in its cargo bed required the construction of wooden racks for its sides and tailgate. Any reasonable volume of dried grass made the height of the load reach dangerous proportions. A gust of summer wind, a pothole in the gravel, or any sudden swerve to dodge an animal crossing that gravel provided rollercoaster-tipping thrills I would have been delighted to avoid.

The normal July and August climate on Vancouver Island is bone-dry, but winter is rainforest-wet. The hay we brought home — at first to feed only one horse and two goats — could sit in a pile on the ground and be protected with a tarpaulin. Feeding two horses, four goats and the bull calf required at least a rudimentary storage barn. At the end of August, in ramshackle fashion, with minimal materials, I helped Jim begin to build one.

DRIED HAY WAS FOR THE WINTRY TOMORROWS: in summer, day to day, our horses had to graze on growing grass. The small field with the blackberries was part of Lim Bang's pig farm — at the corner of Glen Lake Road where I had crashed the Thames into Mr. Bing's vegetable truck — which had a water table close enough to the surface for grass to stay green.

On grazing mornings, one of us would put halters on Misty and Grizzle and walk them as a pair the half mile along the road to spend the day, until we collected them again before sunset. Misty was plodding and placid; Grizzle was always a head-tossing bitch. Too frequently she would nip or kick Misty walking beside her, usually choosing the worst possible moment when there was a mechanized vehicle trying to pass. One July evening, someone decided that Angela was now strong enough to lead well-behaved Misty home. I would handle Grizzle.

I was fed up with walking. I jumped onto Grizzle and gave her a single, very light twitch on the lead rope from her halter. A halter has no bit. With no bit between its teeth, a horse has no incentive, other than good manners, to obey the instruction of its rider. Grizzle had no manners. I also had no saddle on her.

I was riding bareback. She began to trot. A trot produces a rapid jerking motion uncomfortable for the male rider (the discomfort it provides for "budding girls" is a different subject). In an English saddle, the rider can "post" — with feet in the stirrups, lifting oneself upwards in the opposite motion to the horse's spine, then lowering oneself down again — which makes the ride smooth.

Just past James' mink farm, with the last straight stretch ahead of her, Grizzle broke into a gallop. A gallop is smoother than a trot, but with nothing for me to hang onto except part of her mane, it didn't let me feel any more comfortable on her unsaddled back. The uphill slope before our gate slowed her down a little. I squeezed my thighs even more tightly against her flanks.

A futile gesture. If she made too sudden a stop —

She wasn't going to stop. She was going to jump the gate.

It didn't seem possible. The top of the gate was five feet high. When I had had full control — with harness, saddle, bridle, bit and stirrups — Grizzle had never jumped more than two feet. And to approach the gate head on, she had to swerve with a full right angle.

I was going to come off and probably die.

I apologize for the phony melodrama — but it didn't seem phony at the time. How Grizzle made that impossible jump, and how I stayed on her back while she did it, we can call a fluke, disguised as kismet.

I REMEMBER THE DATE OF THAT JUMP so clearly because the day after I survived it, fate came calling again, via Canadian National Telegraph. It arrived in the form of a telegram addressed to: DH GURR RRI LANGFORD STATION NR VICTORIA BC. Spelled out in block capitals, without punctuation, the telegram landed me squarely on the horns of a self-imposed career dilemma:

> THE SECRETARY OF THE NAVAL BOARD TAKES PLEASURE IN INFORMING YOU THAT YOU HAVE BEEN ACCEPTED FOR ENROLMENT INTO THE ROYAL CANADIAN NAVY UNDER THE TERMS OF THE VENTURE PLAN IT IS NOTED THAT YOU HAVE ALSO APPLIED FOR CONSIDERATION UNDER THE REGULAR OFFICER TRAINING PLAN PLEASE ADVISE IMMEDIATELY BY TELEGRAM WHETHER YOU WISH TO FILL THE VACANCY RESERVED FOR YOU IN HMCS VENTURE OR WITHHOLD YOUR DECISION PENDING THE RESULTS OF THE REGULAR OFFICER TRAINING PLAN SELECTION BOARD.

How (you may ask) did I land myself in this Hobson's Choice pickle?

Taking or Leaving a Bird in the Hand

IDIOMS TO THE RIGHT OF ME, IDIOMS TO THE LEFT OF ME: I didn't charge into this decision-making mess single-handed. Although I could have been "recommended" again, and therefore excused from taking final BC provincial university entrance exams, I took them.

For what less-than-nothing it was worth at the time, I received the highest mark in the province for English literature and composition. I had taken the exams, but there was no four-year university closer than UBC, in Vancouver, for me to attend — and even Vancouver would have meant money for board and lodging, as well as tuition, and my parents had no cash.

Which raises the next question: What was Archie Stephenson's part in all this? Scholarships would have been available for a student with my final marks, yet despite Archie's outstretched hand, as he wished me well after graduation, and his grey eyes, above his clipped captain's military moustache and the normally tight mouth beneath it, all now smiling approval at me through and below his steel-rimmed glasses ... he never mentioned the subject of student financial assistance.

Nor, despite that high mark of mine in English literature and composition — reflecting considerable credit for her teaching in those subjects — did Kay Maughan, keeper of Belmont's library, mention it, although she sent me best wishes from herself and Stan at the turkey farm on Rocky Point Road.

UNTIL 1947, THE ROYAL CANADIAN NAVY trained its entering cadets to become officers under nautical nomenclature at *HMCS Royal Roads* — originally Hatley Castle, James Dunsmuir's coal baron's estate at Colwood, overlooked by the Triangle Mountain that I rode up with my mother.

In that pivotal year the Canadian government decreed that to promote cost-cutting and efficiency, air force officer-cadets should be trained alongside the naval ones. A year later, the government tossed in the army cadets as well.

The resultant cadet stew in Victoria was called Canadian Services College, Royal Roads. A former army college at Kingston in Ontario got the same treatment. Both these establishments only accepted cadets with senior matriculation: that is, one year beyond the "junior matric" that Frank and I had from Belmont.

The always delicate balance between the English and French parts of Canada now came into play: both existing colleges were in Anglo territory. The government of Louis St. Laurent created a third cadet-training establishment, this one safely in francophone Quebec, and called it Collège militaire royal de Saint-Jean. And — because economic and educational levels still lagged in Quebec — CMR St. Jean accepted applicants with only junior matric. I could now apply to go there.

The RCN leadership (men like Colonel Max's neighbour, Vice Admiral Rollo Mainguy) had never accepted the idea of a tri-service education for naval cadets. They believed that, from the day they first joined, future naval officers should be part of the working navy.

The admirals in naval headquarters decided to do an end run around the tri-service scheme and recreate the same kind of purely naval college that had trained them, and establish it within the dockyard at Esquimalt. Once the government had been shown how much better the result of such a nautical training truly was, the admirals were sure that they could then get the whole shebang moved back across the water of Esquimalt Harbour, and triumphantly reoccupy Royal Roads.

They had timing on their side. The creation of NATO (which assigned anti-submarine warfare to the Canadian navy) followed by the Korean War had created an acute, if temporary, shortage of officers.

The name chosen for this nautical Trojan horse was *HMCS Venture*. Like CMR St Jean, *Venture* would also accept junior matric. Hence, my need, and Frank's, to choose between them.

His decision was easy: he wanted to speak better French. During our Grade 12 year, he had already attended evening conversational French classes with the Alliance Française de Victoria. I had gone with him to a couple of sessions, but didn't keep it up.

My decision was difficult.

I had already been a Sea Cadet for five years, and the idea of going to a purely naval college — like Dartmouth for the Royal Navy — seemed right. And going to *Venture* would mean staying near home, with the chance of taking weekend leaves at the lake. It would also require me to serve for only seven years, after which period, if I didn't like it, I could leave. Or — Jim's instant advice — take a permanent commission, stay in for the rest of my working life, and retire with a full pension.

On the other hand: St. Jean was more than three thousand miles away, and I would get home perhaps once a year, *but* — and it was an enormous *but:* by some unknowable quirk of regulations, after only one year, because I would be a naval cadet at this uniquely Franco military college, I could switch out of it and be sent to complete my nautical academic training with the Royal Navy, and all its Nelsonian traditions, at the Royal Naval College, designed by Sir Christopher Wren, in Greenwich.

Just before Belmont's graduation day, I went for broke and submitted applications to both *Venture* and CMR. On the day after Grizzle didn't break my neck, decision-making had caught up with me again by telegram.

A bird in the hand ...

I plumped for *Venture* for one other reason, not previously mentioned. Under this brand new "Venture Plan," for each of its two years, and after only three months stuck on dry land in Esquimalt, in order to train naval officers in their proper environment, *I could go to sea*. For four months, aboard an eight-thousand-ton battle cruiser, with six-inch guns.

I sent my acceptance to the naval board. A week later, CMR told me that, like Frank, I could have gone there as well. Instead, on the verge of going our separate ways to sea, we almost drowned together in the Strait of Juan de Fuca.

Beware the Streaming Cirrus

THE CRAZE TO SWIM THE STRAIT was kicked off at five a.m. on August 9th, 1954, by Florence Chadwick from California, co-sponsored by Bapco Paint and the *Victoria Times*, with a prize of $10,000 ($7,500 up front; balance on completion) as part of "the greatest publicity scheme ever seen in Victoria." This heroic swim would cast Flo off from the beach below Dallas Road, see her breaststroke or crawl eighteen and three-tenth miles across the strait, and land her on the sandbar protecting Port Angeles, USA.

Frank suggested that we borrow his father's sport-fishing boat. It was conveniently moored in a little cove off Duke Road, near Albert Head; then, ignoring Flo's early start to catch the tide, we would join the accompanying ballyhoo flotilla, mid-morning, at our leisure. Robbie Robertson somehow caught wind of this excursion and begged to come along as well. The weather was perfect: the sky cloudless, no breath of wind, the sea flat-calm.

The only nautical hitch in our plan was: when we got to the point where we would catch up with it — or rather, with Florence — four and a half miles from her start, she wasn't there.

The attempt was over.

Flood tide, not time, had forced her to quit. (Carl Pendray, boss of Bapco and chief sponsor, gave her the bonus $2,500 anyway, for gallantry.) But still, the day was beautiful. When Frank said, "Why don't we keep going to Port Angeles?" there were lots of boats around us, many wearing the American flag, and the water's surface was calm. On a long low swell, I didn't see any nautical reason to disagree, and Robbie said, "Why not?"

Disappointingly, US Customs and Immigration in Port Angeles found plenty of reasons not to let us ashore, but they only needed the first one to turn us back. The man wearing the badge looked at the piece of paper Frank produced for him and said, approximately:

"This shows someone called Geoffrey Mitchell as registered owner of this vessel. You've signed 'Francis Harris Mitchell.' What gives?"

Frank said: "He's my father."

US Immigration said: "You're under age eighteen. Has he given you written permission?"

Frank said: "No."

US Immigration said: "Do you want us to call your Dad on radio?"

Frank said: "Good God, he'd kill me."

US Immigration said, "You kids better skedaddle. Tide's very strong here," and pointed upwards. "That's high cirrus, streaming. Wind and cross-tide is bad news. Don't hang around, and watch out for a weather change on your way back."

It was five p.m. Sunset wasn't until nine. The boat's inboard motor could make a speed of ten knots. We only needed two hours for the twenty-mile run home in a straight line from Port Angeles past Race Rocks lighthouse to the Duke Road cove at Albert Head. The first five miles out from the Port Angeles hook were smooth sailing — although, once we were clear of it, we had a noticeable side-to-side rock because of the swell.

The Strait of Juan de Fuca runs east–west. The swell from the Pacific rolls in the opposite direction, west-to-east. Florence Chadwick had to give up because the tide had been flooding — which meant that it carried her to the east, when she wanted to swim due south. Now, our tide was ebbing: it was going against the incoming Pacific swell. This generated an opposition of forces, manifesting in confusion of wave action at the surface.

Geoff Mitchell's boat wasn't designed for heavy weather. Its construction was light, and although a small cabin was covered, it was made only of thin plywood. The boat's anchor was secured on top of the cover. As the boat began to roll, the anchor began to flip and flop.

The resultant banging was slight, but the noise made it alarming to Robbie. This passenger anxiety got transferred and magnified in Frank's imagination, and didn't exactly help mine. I felt, with Sea Cadet justification, that I knew more about handling this situation than Frank did, but it wasn't my boat and Geoff wasn't my father.

To reduce the anchor-banging noise, Frank decided to turn into the swell, which meant steering west; but every mile in that direction took us a mile further away from where we wanted to go, and less daylight in which to do it.

Then — I was going to say "with no warning," but the Immigration man had given that to us — the wind predicted by the streaming cirrus cloud hit us with an almost instant gale force.

It was a summer-seasonal product of air from overheated land, passing over very cold water. I had observed the same phenomenon when it howled through the gap of the hills at Glen Lake. Then, if it struck me unexpectedly, I only had to go a few hundred yards in my dinghy or canoe to get the craft home in one piece — and even if it capsized, I could swim. Now, whether any of us we would get home at all was a very real question.

The boat pitched violently. Each time the nose of the bow went underwater the banging of the anchor got louder because the rope that had been holding it was slacker, allowing the pointed flukes of the anchor to bang against the sides of the hull.

If they penetrated the hull, we would sink. I told Frank that we had to turn north; that the risk from rolling would be less than from the pitching; and that, while he steered, I would have a chance to try and secure the anchor again.

We argued. The anchor banged. Robbie cried — I would have, except that I was too angry at not getting my own way. Frank's fear of the weather was finally overtaken by being scared shitless of what his father would say if we didn't get his boat back. He listened to me and made the turn across the swell. The roll was still frightening but while Frank steered, I secured the anchor and stopped its banging against the hull. It was after dark when we reached Albert Head. The police had been alerted.

In the large chunk of my life spent at sea, in all weathers, the conclusion of Florence Chadwick's swimathon was the closest I came to Davy Jones' Locker.

Ave to Adolescence

THIS SAME SUMMER, my mother had decided to sunbathe, topless, beside the lake. If she saw a male — me, or Dickie Proudfoot, for example — coming down unexpectedly to swim, thus catching her unawares, she would cover herself, but not before we had involuntarily seen her breasts.

This maternal toplessness increased friction between my parents. The sunbathing would be followed by a row. My mother would say to me, "We'll just ignore him," and chat about something else.

Jim locked himself into silence, except for the tuneless whistle through his false front teeth as I worked beside him, in my last week at home, on building the hay barn.

I had often ridden up Triangle Mountain. I knew nothing about triangulation: the two-against-one head game that people play within dysfunctional families. Or the countervailing game, when the two enemies in the first round join back again to become the two-against-the-one who was previously an ally.

When my mother drove me in the Thames truck up the drive and away from the lake to join the navy, Jim was working on the hay barn, with his back to us.

I called out, "So long, Dad."

He whistled tunelessly, and didn't turn around to wave goodbye.

Reading Between the Lines

THE VOYAGE OF OUR LIFE is as unpredictable as the surface of the sea. When I joined the Royal Canadian Navy at eighteen, I believed that I had made my own decision. The possibility that my DNA might have anything to do with it was as hidden from me as the invisible currents beneath the flat calm surface of doldrums in the tropics.

When I received my commission to serve Her Majesty, Queen Elizabeth the Second — and with that, the people of Canada — I bought my own *navy blue* doeskin uniform with its first gold stripe, hand-tailored by Messrs. Gieves in Portsmouth, and was given my own sword (by Aunt Nan, on my graduation from *Venture*). I looked forward to driving destroyers on my way to, if not the top, damn close to it.

I did what was needed with no cloud in the sky ... until 1964, when my naval world, the inheritor of Nelson's traditions, began to explode. Prime Minister Lester Pearson — behind the moon face of his Defence Minister, Paul Hellyer — set off the detonation with a white paper proposing the melding of all three branches of the Armed Forces, in a common green uniform. It was instantly branded, shorthand, as Unification. It first took away the "Royal" and after that the Navy, with its White Ensign, and with it my blue uniform, and decreed that I would look and behave like the Army.

My sense of outrage at this "out of the blue" betrayal, and the stripping of what I felt to be a personal identity, seemed irrational. Others of my seniority may have grumbled, but they didn't write letters to the prime minister saying "I quit."

I did. It was immensely painful.

And it was not quick. The process took three years, and in that time I did more than write letters; like my childhood hero, *Just William,* I rebelled in all directions.

I wangled meetings with the Clerk of the House of Commons and the Associate Minister of Defence (this bumped me up against Paul Hellyer himself in a narrow passage). I applied and was accepted to enroll for an MBA at McMaster University in Hamilton — I was part of a computer programming team there for the Navy's experimental hydrofoil, *HMCS Bras D'Or.*

A message from the new Canadian Forces Headquarters, marked Secret, said I was to be arrested if I showed up at McMaster's front gate. Four admirals had already resigned in protest at unification. I should have told the press, been shown clapped in irons outside the gate on the nightly news, and become a media sensation. Instead, I tossed an MBA overboard and wrote my absurd letter to Pearson.

The reaction came from Treasury. The accountants wanted money for an undergraduate degree I had previously received at their expense. In exchange, I had agreed to serve for seven years after graduation. Four had already passed. However, a seldom-used clause of the agreement provided a loophole: in lieu of the balance of time, I could buy my way out.

I said I would.

My unexpected fiscal response produced a pause ... and then Headquarters lawyers flatly said I couldn't buy my way out after all. And then Personnel said if I would just shut up, and stop writing bloody letters, I could go now as Second in Command of the hydrofoil, *HMCS Bras D'Or,* while she was being finished, before becoming her Captain when she finally went to sea — but wearing that hated new green uniform.

I wasn't equipped fiscally for legal battle with the Treasury lawyers. I rejected the Personnel bribe. I served my time and stayed landlocked for those three interminable years in Ottawa. (There is always a funny side: another guy from my Venture college term in similar circumstances went to a shrink, got himself declared mad, was released with full pension, and was hired immediately by IBM.)

I RETURNED TO VICTORIA. In Queenswood, a house that I built for my family on the waterfront, facing Haro Strait, I turned my back on the Navy — literally. From 1972 to 1978, whenever I spotted a warship passing I had to look away.

I had discovered that I could design and build distinctive houses constructed with wood cut from those logs I once birled and rolled with Pat Colclough in Sooke Basin: logs on their way to the mill on the Gorge where Jim had hauled them from the green chain. The supply of old growth Douglas fir and Western red cedar still seemed endless in 1972, but it was their last stand; epitomized by the tiny remainder at Triangle Mountain that I rode through with my mother (now a townhouse development).

At this time, 1976, and my fortieth birthday, I decided to write a book, *Troika*. I thought it was logical that it should be about a ship (but a Soviet one, *Storozhevoy*) and that its protagonist would be a Royal Naval officer. Why I then gave that protagonist a hidden childhood and an almost invisible father — and described a triangular relationship with two males competing for the affection of a woman, ending in doomed love and betrayal — all that seemed logical, the developments driven only by the plot.

Until ten years later, at a delayed fiftieth birthday lunch of smoked salmon, to which my mother invited herself, she said:

"You do know Jim isn't your father, don't you?"

I did not.

Nor that my DNA came to me from three generations of Royal Naval officers. The first, my great-great-grandfather, was a lieutenant, wounded in the War of 1812 which the Americans lost, before he became the sailing master on the ship escorting Napoleon to exile on St. Helena. His son, my great-grandfather, gave his name to Bedwell Harbour, which I first visited as a Sea Cadet. He also painted a picture of *HMS Ganges* at Salt Spring Island, and charted the east coast of Australia.

That digression matches what seemed like an endless numbing of my senses. It was no time at all. My mother went on to say: "I've written about it in a letter."

She began to tell me its contents. I said, "Why now?"

She said, "You're going back to England for this new book. I thought you might ask questions."

The "new book" was *The Ring Master*, my novel about Hitler and his Nazi party seen as an extension of Wagner's operatic cycle and Germany's national psyche. The lead publisher was André Deutsch and the book launch was to be at their office in London. I had thought I would spend half my naval career going back and forth across the Atlantic to interact with the Royal Navy. Instead, I had sailed to every corner of the North and South Pacific. *The Ring Master*'s launch party would be the first time I saw London since I left it.

My mother had been describing to me what was in the letter. It went in one ear — and then God knows where, because she said this:

"I used to call you 'my darling Willum.'"

With those three words; in that tone of her voice; saying that endearment from a past forgotten and buried; that casually habitual phrase of a loving mother to a child brought back through five decades in a single blink of my eye: with her summoning of my first name, the only name I had known for an infant's timeless three years as consciousness is formed ... *William* ... the true name I was born with. In that blink I was there, back with her, the two of us, at Boundary Road.

Jane and "Willum" in Hyde Park

Jane's Letter

Dec. 8. 85
Glen Lake.

Dearest David.

If you are reading this it will mean that death or a physical disaster overtook me. I hope I will have talked with you — but the years at time of writing have not been kind for you and yours. I cannot predict how you will feel as you read on. Sometimes I think you must know or have wondered ...

Anyway I keep waiting for securer times to prevail but must be realistic at 73. So just in case I'm snatched before I'm ready to go it is important I get substance on paper. What I'm working up to & which may not be a shock to you is that James is your adopted Father.

I wanted you to know from an early age but Jim's fragile ego would never agree. He was afraid 'you would love him less' if you knew. He really loved and wanted you but we know now that his personality was in no way equipped to handle the traumas of parenthood or family life —

It is quite difficult to get ages-dates exact but at the age of 19 or 20 I had cast the trammels of the darling Aunts (Dorothea and Elspie) and was living in London. Sister Nan too was there — but she was 5 yrs my senior & all our girlhood we had no common ground, after our parents both died. Nan was above & beyond me — strict, judgmental — disapproving. (This might hurt her but it's how she seemed to me then.) We were poles apart & never saw one another.

I was quite wild, I have to say, men & I were Bees & honey I had a marvelous time discovering that I wasn't just a fat plain little girl in a grey sweater & skirt in winter and a brown Holland dress in summer. Dorothea and Elspie never complimented on appearance — clothing was of the best but not to attract — sex to the Aunts was 'Close your eyes & think of England.'

I shared an apartment flat with a French girlfriend, Pauline. Two parallel streets faced each other and a railed-off garden ran up the middle, about as wide as Douglas Street in Victoria. These were Oxford and Cambridge Terrace — the houses were old & converted to flats — occupied by struggling actors — one of whom was later to take me for evenings of 'chat' and not much to drink to his friends' apartment.

The friends were struggling at the Old Vic in a Midsummer Night's Dream — their names, Olivier, Richardson, Gielgud and Redgrave — we were all poor but no one felt deprived or hard done by — it was a lot less 'gimme' society than now. And then at a party I met a young man and it wasn't long before we were inseparable and madly in Love. In these days we would have just moved in together — Life then was not so simple.

Edward Brisbane-Le Breton (Teddy) lived at home in the suburb of Watford (or was it Hendon) no Watford I'm sure. He lived with his father, an authoritative bitter Vice Admiral — this was a period of restraint for the Royal Navy and he had been axed — and bore a huge grudge. Anyway he ruled Teddy & older brother with a cruel tongue and rigid house rules — In the '30s young men accepted a way of life they would never tolerate now.

Teddy worked in some office capacity as a junior & thro' 'Daddy's connections' for W.H. Wills Tobacco (I think they became Players, not sure.) He was on the Wills cricket team and a Rugby team and so when matches were played or practiced — he didn't go home. By hook or crook we managed lots of weekends & whatever the excuses old Admiral Dad bought it.

We were the same age and to tell the truth I don't think we ever looked at the idea of marrying — we concentrated on having a marvelous time. After cricket & Rugby games there were always parties or meeting in the local pub. To Cambridge for May Week and Ascot for the Derby — always on the cheap and with a group. Teddy had a beat up old Morris two-seater with a rumble seat and we'd somehow pile in and off — in the summer often to the sea, Brighton, Tennis at Wimbledon —

He was handsome in a regular English way —medium height & build — brown short hair, blue grey eyes a flush of colour on his cheekbones — Looked good in browns. Even tempered, easy going conservative, not very ambitious a 'Nanky Poo' sort of young man — with a background and upbringing much like mine — His mother had died when he was about 16 —

Anyway my love — this man who I dearly, dearly loved fathered you. We must (and were) have been incredibly ignorant and naive. I don't recall that it occurred to either of us that we might have a child, we were totally carefree and you my love were the result, but as the country folk would say 'he were a love child.'

How will you re-act? 'Out of wedlock' is almost prestige in 1980's day and age. Your generation long ago moved away from the attitudes of the 30's. In an era of fullest knowledge and matter of fact protection it must seem extraordinary to have gone our blissful way. Of course we were terrified when we knew via Dr. that I was pregnant and we talked about getting married but we had no savings & Teddy as a junior-junior had few 'prospects'.

Finally he talked with his brother who talked to God ('dear old Dad') and the heavens crashed around us. 'Disinherit.' — Without a penny.' 'Leave this house.' and on & on. The man wielded power — he called the shots. Teddy on pain of 'being cast out' was forbidden to see me —

'Daddy' talked to his lawyers who talked to me —unsophisticated, sheltered me — Now I would have fought them tooth & nail by God.

How Victorian and feeble we must both seem to you — Ready cash was a very real factor & young men did obey in those days — there were _no kindly social work ladies_ to strew rose petals along the rocky path..

I was lucky that I remained extremely well & 'didn't show' so I could go on working till birth day. I was on call for two or three French fashion houses in Chelsea — Funny things you remember. I travelled of course by bus (few of the young had cars) & I ran and jumped on as always. Sometimes if the conductor didn't catch my arm I wanted to say 'Don't you know I'm having a baby?' I thought I should receive the respect due my interesting condition. It was possibly in Dec. or Jan. that my roommate Pauline panicked and spilled the beans to Nan.

It must have been a huge shock to 'schoolteacher, straight laced Nan'. But sister rose to the occasion and never scolded or preached as we planned and replanned the future. We decided quite firmly that you would be adopted — prior to birth it was pretty easy to be dispassionate — as the best and only solution.

Teddy would make time we could be together but Daddy's shadow was over us and we couldn't see a future.

Nan & I had a gruesome day (funny in retrospect) when the Aunts wrote that they were coming up to London from Whitchurch and would we lunch at their club in Cavendish Square. God knows how we got through the day — I know I had a Jaeger Top Coat 3/4 length and loose in large check tweed — guess I kept it on all thro' the meal — anyway the visit was happy & the old darlings went happily off to the Albert Hall.

Time was flying and we had to decide where I was going to live before and following your birth. Pauline, a good R.C., knew some Nuns who had a House of Retreat and always room for 3 or 4 young mothers. This proved an excellent solution. The Nuns were kindness itself with a great sense of fun — no preaching — rather Aunt Elspie people.

In the late afternoon of Feb. 4th labour began. After an hour or two the Sisters put on their capes and matter of factly said we would walk to the hospital — they assured me that walking was the finest exercise for me at this point. So in the clear, frosty very cold London evening, a Sister comfortably on each side of me we walked twenty, twenty five minutes — I don't know. I do know I was totally unprepared & ignorant of what to expect thro'out the birthing process.

Anyway love you made your way into this world around 6.30 a.m. Feb. 5 1936 in Queen Charlottes Hospital. Marylebone — London.

They didn't put babies in separate rooms then — little bassinettes hung at the foot of each bed — if you stretched with your toe you could rock the cradle if your baby cried. We were all hospitalized for two weeks — you were breast fed and I realized that I could never let you go for Adoption.

When I broke that news to Nan she was very good & never tried to persuade me otherwise tho' I imagine she was worried sick how we'd make out. She arranged for me to stay with her best friend Kita Corbett in Surrey while we sorted things out.

You were duly christened William Brisbane Le Breton Harvey. I wanted to Register you without my Maiden name but the old Clerks were very intimidating as to legalities, 'No hyphen with Brisbane.', and dire punishment to use the father's name last unless you were married — Nowadays of course one would demand 'one's rights'.

I have thought you should use William Brisbane Le Breton as a nom de plume — it's legally yours — or just William Le Breton sounds good to me ('a Proper writer's name for a Proper Novel,' Dorothea would say. I've often wanted to do a Harlequin myself.)

I found an apartment near Marble Arch on Cambridge Terrace. A Scottish widow lady 'Auntie Rita' owned the big old house — She lived in the basement. A dignified Frenchman, Monsieur Laurillard (funny the things that are recalled clearly) a part-time something to do with Freud, was on the main, he used to call you 'mon petit Guillaume'. He was a Warden in the Blitz — Upstairs Dorothea Clayton a violinist and teacher (a 'Brown Owl' type) — I had known her for some time & she was your Godmother.

Next there was you & me and up in the very top an aspiring young Shakespearian actor — Teddy Bach, who would introduce me to the Old Vic (tho' I never liked Shakespear) & his friends.

The old portable H.M.V record player you used to play endlessly was Redgrave's — Michael asked me to house it when he went on tour as his landlady wanted it in lieu of unpaid rent.

Our flat had very good high windows and a small balcony big enough for plants and a nine inch railing, there's a story.

One day I was tidying the mantelpiece and looked into the mirror. In it I saw you outside the window settling down in the tiny balcony. I've never moved so fast before or since & without a word snatched you back. When Monsieur L returned from whatever he did by way of real work Auntie Rita had him nail the bottom of the windows firmly shut.

It was a companionable house and the tenants welcomed & loved you. It didn't cost much to live quite adequately. I had an odd variety of jobs — modelling again — cashier in an Odeon — I don't remember.

Granny Monk was a prop & stay. She lived in a tiny, cluttered little house in a lane that ran at the back. She was neat as a pin & short & plump. She loved you. I have a picture of walking in one afternoon — you were bare naked leaping up & down on her sofa while she rocked in her chair and knitted — 'Carnt do nuffin' with him mum' she said placidly.

We walked lots, Dorothea Clayton me & you in the pram into Hyde Park, beside the Serpentine to feed the ducks, and play by the Peter Pan Statue. We sat on the benches comparing notes with other young Mothers — and uniformed nannies who offered firm advice to us silly young things.

And then Teddy began to drop by.

He had got our address from Pauline. He was fascinated by you and the idea of having a child but frightened of the implied responsibilities of this — It's probably hard for you to believe that we did love one another so much yet he couldn't go against his father. We didn't waste time on post mortems or talk of marriage. We three walked in the park or into the country in his same rattle trap little Morris —

Now on a side street near Granny Monk there was a small restaurant in a house run by two sisters — home cooking. It was always packed — Medical students from St Mary's Hospital and the assortment of us who lived nearby — people squeezed onto a chair and sometimes shared one. And so on occasion we shared a table with a man who was quite different in dress & deportment from most of the regulars — the owner ladies fussed over him 'dear Mr. Gauer' he left large tips on the table, most of us left pennies (sixpence was a lot). Debonair & sophisticated best describe him — he wore good suits starched white shirts & was immaculate obviously a man about town — tho' Nan loathed, and called him a 'lounge lizard' because of his Brylcreem hair.

He had a good new car — a Vauxhall — and took me to concerts. (I was bored with some.) The Music Hall became a regular Saturday date — we listened to the speakers in Hyde Park on Sundays — he paid you a great deal of attention — played games & bought presents. He lived near us where Oxford & Cambridge Terraces became Sussex Gardens which had slightly larger flats and Professional people as tenants and felt itself superior.

He loved to take you around with him & I suspect even then he introduced you as his son — and later when he came to the idea of marrying I believe he wanted a son much more than a wife. (Looking back that is.)

He had been married twice. The first at about 18 to a woman

nearly double his age — Mickie — It didn't last long & she divorced him and married an Australian — it seems to have been a Mother/son affair & they parted I believe amicably. Then he married a concert singer Gladys Knight — that was very unhappy — two temperamental people and he divorced Gladys.

He was just coming up for air about the time we met and certainly we never talked marriage. He gradually assumed more & more of my time — was immensely jealous of Teddy & couldn't countenance any continuing contact between Teddy, you or I.

He encouraged me to quit working and we took the flat in Boundary Road — it was a good time — plenty of Jim's friends — parties — a nice garden for you to play in. It is hard to sort out time spaces over that period — War was creeping up on us. We were desperately ashamed of not going to Czechoslovakia's help and when Hitler went into Poland there was only a huge feeling of relief when at last we acted. It's interesting to see, looking back how one got emotionally ready to go to war.

When Jim did begin to talk of marriage it seemed like a marvelous thing for you & I thought I loved him — never like I loved Teddy (most of Jim was I think the glamour of new experiences & Man about Town bit). His friends begged us not to — said they'd give us a year or less.

I was no judge of character and knew nothing of neuroses, psychosis etc. etc. There was an episode only once in the period before we married but I couldn't read the signal. One evening on no pretext he flew into an ungovernable rage, threw things and then didn't speak for two days. I had never seen such behaviour but it carried no message to me —no danger signals waved.

Ah me what if I had taken you and run —

In this period Teddy phoned and asked to meet — We did and he seriously asked me to marry. With all my heart I wanted to but I was afraid he might fail me that in the crunch 'Daddy' the Admiral would once again prevail.

Jim seemed to offer the best security for us — he certainly loved us, you particularly — who could guess at the underlying shattered ego? The need for everyone connected with him to be perfect. He wanted so much to be his own ideal: a generous, sensitive loving parent and husband — luckily for him he believes he has achieved this.

Anyway I made my choice and let Teddy go out of our lives. I'm sure he joined up right away — R.N. perhaps because of his father, but I suspect it was a Commando Unit or Air Combat. I never knew if he survived the war — he was the sort of young Englishman who died in their thousands.

He hoped in the face of all our problems something would work out for him, you, and me. But Jim couldn't share, it was too threatening, not even to keep pictures — and he has always been dead against you knowing he adopted you — as I say, fearing you would 'love him less'.

Adoption in England was a simple and straightforward affair — no investigations, <u>no social worker report</u>. We went with you before a little old Judge in the local Marylebone Court. He asked a few questions, we were in & out in ten minutes & you were re-registered with names of Jim's choice — I would have liked to keep my Darling Willum at least, but no.

We must have been married before that (the certificate is in the safety deposit in Langford Commerce Bank) — I can't set the year but know it was Jim's birthday, June 20. in Marylebone Registry

Office. (All the theatre stars got married there because of course they'd all been divorced and Churches wouldn't marry you at that time.) Nan was there and Jessie Franks the buyer from Paris you liked, she taught you French. And Marjorie & Timmy Vaughan — a charmer who elected himself your Godfather, died in one of the Bombing raids.

And now you begin to see the pattern —

Out of the blitz to your old friend, Ann Crow at Reigate, and then when Jim was called into the Royal Marines the Aunts suggested we go up to them, near Monmouth —until then they had not met you or James. You know how much they loved you but they never really accepted Jim. His ways were quite foreign, his world a strange one to them. In their old fashioned way they had always the feeling I had married 'into trade', 'beneath me'.

They were good solid years with the Aunts — then Bunna was born before Jim was posted overseas. The Aunts sold Barton-Olivers 1 at Whitchurch and bought B.O.2 in Burton Bradstock to be near their sisters Margery & Rhoda in Dorset. During the move you & Bun went to Ann Crow again while everything settled in — and we stayed with the Aunts till it was the time (by English standards) for you to go to prep school at Sherborne.

~~I cannot predict~~

Don't feel belittled — you had an awful lot of loving people around you, most of all probably Nan. But Dorothea as well, reading you Don Quixote or Pilgrims Progress and Dickens Bleak thing — rather rich at six. Even Great Aunt Kythe — how furious she got when Jim called her Old Trout. — who filled you up with all that Hundred Years in the Highlands rubbish about being descended from Kings of Scotland on our Gairloch MacKenzie side, tho' you did look simply adorable in your Hunting Tartan kilt. And your stuffed animals — Panda and Rabbit. 'P&R' as you called them.

Of course I have wondered what our lives would have been had we been with Teddy — a very conservative English pattern of upper middle class, predictable and happy because we were both pretty equable temperaments. Living with Jim — well you know his oddities & problems but that's not to say I haven't had a happy and satisfying life.

I've loved Canada — after Duncan, on the farm, where you saved all our lives from the stove gas and shot Bun with the arrow. I enjoyed the childhood & growing years at the Lake, being a parent, my work, good friends — the many loved real animals — the outdoors of us riding together up the Old Pipeline Trail and latterly Nan as a friend, a great Joy.

Apart from Jim — who I did love in the early days, but I think the gap of war service, as with so many families was too great to cement our marriage firmly — there was all the adjustment for him of coming back not to almost babies, but children with minds of their own. He was always at his best if we were all totally dependent.

I have always liked & attracted men three stand out in my life as lovers: Teddy my one & only true love as the stories go. Dickie B, an American wartime fun fairy tale but painful too. And latterly Arthur in Qualicum Beach — the world is exactly right for us when we are together but Arthur loves his money & in B.C if he separated he could be taken for half his worldly goods. — The fishing tackle shop — and love me as he protests, no woman could be worth that sacrifice to Artie.

I have been blessed with excellent health and all in all the balance of the years weigh out on the positive end. This go around I have loved, and as I am a firm believer in re-incarnation I am very ready & interested in the next Turn of the Wheel — what indeed will our roles be? — there will be the feeling of familiarity tho we won't know how we have met before.

No Aunts' Version of the prayer book, please. Just Memorial Society cremation and my ashes in a flower bed (it's all paid for) but maybe, and depending if you intend to share this — I'd love to see the kids' expressions when they learn what a wild one I was.

We've not been very demonstrative — our actions more than words, but you have been my very dear son. God bless.

Your
loving Mother.

Lifting the Fog

"My Darling Willum" ... the shock caused a shiver. The effect was profound. My mother and I parted. I wasn't saying much. She dabbed at tears. I retrieved the letter from Nan, who was almost equally shocked — but at the fact that her sister hadn't told me the truth decades earlier.

The letter itself takes up thirteen pages, handwritten on lined, yellow, legal-size sheets. When I read it, the reasons for my exaggerated reactions to things that I sensed as betrayal — "unification," or having Scotty stolen from Jim's car, or Sammy the Pekingese grabbed back by Dorothea — began to emerge from mist, as land does when approached from seaward, through lifting fog.

And on the other, lost side of that fog, looming large in my consciousness as the Rock of Gibraltar was the flat at Boundary Road where a piano-playing man from the music halls turned into a Black Magic act to obliterate Willum and replace him as Snod.

After our lunch of scarcely touched smoked salmon, my mother got into her car. She said, by way of farewell explanation of the letter and why she had left it with Nan:

"I didn't want it to upset Jim."

A Note of Appreciation and Acknowledgement

Only the keen eye of such an expert pruner as George Galt allowed this book to emerge from the thicket of overgrown memory in my antique head. The touch of an equally gentle yet ruthless finishing trimmer, Mark Abley, removed the last thorns. I thank them both, considerably. As do I to good friend, Charlton Bullock: an artist skilled enough to take my octogenarian's scribbled Map of Glen Lake in hand, and make it look more genuinely childish.

Written at Ansell Road, 2024

About the Author

David Gurr is the acclaimed author of several novels, including *Troika, The Voice of the Crane,* and *The Ring Master,* which was shortlisted for the Governor General's Award. Before launching his literary career, Gurr served with the Royal Canadian Navy as an executive officer and computer systems analyst. He subsequently alternated between writing books and building distinctly West Coast houses. He lives in Victoria.